At Smith's House

At Smith's House

The Search for Meaning in a Postmodern Age

Jay Trott

Resource *Publications*
An imprint of *Wipf and Stock Publishers*
199 West 8th Avenue • Eugene OR 97401

AT SMITH'S HOUSE
The Search for Meaning in a Postmodern Age

Copyright © 2007 Jay Trott. All rights reserved. Except for brief quotations in critical publications or reviews, no part of this book may be reproduced in any manner without prior written permission from the publisher. Write: Permissions, Wipf and Stock Publishers, 199 West 8th Avenue, Suite 3, Eugene, Oregon 97401.

ISBN 13: 978-1-55635-438-0

Manufactured in the U.S.A

Contents

Foreword / vii

Chapter 1: The Sublime and the Beautiful / 1

Chapter 2: Absolute Dilemma / 13

Chapter 3: What Kind of Sign? / 29

Chapter 4: Exquisite Stranger / 45

Chapter 5: Asymmetry, Mathesis, 'The Good' / 57

Chapter 6: Sanctus / 73

Chapter 7: Seasons of Creativity / 91

Chapter 8: The Law of Desire / 107

Chapter 9: Something of Substance / 123

Chapter 10: Indomitable Being / 141

Chapter 11: A Case of Mistaken Identity / 161

Chapter 12: Life and Culture / 175

Foreword

How I Got There

THE BOOK you are holding in your hands right now may be something of an oddity: an unintentional manuscript.

It grew out of an attempt to reconstruct several enjoyable conversations I've had with Professor Robert W. Smith, an old friend and formerly a colleague in the English department at Norman College. Several years ago Smith's wife Jane died rather suddenly of cancer—apparently she had been concealing the symptoms for some time. Not long after this tragic event he retired and seemed to retreat into a shell. He rarely appeared at the college, declining repeated invitations to speak on subjects that had once seemed irresistible. Those of us who saw him socially thought he looked a bit unkempt. Most disturbing, he stopped publishing for the first time in forty years, thus becoming a favorite topic of conversation in department offices as even former rivals vied to articulate various degrees of apprehension with regard to his state of mind.

In short, everyone was complaining about Smith's psychological weather but no one seemed to be doing anything about it. And to tell the truth, he is not exactly the sort of person you can approach with hand-wringing and a sympathetic tear. I had a nagging feeling that I was the one who should take the initiative, however. I was probably as close to him as anyone else on the faculty, in spite of our age difference—most of his contemporaries had long since retired and moved away. Also we happened to be members of the same ecclesiastical institution, which added a certain sense of obligation. Yankees don't cotton to busybodies, but it seemed natural for me to drop in from time to time, especially since I drove right by his house on my way home from work. I could always bring along something interesting to break the ice (or melt it).

What exactly I hoped to accomplish through this devious plan is a little hazy now, except perhaps to demonstrate that I had spent too much time reading Henry James novels. But I decided to put it into action the very next day, on a bright afternoon in October, having stopped first in town to pick up a decent bottle of port, which I knew he loved. I still had misgivings as I pulled into his driveway and in fact did not fully commit myself until my index finger actually touched the plastic surface of the doorbell, but Smith made these reservations seem foolish by giving me a grand reception and ushering me into the den, where we sat near the woodstove and commenced a lively conversation that lasted somewhat longer than the fortified beverage.

After that I made up my mind to stop by on a regular basis. Smith seemed to look forward to these visits, which was gratifying, but I was surprised to find how much they came to mean to *me* as well. A remarkable degree of freedom developed between us, unshackled as we were by the artificial environment of the college; the most trifling remark seemed to provide an excuse to go plunging into some deep discussion, as if by unspoken conspiracy. It was a rediscovery for me of the pleasures of conversation. Many were the times when I found myself almost longing to get to the old red house to talk over something I had seen or simply to vent my frustrations.

In the meantime I had been preserving the highlights of these conversations in my diary and had even given some thought about turning them into a book. Smith's thesis—that philosophy is divided by divided loves, but that love itself provides a way to go beyond the limitations of philosophy and its concepts of value—certainly seemed timely in the wasteland in which we now find ourselves. But I was so intrigued by a conversation we had about aesthetics one wintry night that I sat down at the kitchen table and tried to reconstruct it in detail. I had never attempted to write dialogue before and was surprised at how easily the words seemed to pour out of my pen. In fact the exercise was so gratifying that I began to jot down *any* conversation with Smith that seemed noteworthy.

After three or four of these exercises I began to realize that the book seemed to be writing itself. I must warn the reader, however, that the resulting portrait of Smith is a bit one-sided. Much of the book is taken up with the discussion of philosophy and the limitations of its value judgments, as if that were the only thing Smith ever talked about, when it would probably be more accurate to say that it was *my* prevailing interest at the time. I seem to have been on something of a spiritual journey in recent years. More than once I have had the unsettling feeling that my career was at a dead end; meanwhile I have often been tempted to wonder if it makes any sense to continue to believe what I believe, especially in the face of the monolithic indifference and sometimes outright antagonism encountered in the academy.

Foreword

Call it a mid-age crisis or what you will, but any obsession with philosophy was probably my own. It has been wonderful to talk openly about such matters with someone who is able to take them seriously and has interesting things to say; but their prominence in the following pages may remind the reader of Dr Johnson's seeming fascination with ghosts, which finally drove the great editor to comment that Johnson was not particularly *prone* to talking about ghosts but was simply trying to accommodate Boswell's morbid interest. In real life Smith is just as happy to talk about fly-fishing or football as Kant and Descartes, and many a discussion about literature and other interesting topics did not find its way into the following pages simply because they were not foremost in my mind.

Speaking of Boswell, my dear wife, upon reading the manuscript, has raised an interesting question: how much did Smith know, and when did he know it? As I gradually became immersed in the project I fell into the pleasant habit of dropping what I thought were obvious hints about the existence of such a manuscript, but Smith seemed quite unhappy when I showed up one day with one in my hands. He did not want me to send it to my publisher and still has not read it. I will leave it to others, then, to puzzle over the dynamics of our relationship and what effect they may have had on our conversations.

My wife also questioned the *prominence* of Smith's voice in my recreations, knowing full well that I rarely miss an opportunity to make my own feelings known. I will freely admit that I left out a great deal of what I said during our visits. I am intrigued by Smith's analysis of the demise of "the good," which is the centerpiece of his thinking, and by his attempt to recast the good as the absolute desirability of life. As far as I know, the concept is new—in fact it could only have come into being in a postmodern context. Since Smith has not made any attempt to put these concepts into writing, it seemed important to me to communicate them as clearly as possible.

Which reminds me—Smith is known in certain circles as "the curmudgeon"; and indeed, I am conscious, as I reread these too-solid pages, that my eagerness to give him center stage may make it seem like he deliberately pushed me to the side. This was not the case at all. Smith has always been gracious and more than willing to listen. Since the full panoply of his character seems to have been obscured by my clumsy pen, I can only hope that it will be revived in the charity of my readers, who must look upon the following pages as an experiment in talking without stopping first to chart a sure course.

J. W. Moore
Norman College

Chapter 1

The Sublime and the Beautiful

It was the second nor'easter in a week. I was glad to have the heavy-duty snow blower I had picked up at a tag sale the previous summer as the forty inches of snow that fell between the two storms kept multiplying with gale-force winds. An old farmhouse across the meadow looked permanently sealed off from the world by drifts at least ten feet high.

Smith always insisted upon doing his own shoveling, in spite of the heart problems he'd had in the past. I drove over with the snow blower as soon as the storm started to let up, but he had already cut a narrow tunnel into the towering wall that surrounded his walk and driveway. He had not done anything about the black ice concealed by constant drifting, however, as I discovered by taking a ludicrous fall near his mailbox and bruising my arm in an attempt to protect a bottle of rather good apple brandy I had brought along for the occasion.

Smith emerged from his cellar just as I stumbled in the back door, looking a bit like a lumberjack in flannel shirt and thick, lined khakis.

"Oh!" he said, dropping a load of musical ash near the wood-stove. "It's you."

"Whom were you expecting?" I said, pretending to be offended.

"The man across the road," he grunted, picking up a log and tossing it in the fire. "He comes over to borrow a shovel every time it snows."

"Perhaps he has not yet realized he lives in New England."

"Perhaps," Smith replied. "But what are you doing out in such weather? I haven't seen a car in hours."

"Rescue mission," I said, handing him the brandy and stamping the snow off my boots in the flagstone entryway. "Not Napoleon, but the best this unsaintly dog can do from his limited private stock."

"Very nice," Smith said, inspecting the bottle. "It should prove useful tonight. I don't seem to be able to get any heat out of this thing. Pipes probably need a good cleaning, but I hate taking them apart."

Smith fetched a couple of plain tumblers and led the way unceremoniously to the den, where he sat in his red leather chair and stared out at the snow.

"Quite a storm," I observed as I unscrewed the cork with my jackknife and poured some of the strawy nectar into stout glasses. "Every year Mary and I talk about moving to a gentler climate, and every year we still seem to be here when the snow flies."

"I wish you snowbirds would all move south and leave the rest of us in peace," he growled. "Maybe then these blasted contractors would stop building houses in my woods."

"Come now—don't tell me you actually enjoy this sort of thing," I said, knowing full well that he did. "Wouldn't you rather be sitting in Symphony Hall right now, listening to some cheerful concerto and looking forward to what you're going to drink at intermission, than suffering the indignity of winter in these desolate western hills?"

He shook his head. "There are few things I enjoy more at my age than having my bones rattled by a good blizzard. A winter storm is tonic for the soul. There is something invigorating about the north wind swirling through the pines, blowing away the illusions of these lightless days; something profound in such ghostly howling, if only we could understand what it means."

"Allow me to interpret. My wife's van won't start in the morning, there'll be ice dams a foot thick on the north roof, and half the trees in my little orchard will be flattened when the front finally blows through."

"Ah, but the storm is beautiful," Smith replied with a smile.

"Some people may be more inclined to find *beauty* in great music than in howling winter winds," I teased.

"Why, then, they must be young like you and still living in the realm of possibility," he replied in the same tone. "There is something about beauty that causes us to want to make art, and something about art that makes us think we are unusually important; this is why we wax eloquent over the arts, as if it were possible to make them last forever. But such high-powered talk begins to seem ridiculous in old men like me. Oh, yes; youthful enthusiasm is replaced by a colder frame of mind as the energy of life ebbs away."

"I can feel the chill. But then you must be one of those famous enemies of beauty that we hear so much about these days."

"Not at all," he replied laughing. "I long for the day when the prisoners are set free from the reigning orthodoxy and its tedious resistance to beauty. But we are the ones who are responsible for the loss of beauty—we are the ones who made the word *beauty* seem small through all of our empty prattling about 'the good.' We tried to make ourselves seem like masters of being by claiming that beauty is the product of pure intellect or a synthesis of intellectual and material causes; and then we grew so tired of the dividedness of such valuations that we decided to negate beauty as if it did not exist at all."

"We sought *identity* in the love of beauty," I suggested. "We tried to use the great pleasure provided by beauty to obtain knowledge of being and transcend our nothingness through our methods of judging value—but those methods led to dubious results."

"The power that makes beauty valuable is love, without which it is nothing, but the philosophers were in love with the force of judgment found in intellect, which leads to divided values. Plato realized that the great pleasure provided by beauty intimates the existence of 'the good,' a transcendent value; but he was not content to enjoy the goodness of beauty for its own sake. He wanted to beautify himself and become known as a philosopher, and he sought this transcendent identity in intellect and its capacity to make value judgments about the nature of beauty and the good. But Plato also happened to be in love with the concept of pure intellect, a love that caused him to attempt to describe beauty as the product of the resistance of divine intellect to the formlessness of matter, and to claim that the love of beauty was really therefore the love of intellect, an ethereal love that can be consummated by negating the combination of intellect and matter he thought he saw in existence."

"Which results in the negation of the beauty that actually exists and produces nothingness—not 'the good,' or that which is absolutely desirable. This left an opening for Aristotle and the concept that beauty and the good are synthetic values."

"Aristotle also wanted to be known as a philosopher who had found the secret of happiness. He saw that pure resistance leads to nothingness, but he thought he could overcome this limitation by grounding the seeming purity of intellect in existent values. He fell in love with the concept that divine intellect has overcome the difference between itself and matter through pure action—that the beauty of the sensuous universe actually contains the goodness of intellect because it comes into being at the point where the difference between these two 'causes' disappears. But that difference cannot be made to disappear without depriving intellect of the purity of its resistance to divided values."

"Aristotle's method is incapable of reflecting the transcendent value that beauty intimated to Plato; thus our descriptions of 'the good' are divided by the difference between the value of existence and our consciousness of a force of resistance to its limitations, and have been from the very beginning."

"The philosophers began by embracing the goodness of beauty—its great desirability—but the dividedness of their value judgments about 'the good' led to the loss of beauty in the end. Descartes set aside any explicit discussion of beauty or the good in order to avoid the divide between Idealism and Realism. He thought he could go beyond the limitations of traditional philosophy and obtain knowledge of transcendent being through science, but science and beauty have nothing to do with each other."

"Beauty began to fade from philosophy with Descartes because he was trying to avoid the dividedness seen in Greek philosophy and its concepts of the good."

"Descartes attributed transcendent value entirely to intellect; there is no sign of the gracious old love of beauty in the cogito. But setting aside beauty did not enable him to supercede the dividedness seen in Plato and Aristotle. It turned out that the cogito had exactly the same limitations as Idealism—it was rooted in a love of pure intellect and resistance, and this love leads to nothingness. Hegel attempted to overcome this nothingness by synthesizing it directly with being, but his method had the same limitations as Aristotle. It is impossible to describe such a synthesis without putting a limit on nothingness and its capacity to resist the unhappiness of existence. And this is why Nietzsche decided to try to embrace nothingness for its own sake—not merely to set aside beauty and 'the good,' but to annihilate them in the hope of obtaining transcendent value through the will to power."

"The Nihilists thought it was possible to go beyond the dividedness of philosophy by negating the good and embracing existence for its own sake. But this ideology resulted in the foolish embargo on beauty seen in modern culture."

"Beauty cannot be good if 'the good' does not exist; hence both beauty and the good are dead to philosophy in the modern age. At one time philosophers were burning to talk about such things, but now the mere mention of them elicits a condescending smirk from the lowliest sophomore who reads little and knows less. And while it seems doubtful that such smirking is a sign of greater intelligence than Plato and Aristotle, it does indicate a collective consciousness that the attempt to use beauty to glorify intellect and its concepts of value leads to divided values and cannot make us happy."

"So in your view, the negation of beauty reflects our frustration with our own methods of describing value. We cannot be satisfied with a divided identity, but we also know at this point in history that it is impossible to use the force of resistance found in intellect to make value judgments about the goodness of beauty without producing divided results."

"We find ourselves in a bit of a dilemma at the end of the age," Smith observed. "We can hardly walk out of our houses on a winter night without experiencing a great longing as we gaze upon the beauty of the thick galaxies and far-flung stars—the same longing that leads to the attempt to obtain a transcendent identity through intellect and its capacity for judgment. But the divided value judgments seen in philosophy are incapable of satisfying this longing. The philosophers seemed like giants in their own time, but they all succumbed to foolishness in the end. Hegel wanted to be known as a 'superior man' because of his love of synthetic valuations, while Nietzsche thought he was a 'superman' because he was in love with pure resistance. They managed to conquer the world through their methods of describing value—but they divided its greatness between them."

"There was a last-ditch attempt to rescue beauty for philosophy through the 'Transcendental Aesthetic,' but this too led to divided values, since Kant's method is basically the same as Aristotle's."

"Actually it led to a far more serious problem than Aristotle because Kant tried to set aside the transcendent. Kant wanted to seem thoroughly modern and scientific. This is why he went out of his way to distance himself from the teleology of Aristotle and especially from Scholasticism, which led to dubious results in science. The old description of nature as a coming-together of intellectual and material causes seemed hopelessly out of step with the scientific naturalism of the modern age, which is why Kant threw up a firewall between Transcendentalism and any invocation of the transcendent as a means of accounting for the goodness of nature."

"Aristotle's concept of being began in the mind of the Supreme Being, but Kant made a great show of setting aside the transcendent being and describing a 'transcendental' synthesis that occurs in the mind for its own sake—a synthesis of its own concepts of being and the resistance to their limitations seen in Rationalism; a purely natural synthesis that does not require any direct reference to transcendent causes."

"Yes, but the problem with this purely natural synthesis is that it precludes any intimation of the good. Kant thought he could overcome the nothingness caused by Rationalism by setting aside the transcendent and seeking transcendental value judgments in the goodness of nature for its own sake—but the very concept of goodness begins to lose its significance as soon as we agree to set aside the transcendent, 'the good.'"

"Far from overcoming the problem of nothingness, the Transcendental Aesthetic made us more aware of it, leading directly to Nihilism and its antipathy to the good."

"Nothingness is not merely the result of methods rooted in pure judgment; it also reflects our own mortality. Synthetic methods cannot dispel our feelings of nothingness because of the great longing we were talking about before—the longing for a transcendent identity. Aristotle and his followers attempted to overcome the problem of nothingness by seeking knowledge of what is good in the goodness of nature, but nature is not the good. Nature is 'very good'—highly desirable for its own sake—but it is also mortal and cannot satisfy any transcendent longing."

"The synthetic method attempts to provide happiness by reconciling us to existence and the goodness of natural values—but this is impossible because we desire something more than what is seen in nature. We desire life."

"This is the fundamental flaw of the method. It attempts to make us happy with something that cannot satisfy our higher longings. It attempts to overcome the nothingness caused by Idealism by drawing transcendent value into existence, by making it immanent, but no immanent value can satisfy our desire for life. A howling storm—a thing of nature—can intimate transcendent value by reminding us of our limitations; but the transcendentalists cannot reconcile us to nature and also retain the power of the storm to intimate transcendence."

"The terror of the storm reminds us of our nothingness and the difference between existence and transcendent being; but then Transcendentalism deprives the storm of its dark pleasure by proposing a construct of nothingness and being."

"The Transcendentalists took the thunderer out of the storm by setting aside the transcendent. They tried to reconcile us to the storm, as if its pleasures were not beyond the pale of reason, but then reason turns the thunder pale and deprives it of its suggestive power. The synthetic method cannot make us happy by glorifying nature and attempting to reconcile us to present being when the thing we desire most is life. The Transcendental Aesthetic seemed impossibly exciting because Kant was a great writer, a great propagandist, and was able to conceal its limitations. But in execution it produced hopelessly tedious results that were not commensurate with the desire for life."

"So it seems the basic limitation of the synthetic method is that it tries to placate the very resistance that is essential to great pleasure."

"This is the resistance we experience in the tears of the 'Lacrymosa,'" Smith claimed, nodding toward the radio, on which Mozart's tenderhearted masterpiece happened to be playing at that very moment. "Transcendentalists want to dry our tears. They must overcome the tears that reflect a consciousness of our mortal limitations in order to convince us that it is possible to find what we are looking for in existent values—that 'the good' can be known to us through the beauty and functionality of nature. But there can be no doubt that the tears of the Lacrymosa are highly desirable, or that the most soulful music is found in the largos and adagios in their mournful minor keys."

"Those tears indicate our consciousness of the value of *life* and the resistance of this value to our own mortality. Therefore it is not desirable to suppress them."

"There is something refreshing about the hot tears that sometimes overcome us when we listen to sorrowful music. They etch our cheeks with their saltiness and leave us feeling cleansed and strangely satisfied. But the purpose of synthetic philosophy is to chase away those tears and make us conceited about our methods of judging value. According to Kant, it is possible to find what we desire by setting aside the transcendent and seeking knowledge of 'transcendental' values in the goodness of nature—but to set aside the transcendent is to give up the hot tears that flow from the difference between the immortal realm and our fleeting existence."

"All for a pot of porridge, as they say. In order to justify his concept of what is good, Kant must convince us to give up the resistance that reflects our consciousness of the value of life, the strange exaltation we often experience in tears. But then it is impossible to find the happiness we are looking for in his method."

"The philosophers staked their claim to greatness on the power of their methods to equip the will to obtain happiness—but this is precisely why philosophy cannot make us happy. We are mortal beings and cannot satisfy our desire for life through any power we ourselves have. It is possible to experience an ecstatic moment in the hot tears of the Lacrymosa, but this ecstasy has nothing to do with human will or how powerful we might imagine ourselves to be. In fact in order for those tears to be truly hot, they must spring forth from the reality of our limitations."

"They are hot for the very reason that they reflect a higher longing—a longing that cannot be satisfied by philosophy and its methods of judging value."

"We are mortal beings with immortal longings. All philosophers shared this longing; otherwise they would not have been so eager to obtain the exalted identity of philosopher. They pursued such an identity by glorifying their theories about the good; by trying to make us think they had discovered a method of obtaining this transcendent state of being. But if they really are masters of the good—transcendent beings—then they cannot enjoy the hot tears of the Lacrymosa, which indicate our mortal weakness."

"They cannot have the happiness they claim to have and also have hot tears. Those tears indicate that we have not obtained what we desire by our own means."

"The philosophers wanted us to believe it was possible to obtain the good of happiness through some method of thinking about value, of judging what is 'good,' but it is a paradox of human existence that the hot tears of the Lacrymosa must come against our will and better judgment in order to be truly ravishing. No one chooses willingly to experience the suffering that causes such tears to flow; but then it should be clear that the soulful pleasures of the Lacrymosa have nothing to do with the appearance of supreme self-possession and rationality affected by the philosophers."

"In order to have those pleasures, it is necessary to go beyond reason; to give up the vanity of self-possession for the possibility of obtaining something greater than what we see in philosophy."

"Philosophy and its methods of judging value lead to slavery to small and divided values," Smith declared. "Intellect is good, just as the philosophers said; indeed, its qualitative force of resistance is astonishing. But this same force of resistance divides it from the sensuous universe, which is also 'very good.' Thus any attempt to use intellect to determine what is good leads to divided values. The Transcendentalists felt a strong attraction to nature. They could not be satisfied with Rationalism because the love of pure intellect tends to minimize the goodness of nature."

"The Transcendentalists tried to reinstate nature by describing being as a coming-together of intellect and sense; but as soon as this coming-together comes into being, it negates the freedom found in intellect and its force of resistance."

"Constructive methods cannot make us happy because they enslave our concept of value to the goodness of that which already exists—and existence is a mortal value. Synthetic philosophers must attempt to read intellect and its ways of conceiving of value into nature in order to justify their concepts of what is good. Typically this effort leads to some form of causal reasoning, since happiness in men is an effect. A modern version of such reasoning is seen in the chemical aesthetic, which attempts to account for the great pleasures of music through molecular actions and reactions in the brain. This concept of value seems reasonable enough, since music is made of sounds and the brain is a physical thing; but it cannot account for the hot tears of the Lacrymosa, which indicate a highly desirable force of resistance in the mind."

"This resistance is *subjective*. Interpretation is a matter of vital importance in music and the pleasure it provides, and interpretation is not something that can be quantified or fixed precisely."

"By the relentless logic of the chemical aesthetic, it should be possible to guarantee great pleasure from the Lacrymosa by putting together the best-sounding players in the best-sounding hall and waiting to be ravished by their performance. But this is not the case. The point of the Lacrymosa is hot tears, and the truth is that a sensitive reading by the local choir might move us to tears more readily than the cold fiddling of a pack of indifferent virtuosi."

"Arvo Pärt said that Schubert's pen was part ink and mostly tears; and a conductor who is incapable of tears is unlikely to wring any great pleasure either from Schubert or the Lacrymosa, no matter how technically accomplished he might be."

"The chemical aesthetic cannot make us happy because it cannot incorporate subject and its force of resistance into its valuations. But of course this is just where the synthetic philosophers attempted to distinguish themselves from mere empiricism. They did not regard themselves as physical scientists; they were interested in metaphysics—in the good of happiness, which they attempted to ground in the goodness of nature. Happiness is a subjective value, which is why they found it necessary to incorporate subject and its capacity for resistance into their valuations. But subject cannot be fixed without depriving it of this highly desirable quality."

"The synthetic philosophers positioned themselves as lovers of freedom who had overthrown the tyrannical nothingness of pure intellect by rooting their concepts of value in sense, but this is impossible without equating 'the good' with specific, fixed values found in existence."

"No such valuation can make us happy because we are conscious of the value of life, which resists the desire to fix value within the mortal realm. This becomes clear as soon as we attempt to apply the synthetic method to the Lacrymosa because of the troublesome variable of interpretation. According to Kant, the Transcendental Aesthetic has the power to furnish authoritative 'judgments about taste.' Synthetic methods lend themselves to speculation about aesthetics because aesthetics are the actual content of art. But the only way to obtain a 'judgment about taste' with regard to the Lacrymosa is to identify an authoritative interpretation—in short, to overcome the potential of subject for resistance to the limitations of existent values."

"The very process of seeking such a judgment requires us to put a limit on this variable and specify a particular interpretation as the authoritative one. And the obvious problem with this approach is that different people like different interpretations."

"The grandiosity of the Transcendental Aesthetic reflects our consciousness of the value of life. We desire an identity that reflects this great value, and we are infatuated with intellect and its capacity for judgment because it seems to have the power to distinguish us and provide such an identity. But it is impossible to obtain an immortal identity through our methods of judging value when we ourselves are mortal beings. The desire to make 'judgments about taste' is linked to identity—to what we like and the vain desire to see our pleasures enshrined in the larger culture—but then it is impossible to obtain what we desire through intellect and its capacity for judgment, since different men have different pleasures and different notions about what is good."

"Judgment appears to have the power to render us an immortal identity through its dividing power, but in reality it does nothing more than reveal our dividedness."

"It is a strange fact of existence that two music lovers can sit and listen to the same performance and have widely divergent reactions to what they hear. Transcendentalism led to the celebration of 'organic' values in art and the resistance of nature to the emphasis on form seen in Neoclassicism. Those who identify with the concept of organic values may gravitate to interpretations of the Lacrymosa that are more fluid; that resist the tyranny of formalism by emphasizing a strong legato and sense of gesture, as seen in the Romantic conductors. But there also aficionados of Karajan and Bernstein and their dynamism; and now there is the period performance movement, which gives the nod to authentic instruments and smaller forces with faster tempi and greater clarity."

"It is impossible to overcome the differences between these warring factions by attempting to identify one single recording of the *Requiem* as the ideal. The Internet is full of this sort of thing," I admitted.

"Hence the larger premise of the Transcendental Aesthetic—that it is capable of furnishing a transcendent identity through its capacity to render authoritative 'judgments about taste'—is nothing but a pipe dream. We are finite beings, and such methods make us slaves of our own limitations. But neither does the Transcendental Aesthetic seem to have much *practical* use, frankly. We know it is impossible to identify a performance of the Lacrymosa that is ideal for all men, but the method also seems to lack the power to identify such a performance for *ourselves*. We can make a good case, by the light of the Transcendental Aesthetic, for the Walter recording with the Philharmonic, since he was one of the last of the great Romantic conductors—actually knew composers from that era and studied with them. Nor would it be difficult to make the argument that his conducting style represents a middle ground between, say, the totalitarianism of Toscanini and the excessively sensuous gestures of a Mendelberg—the golden mean that Aristotle and his followers recommended."

"It is possible to make such determinations and to support them with sound reasons—but this does not mean we will always be able to obtain great pleasure from the performance that we ourselves have singled out as the ideal."

"We cause two problems for ourselves though our eagerness to make such value judgments. First, the very fact that we have singled out a particular recording as our exalted ideal may make it difficult for us to enjoy it as much as we would like. It seems we are not able to evade the poisonous influence of vanity even in the small task of choosing a favorite recording for ourselves. As soon as we have done so, we find ourselves investing our designated favorite with transcendent significance; and then it becomes impossible for us not to become aware of its limitations."

"We use the recording to justify ourselves and our likes and dislikes, but no recording can measure up to our desire for life."

"The second problem we cause ourselves is that we close ourselves off to other possibilities through the value judgments that we make. As soon as I talk myself into believing that I have identified the ideal recording of the Lacrymosa, I find myself in a position of having to support this decision by discounting all others. The choice I have made becomes personal, a matter of identity, but then this choice also makes me defensive and prevents me from being open to other possibilities; from maintaining the vulnerability that is absolutely necessary to the hot tears of the Lacrymosa."

"It becomes difficult to remain open to experiencing something new when we are still clinging to that old, familiar thing."

"I am often reminded of this through the glorious anonymity of the radio," Smith noted. "I rarely know the identity of the performer I hear murmuring away in the background, and this can be the cause of a good deal of foolishness, for I often find myself enthralled by a certain performance only to discover that it was by someone I had been in the habit of dismissing as bit of a lightweight to all of my friends and relations."

"The same thing happens to me," I said with a laugh. "The desire to make such judgments is linked to vanity, which is why they deprive us of the happiness we seek."

"The anonymity of the radio affords us the freedom to put aside the problem of identity and react to the music on its own terms. It strips away the armor of judgment and makes us vulnerable again to the hot tears of the Lacrymosa. And such freedom should be precious to us, now that we have become fully aware of the limitations of our methods of judging value. At one time we thought that the Transcendental Aesthetic had the power to make us happy, but now it seems all such methods of judging value have lost their power to beguile us. The only way to restore great pleasure is to go beyond the love of judgment seen in philosophy and reclaim the freedom we willingly threw away."

Smith swallowed the remainder of his brandy. I did the same, surprised at where the blizzard had taken us and wondering what exactly he had in mind by "going beyond."

Chapter 2

Absolute Dilemma

Because of course Nietzsche *also* talked about "going beyond." Apparently Smith was aware of this ambiguity and pounced on an innocent little comment I made the very next time I went there to assure me that he was no more impressed with the modern age and its worship of the will to power than with Transcendentalism.

It was a cold and sunny afternoon in February, and I had to knock six-foot icicles off the gutter before I was able to squeeze through the porch door, stopping first to admire the lucid rainbows of color. Smith seemed phlegmatic, as if the raw weather had affected his blood flow. A glass of sherry did nothing to break the chill, so I tried to jump-start the conversation by bringing up a vintage recording of *Don Giovanni* that had recently appeared in my mailbox.

"The genius of the composer has never seemed so clear to me before," I chirped, hoping to pick up on the salubrious vibrations of our previous discussion.

"Genius," Smith snorted inexplicably.

"What—you don't think Mozart was a genius?" I said with some surprise.

"I'm sure he was, but frankly there is hardly anything in this old world that bores me more than its geniuses. We have just suffered through an entire age of self-proclaimed geniuses and intellectuals and other freaks of nature; one would think the interminable dreariness of it all might have cured us of such droll enthusiasms."

"You're suggesting there is something wrong with genius?"

"Nothing except our insufferable vanity," he replied with a chuckle. "The word 'genius' indicates transcendent value and is used to make us think highly of ourselves and our favorites—but there is something troubling about this value when we encounter it in a Don Giovanni. Apparently 'genius' can be cold and unforgiving; genius can be nasty and cynical and bloodthirsty."

"Don Giovanni is an evil genius. So genius, in itself, is value-neutral."

"The transcendent glow that attaches itself to the word *genius* used to reflect a consciousness of the difference between divine intellect and our own foolish existence, between a gracious immortal realm and the littleness of men. But after negating transcendent being, the superman forgot to be modest and appropriated the word 'genius' for himself. Hence Mozart, the prototypical genius, is depicted in modern iconography as a brilliant wastrel who cared for nothing but himself and selfish pleasures—his art, his carousing, his apotheosis—a Dionysus whose will to dominate is said to have been intimated in the mocking, rapacious Don."

"Not a very appealing figure, at least in the mind of Hollywood. Giovanni is a genius among fools, according to Shaw; unfortunately he is also a cold, cruel man who thinks nothing of destroying the happiness of others in order to gratify his desires. And this puts a certain limit on the desirability of his genius."

"The measure of genius in the superman is based on the will to power and the negation of the good, which also negates such values as pity and kindness as well as simple common decency and respect for others. But then the soulfulness of those values prevents him from obtaining the transcendent identity he desires. Now of course Mozart followed the old morality tale and gave his evil genius a comeuppance in the end, thus announcing himself to be on the side of love and kindness. But to the followers of Nietzsche, Don Giovanni was a prototype of the superman and worthy to be praised."

"Mozart condemned the evil genius by packing him off to hell with the wail of trombones, but the demise of God led to a change in our view of Giovanni, as seen just a few years later in Byron. The sensuous don has become a hero, and his heroism is based on resistance to any thought of 'the good' or goodness."

"Byron and Shelley openly identified with Milton's Satan, whose genius for resistance seemed preferable to the highly formalized conception of the good seen in Idealism and its icy Northern stepchild, Puritanism. In the modern age, genius became associated with absolute resistance to 'the good' and the dividedness of this value as described by the philosophers. But 'the good' also entails goodness, which is rooted in the value of life and not intellect—and it is impossible to obtain a transcendent identity through resistance to goodness. Giovanni's genius is predicated on his skill as a despoiler of women. Those who despoil women in order to gratify selfish desires obtain the status of superman by defying 'the good' and the concept of morality known as goodness; but the misery they visit upon others through their selfishness prevents them from obtaining a transcendent identity because we are conscious of the value of life."

"'Genius' indicates a transcendent force of resistance, and in Nihilism this became translated into absolute resistance to the good. But then genius loses its transcendent significance in the modern age, since the value of goodness in our relations with others is self-evident."

"The superman overthrew Transcendentalism and its synthesis of being and nothingness by clinging to Nihilism, or nothingness itself, but he could not overcome the dividedness of philosophy. He could not go beyond good and evil through absolute resistance to 'the good' because the negation of the good results in evil. Nihilism was supposed to be something new, but it has the same limitation as all identities rooted in a love of resistance: it negates existent values. Plato founded Idealism on the beauty of nature, a great and gracious value, but his first love was intellect and its force of resistance—which intimates the possibility of obtaining absolute values—and totalizing this resistance as pure intellect leads to the negation of nature as well as all existent beauty."

"Plato claimed that the force of resistance found in unhappiness was a sign of the good, an absolute value, and that it was possible to obtain the good by totalizing this resistance; but if the good of happiness is pure resistance, then the only way to obtain it is to negate all existent values—which leads to nothingness and not 'the good' or any undivided value."

"The same problem is seen in Descartes. He lived in an age when Scholasticism was in its dotage and inciting disgust and irreverence through its ornate constructs of being. Like Plato, he was a lover of resistance and absolute values, but he knew he had to go beyond Idealism if he wanted to be taken seriously. The attempt to revive Idealism in the Renaissance had failed, while the discoveries of Copernicus and Galileo were beginning to make Plato's cosmology seem quaint and old-fashioned. But the new science provided Descartes with a way to recast the love of resistance as a tool for obtaining a pristine scientific understanding of being."

"Pure intellect was supposed to make us happy by cutting the Gordian knot of Scholastic metaphysics and producing clear scientific value judgments. But pure intellect is incapable of furnishing any substantive value judgments about transcendent being in its own right because it is nothing more than a force of resistance."

"Like Plato, Descartes thought that the transcendent being was intellect in its essence and that pure intellect had the power to reveal the imprint of this being on nature and make us happy by sanctifying our thought-existence. He claimed to be able to use intellect and its force of resistance to reform science by shining its doubting power upon Scholasticism and its metaphysical constructs of being. But linking transcendent being to the resistance of intellect to the limitations of its own constructs of being leads to nothingness because of the difference between that force of resistance and existent values."

"Some sort of construct of intellect and sense is necessary in order to overcome that difference and arrive at any positive conclusion about being, and the cogito was specifically designed to resist all such constructs by linking its doubting power to being itself. This is why Kant suggested setting aside the transcendent in order to overcome the nothingness produced by the cogito—which opened the door for the 'blond beast' and the concept of absolute resistance to being itself."

"Nihilism *seemed* different from Idealism and Rationalism because it negated 'the good'—but it is rooted in the same love of resistance and absolute values. It is based on the concept that absolute resistance to the good has the power to produce transcendent value, which is an inversion of Idealism, but it leads to the same nothingness as Idealism by negating goodness itself as well as the goodness of existent values. Our supermen are more puritanical than the most rabid Puritan. They hate storytelling because it implies being; they hate representation because it indicates value in things that have nothing to do with the will to power; they shun melody, harmony and rhythm because they are opposed to the notion that any existent value can be 'good'; why, some of them have risen to such an exalted level of resistance that they even claim to hate the pleasures of nature!"

"Nihilism must attempt to negate the goodness of such things in order to justify its negative ideal of absolute resistance to the good—but it is impossible to obtain a transcendent identity through resistance to the goodness that actually exists."

"Existence is a mixed value because we are living beings who are conscious of the value of life. We recognize that life is good—absolutely desirable for its own sake—and therefore we are also aware of the evil or dividedness of mortal existence. This mixed value cannot make us happy, but any attempt to obtain happiness by negating it results in nothingness. Just as Plato attempted to obtain the putative happiness of pure intellect by negating the mixture of intellect and matter he thought he saw in existence, so Nietzsche tried to obtain what appeared to him to be the transcendent value of pure existence by negating any thought of 'the good,' an immortal being. But the negation of 'the good' does not result in supermen or knowledge of transcendent value because it is impossible to negate our consciousness of the value of life."

"Instead it produces an age of anxiety by making men aware of their nothingness. Nietzsche thought negating 'being' and 'the good' would liberate the overman from the bondage of Transcendentalism, but it resulted in a new form of slavery because nothingness for its own sake is a highly divided value."

"All methods rooted in resistance lead to a loss of freedom in the end—to totalitarianism—because pure resistance is pure form. And this is ironic, since their initial appeal is usually based on extravagant promises of freedom. Idealism was supposed to liberate the philosopher from the murkiness that resulted from attempting to blend intellect with sense, form with matter; but its celebration of pure form leads to the rigid behaviors described in the *Republic*. And the superman was based on a similar promise of freedom. Anyone who turns from Hegel to the *Will to Power* will immediately see why Nietzsche became popular—the clarity of the master's prose provides a refreshing break from the 'science of logic' and its incomprehensible ratios of being. But the same love of nothingness that liberated the superman from Transcendentalism and its construct of value also enslaved him to a rigid antipathy to being."

"He had to totalize nothingness in order to obtain the appearance of a transcendent identity; he had to annihilate any thought of the goodness of being, which was the subject of traditional philosophy. This is why Nihilism led to such gray monstrosities as Existentialism in the end and the notion that the overman finds nature to be repulsive."

"If such gloomy creatures really do exist, then they should be in asylums, since the beauty of nature is obvious. And it is worth noting that this was not what Nietzsche had in mind. Nihilism was not supposed to negate the value of nature; it was supposed to restore it in a purer way by purging the mind of Transcendentalism. But Nietzsche did not anticipate the collateral damage of his love of resistance. In his mind, Nihilism would enable the superman to dance in the shining fields of Elysium and recapture the joyfulness he attributed to man in his natural state, before the philosophers and religionists came along and loaded him down with guilt and a lot of false talk about the good."

"For some reason it did not occur to him that absolute resistance to the good also negates the goodness of existent values."

"Nihilism cannot make us happy by negating 'the good' because the word *good* indicates more than the concept of 'the good' seen in philosophy. In its purest sense, it simply indicates that which is desirable; therefore by negating the good, Nietzsche inadvertently negated desirability as well. He was right about philosophy and its descriptions of 'the good': they were based on divided pleasures and not any transcendent value. Plato was in love with pure intellect, with the very concept of its purity and the freedom it provided from fatiguing constructs of value, while Aristotle was in love with nature and the concept that it is possible to overcome the nothingness of pure intellect by describing the good as a ratio of intellectual and material causes. But the fact that their descriptions of 'the good' were hopelessly divided does not mean that goodness does not exist; and the attempt to obtain a transcendent identity by negating the good cannot lead to transcendent results when there is a great deal of goodness in existent values."

"The goodness of nature stands as a rebuke to the overman and his attempt to annihilate any thought of the good. But you believe that the concepts of 'the good' seen in philosophy deserved to be negated because they reflected little more than one's own pleasures; in fact that the guiding spirit of philosophy was vanity and not 'the good.'"

"The self-serving nature of philosophy was concealed somewhat in the past through the devotion to 'the good' described by Plato and Aristotle, a value that is clearly not the same thing as themselves—although it could be seen in such odious notions as the four metals. But it began to surface in the modern era through the cogito, which shifted the focus of philosophy from the mind of God to the minds of men; and it became quite obvious when we agreed to set aside the transcendent and glorify human genius for its own sake—when men tried to turn themselves into 'superior men' by synthesizing being with nothingness or 'supermen' by using nothingness to negate being."

"And this is what troubles you about the modern infatuation with the word 'genius.' Men are too full of themselves. We do not believe in guardian spirits anymore; when we talk about Mozart's genius, we quite literally mean a power found in Mozart himself."

"According to Mozart, the genius of music is 'love, love, love,' not intellect. But not everyone is as humble as Mozart. Descartes lighted the bonfire seen in the modern enthusiasm for 'genius' by changing the focus of philosophy from the good of happiness to the attempt to find happiness in good science—a seismic change that magnified the philosopher and his ability to think. In Greek philosophy, 'the good' is an omnipresent force that directs all thought upwards and makes our own minds seem relatively small and weak in comparison. But good science is not so far off—or at least it did not seem that way to Descartes, who had no concept of the difficulties that would emerge."

"The earth-shattering discoveries of Galileo made him feel optimistic that it was possible to obtain a perfect scientific understanding of being; and since he believed that the universe reflected the invisible qualities of the creator, it seemed to him that such knowledge would lead to the happiness of knowing the mind of God."

"It was an age of great optimism about the potential of science to make men happy," Smith agreed. "Descartes and Bacon and Newton and Locke all started with the same premise—that science had the power to redeem human existence by overcoming the limitations of philosophy and its divided descriptions of the good. Copernicus had proven that Scholasticism produces false value judgments about nature by attempting to mix science with metaphysics, and his discoveries were so cosmic in scope that they gave birth to the notion that science had the power to provide enlightenment and happiness by directly disclosing the nature of transcendent being, without the help of syllogisms."

"This giddy optimism is seen at the beginning of Descartes' book, where he claims that the new science has the power to go beyond the old divide between 'synthetic and analytic methods.' But his faith in the redemptive power of science was misguided, since his love of pure judgment also led to divided results—as seen, for instance, in the difference between his own analytical geometry and Newton's synthetic geometry."

"Descartes' infatuation with intellect and its capacity for resistance led to the same divided results in 'natural philosophy' as in classical philosophy; but at the same time his willingness to set aside the good for the sake of good science also introduced a certain coldness into the cogito and its celebration of human genius that was not evident in the ancients. According to Descartes, it is possible to obtain knowledge of transcendent being by using intellect to acid-test all constructs of value—but this hardheaded concept of philosophy is nothing like the smiling humanism seen in Castiglioni or Erasmus or the enchanted notions of being produced by Scholasticism."

"'Genius' begins to lose its gracious connotation and becomes associated with the hypercritical attitude seen in modern science."

"Kant compounded the problem by setting aside the transcendent. The pursuit of knowledge of transcendent value was no longer directly linked to a gracious transcendent being in the Transcendental Aesthetic but was said to occur purely in the human mind for its own sake. The constructive method is rather cool by nature; much of its appeal derives from the contrast it draws between its moderate method of reasoning and the nothingness that results from Idealism and its fiery force of resistance. This coolness is evident in Aristotle as well as Thomas—but it became a salient quality of Transcendentalism after Kant set aside the transcendent."

"The possibility of ecstasy implicit in Aristotle and Thomas and their forthright pursuit of the good is lost as the method is used in an attempt to obtain a purely objective construct of being in the mind per se; of its own concepts of being and its capacity for resistance to the limitations of those value judgments."

"There was still room for warmth in the notion of genius in the Transcendental Aesthetic because Kant did not negate transcendent being or its graciousness. Quite the opposite—setting aside the transcendent was a ruse for reintroducing it in a new way. In fact 'genius' is simply a positive assonance in the mind to the goodness of nature, according to Kant, which makes it subordinate to transcendent being and its graciousness. The age of Romanticism inspired by Kant was capable of a great deal of graciousness because it was rooted in the goodness of nature, a value that was believed to reflect a benevolent Creator; but all warmth disappeared from philosophy and the notion of genius when Nietzsche decided to negate the good and seek transcendence in the will to power."

"This value explicitly excludes the possibility of graciousness."

"Hegel had failed to overcome the unhappiness of existence through his synthesis of being and nothingness, so Nietzsche took up nothingness for its own sake and claimed that it was possible to transform ourselves into supermen by annihilating any thought of being. Nihilism was supposed to burn away the fog of metaphysics and produce a race of jolly Dionysuses for whom nature was perfectly natural and who were happy for the very reason that they did not waste their time fretting over the difference between transcendent being and themselves. But the negation of 'being' produced exactly the opposite effect because men are mortal beings and cannot be happy with their own mortality."

"The grave is a fairly frosty habitation, which may account for the cold quality of 'genius' as it is encountered in the modern age."

"Nietzsche annihilated Transcendentalism and its devotion to being by taking up the same sword of evolution that Hegel had used to prop up his scientific synthesis and turning it against him. Hegel knew he had to find some way to justify his claim that being is a synthetic value without resorting to the teleology of Aristotle and Thomas, which by his time had been widely discredited, since it produced divided values and conflicted with the modern enthusiasm for science. His way of setting aside any explicit teleology was to tap into the evolutionary currents that had begun to swirl at the end of the Enlightenment through the concept of the great chain of being."

"Lucretius became popular again as the cognoscenti began to cast about for naturalistic ways to account for the existence of the universe, and Hegel exploited these currents to describe the synthesis in evolutionary terms."

"He was not interested in the old description of being as a synthesis of intellectual and material causes. Instead the Absolute Idea was said to be precipitating an evolution in our *understanding* of being and drawing us to itself by overturning all limited constructs of value. The nothingness produced by Rationalism was characterized as nothing more than our consciousness of the resistance of the Absolute Idea to the limitations of those constructs. Hegel claimed it was possible to supersede it by recognizing that the process of obtaining knowledge of being was evolutionary and incorporating nothingness into a new kind of synthesis as itself—a synthesis of nothingness and being. But then Darwin came along and provided relief from the prohibitive difficulties produced by the 'scientific synthesis' by describing a new kind of evolution that appeared to lead to desirable results without having to invoke transcendent being at all."

"Darwin's method seemed to validate nothingness itself, as opposed to 'being.' And since Hegel's description of being had failed to make us happy, in fact was almost impossible to understand, it was easy for Nietzsche to turn evolution against it by using Darwin to justify Nihilism, or the annihilation of being."

"Darwin attributed the goodness of the species and all existent values to the survival of the fittest, not to the creative power of a transcendent being. This clever phrase suggested a certain vitality and strength to ears that had become weary of the ephemeral metaphysics produced by Transcendentalism. It also intimated a transcendent value found in nature itself that could be used to pursue happiness—which Nietzsche rendered in philosophical terms as the will to power."

"This value was supposed to make us happy by purging the mind of the pale cast of thought caused by the scientific synthesis as it attempted to mediate between being and nothingness."

"Synthetic methods decrease the power of subject by relegating it to the role of observer—which led to a crescendo of complaints in Nietzsche's day about the loss of 'personality' in Transcendentalism. The will to power seemed to provide a perfect antidote to this passivity and sense of helplessness. According to Nietzsche, it is possible to go beyond Transcendentalism and its paralyzing ratios of being, its fully determined values, fixed by existence itself, by embracing nothingness and seeking a transcendent identity in the will to dominate, just as this same will appeared to be responsible for the great values found in nature."

"But then 'genius,' in the overman, becomes explicitly linked to the will to dominate, a coldhearted value. It is not the transcendent value that our overmen would have us believe because it excludes the graciousness of the good."

"In the past, domination was left to the dominus. Philosophers had the freedom to be gracious and exhibit a good deal of warmth because they were not compelled to try to justify themselves through domination per se. Nietzsche's favorite god made no attempt to dominate—he left that odious burden to the thunderer. Indeed, it is his lack of a will to dominate that makes him seem so carefree and appealing. But if we negate the dominus and our faith in its ability to justify existence, then it becomes necessary for us to take up the mantle of domination ourselves in order to obtain a desirable identity."

"At which point the coldness of our concept of genius becomes evident. The overman must annihilate any thought of being or the good and dominate those who have the temerity to see goodness in nature in order to justify his identity."

"The superman predicated his domination of the 'superior man' on absolute resistance to transcendent being and the good; but this reveals the limitations of his notion of genius, since nature is in fact 'very good,' and it is impossible to account for this goodness without invoking transcendent being. Our modern geniuses often find themselves in the impossible position of attempting to deny that nature really is good, as was seen in the Existentialists and is now also seen among the Neo-Darwinists; but then the self-evident goodness of nature becomes the natural limit of their genius for resistance and their claim to have obtained transcendent status through pure naturalism."

"Darwin was fully aware of the problem of beauty and what it implies," I concurred. "In fact in one sense the whole purpose of his book was to try to explain how the beauty of the species could have come into existence without the help of a transcendent being. He attributed this strange phenomenon to the power of sex—supposedly wild creatures have the ability to select the most beautiful mate, and therefore beauty makes them more fit for breeding. But nature's creatures do not exhibit any such lofty capacity for discernment, as he himself admitted in his prologue."

"No power to discern beauty is evident in the animal kingdom. Left to their own devices, domestic animals seem perfectly happy to forsake the beauty that men breed into them and revert to a less differentiated form. And Darwin stumbled into the realm of the ridiculous when he attempted to use sex to explain the beauty of inanimate things. The mysterious force of aesthetic attraction that he attributed to nature was used to account for the beauty of trees, as if bees were little Rembrandts, painting the forests with their waxen thighs."

"Such a poetic affinity between bees and trees seems highly unlikely, in spite of onomatopoeia," I agreed.

"The very absurdity of these rationalizations has led to their suppression. No longer is Darwin permitted to speak for himself; his love of beauty and faith in the power of nature to produce the goodness seen in the species by its own means are strangely absent from the official retelling of the story. The poetic warmth of 'natural selection' has been supplanted by the survival of the fittest and the need to negate any implication of the goodness of nature in order to justify the prevailing cultural identity."

"So Nietzsche tried to restore the pleasures of nature by wiping away the cold abstractions of Transcendentalism, but in reality the will to power added a frigid quality to intellect and the modern notion of genius."

"In order to justify their belief that the will to power has transcendent value, our supermen find it necessary to claim that existence is nothing more than a desperate struggle to survive and nature nothing more than a bleak contest for domination—in short, that graciousness does not exist. But this is not what we see when we actually look at nature. For one thing, nature is overwhelmingly beautiful. Beauty is a gracious value, and there is nothing in the creation story of the superman that can account for the beauty of nature. Nor is the will to power as evident in the animal kingdom as our supermen would have us believe. No desperate struggle for domination is seen in the graceful deer as she grazes in our meadows in the evening hours, or the butterfly as it flutters about our bushes, or the magnificently lazy turtle, or the fat woodchuck basking in the sun near his den."

"What about the shark?" I said.

"The shark may come closest to the concept of existence seen in the superman," Smith admitted. "Let him swim with the sharks, then; he has enough blood on his hands. The clever sages of the Zeitgeist are resisting the inference of design by exclaiming over the 'horror' of the natural world—a new form of Platonism that seeks to demonize nature in order to deprive it of transcendent resonance. But they are fighting a rear-guard action. Design is not Dasein, and nature cannot be made to fit the value judgments men use to flatter themselves and their genius. The tender patience with which the robin feeds her young can supply a powerful identity to the imagination, but it is not the identity of the superman. Many different identities might be adduced from the playfulness of the cub, the swallow's fantastic indulgence of flight, the beaver's ingenuity, the swiftness of the eagle, the fastidiousness of the raccoon—not merely the will to power. And in fact even the shark and the lion do not make any apparent attempt to dominate. They kill only to eat; there is no other significance to their actions."

"The will to power is found in men, who use it to overcome their nothingness, but it is not found in the animal kingdom as itself; and the attempt to read it into the behavior of the shark and lion amounts to a pathetic fallacy. So your point here is that the gracious pleasures of nature indicate the limitations of the overman and his resistance to the good and prevent him from obtaining the transcendent identity he desires. But then would you consider yourself to be some sort of creationist?"

"I would consider myself to be someone who is looking for freedom from the vanity of our excessive love of intellect and the small value judgments this love produces," Smith replied with a sigh.

"But this freedom cannot be found in creationism, I take it?"

He shrugged. "Too often creationism seems to go hand-in-hand with the same antipathy to nature as is now seen among the Neo-Darwinists. They appear to be bitter enemies but are quite similar in one respect—their theories of value reflect a love of pure judgment and absolute values. And this is probably why they are both attracted to the question of origins. Now according to Kant, such questions have nothing to do with science, since origins cannot actually be observed. But a consuming interest in origins leads to a more serious problem in our pursuit of knowledge and concepts of value because it is often linked to some form of dualism."

"It reflects the trope of the golden age," I suggested. "In this view, there was a time when things were much simpler than they are now, which makes it seem possible to regain that simple happiness by negating the complications of existence."

"The prime example of this type of storytelling was Plato himself. He claimed that the good was intellect, and that we were happy as long as our souls were merged with the universal intellectual soul. Supposedly those souls lost their purity and became unhappy when they were mixed with matter—which suggests the possibility of restoring the purity of our original state through the power of intellect to negate existent values."

"Plato's love of pure value judgments and simplicity results in dualism. In his view, intellect is good and the material realm is evil."

"The same result is seen in both Neo-Darwinism and Creationism," Smith claimed. "Both reflect a strong desire for simple stories and simple valuations—thus both lead to dualism. Creationism has the effect of miniaturizing the act of creation and making it seem small and manageable, not unlike the Cartesian coordinates. Too often it uses the simplicity of the origin story, which is soulful, which is poetic and large, to resist the complications of existence and produce a harsh theology in which there is very little soulfulness at all. It totalizes this resistance in order to justify absolutism and the characterization of God as a force of pure resistance to existent values—but then it has the strange effect of negating the value of the universe that God himself has made."

"It attempts to glorify God by devaluing his handiwork," I said with a laugh. "The type of theology seen in creationism often indicates that nature was idyllic in its original state and became totally depraved after the fall. This simplifies matters considerably, but only by introducing a highly restrictive concept of value. But in what sense is Neo-Darwinism dualistic?"

"In the sense that the Neo-Darwinists now find themselves compelled to try to convince us that nature is evil; in the sense that the love of resistance to 'the good' enshrined in Nihilism leads to a need to negate the self-evident goodness of nature. There was a time when the followers of Darwin clung to his own sunny outlook and claimed that evolution was rising upward to transcendence and happiness; that nature was essentially good and would lead to good ends. But there is a problem with this optimistic view because the goodness of nature cannot be assumed from the postulates of naturalism."

"That goodness seemed axiomatic to Darwin, probably because he lived in an age that almost worshipped nature. But if we take the axiom that nature is good out of Darwinism, we are left with a very different view of physical reality—a view that is necessarily devoid of goodness."

"Darwin's naturalism was supposed to make us happy—turn us all into Dionysus—but the wars and horrors of the twentieth century tended to sour this shimmering expectation. It became necessary to reexamine Darwin's axiom in order to perpetuate his origins story, which is the basis of Modernism; and an honest reexamination, as seen in such proponents of Neo-Darwinism as Gould, leads to the inevitable conclusion that Darwin was unnecessarily optimistic. There is no reason to assume that nature is good in any sense of the word if 'the good' quite literally does not exist, nor is there any good reason to assume that evolution is leading naturally to a happier, more desirable result."

"The dualism produced by Neo-Darwinism is seen in its purely negative view of the value of nature. Not only is nature not 'good,' but a frank negation of the good leads to a tendency to describe it as something that is positively evil."

"The prevailing view today seems to be that nature is devoid of any intrinsic goodness and often evil, but that it is possible to use the analytical tools supplied by Neo-Darwinism to expose its shortcomings and thereby to eradicate them by rational means—as is seen in so-called evolutionary psychology. But then Neo-Darwinism leads to a very similar view of nature as is seen among many Creationists. And the reason for this is that a love of pure resistance and absolute values leads naturally to an attempt to negate the mixed values that actually exist."

"So to sum up, the problem with philosophy in your view is that it is rooted in a love of judgment, which the philosophers use in a futile attempt to build up themselves and their concepts of value at the expense of others. Transcendentalism, Neo-Darwinism, Creationism—all of these identities reflect the dividing power of judgment itself, and therefore they themselves are highly divided."

"The value judgments seen in philosophy are divided because they are rooted in divided loves. It is not known why Plato was in love with pure intellect or why Aristotle was attracted to constructs of value, but these divided loves became translated directly into their theories of value. Philosophy is dead and cannot be revived because we have seen the limitations of its value judgments. But it may still be possible to go beyond the dividedness of philosophy—by seeking knowledge of value in a greater power than intellect and its divided loves; in 'love itself,' as Augustine called this power in order to distinguish it from mortal loves."

"The way to go beyond the limitations of philosophy, in your view, is to give up the dividedness and unhappiness caused by philosophy and its excessive love of intellect and explore the transcendent possibilities of love for its own sake, as indicated by the formulation *deus caritas est*."

"This is the power revealed through desirability, the power that accounts for goodness. And it is of a different order of power from the divided loves seen in philosophy because sense and intellect are both 'very good'—because it is sense that enables us to enjoy the goodness of nature, and because it is intellect that makes happiness possible through its consciousness of this goodness. And only this power can provide the freedom we are looking for and cannot find in philosophy. It does not compel us to give up what we love, as if we could help being who we are; nor does it compel us to divide our concepts of value between Plato and Aristotle and Nietzsche. All that it prohibits is the attempt to use intellect and its force of judgment to glorify ourselves."

"Which makes 'love itself' rather hard," I observed with a chuckle.

"The intrinsic graciousness of this value goes against the very marrow of our divided existence," Smith agreed. "And yet it is the only hope left to those who have not given up hope and are still looking for happiness. Philosophy has begun to seem like a foolish dream to us now. It is no longer possible to believe that Plato or Aristotle or Descartes or Kant is as great as they once seemed because we are fully conscious of their limitations; and Nietzsche will soon be added to the list of the once-great by the dismal failure of Nihilism to provide a transcendent identity. Philosophy is dead—but we can find a way out of the wilderness we created for ourselves by giving up our excessive love of intellect for the sake of something greater."

Chapter 3

What Kind of Sign?

All of which seemed to be trending in a particular direction, but I was perplexed by Smith's apparently dismissive attitude toward the religious impulse. Did he feel it was no more capable of providing happiness and a reason to live than philosophy?

In any case, he looked positively ruddy when I dropped in on him one fine afternoon late in the blustery month of March. There are few things he loves more than gardening, and he informed me, rather proudly, that he had just finished planting a row of peas in the rustic vegetable garden he kept out back.

"Isn't it too soon for that?" I said. "I don't see how the frost could be out of the ground yet, with the winter we've just had."

"Oh, the ground is still quite cold and wet," he agreed as he carried the pot of tea he had brewed out to the porch. "I will probably lose them, but it was such a mild day that I couldn't resist. Besides, you have to plant early if you want peas on the Fourth of July. I mean real peas—not those Chinese abominations."

"You seem unusually cheerful for someone who expects to be defeated by nature," I told him. "I assume you've found something better than the overman or absolutism to sustain you in your struggle with our famously stingy soil."

"To tell you the truth, I did have an interesting experience last night; a sort of baptism or easement against nature and her unforgiving laws, of which I received confirmation in my morning labors."

"At vespers?" I said, becoming interested.

He nodded. "I was feeling somewhat oppressed as I sat there dully in my pew—by the mocking insubstantiality of words. It occurred to me that there is a strange force of resistance built into words. Oh, we think we can make them serve us and glorify our methods of judging value; that is what keeps us going—the perennially unrewarded hope of obtaining a desirable identity through the power of words. But the goal for which we are striving is like a mirage that seems to recede as fast as we approach. In the end we begin to realize there is something strange about the words we pour into our methods of describing value. We are not able to appropriate their power to our divided ends—make it serve our love of judgment—because that power does not belong to us any more than it belongs to those who happen to have other pleasures."

"I take it the sermon was not terribly edifying. But this goes back to your belief that method is rooted in divided desires. We sense a great power in words, but for some reason we are not able to harness that power into the divided streams of judgment."

"No, and we find this frustrating. 'Beauty,' for example, is a word that indicates great pleasure, and on that basis we have no doubt about what it means. But its significance becomes maddeningly elusive as soon as we attempt to appropriate that pleasurable power for ourselves and our methods of describing value, as in Idealism, where Socrates strains to turn beauty into something it can never be. We use method in an attempt to capture the power signified by a word such as 'beauty'—a power that is not our own—and use it to adorn ourselves with a transcendent identity; but this vanity comes between us and the real power or significance of the word and deprives us of great pleasure."

"Now you sound like one of our Postmodernists," I said laughing. "Are you saying our words are merely signs of divided pleasures?"

"The significance of a word such as 'beauty' is established through desirability, an undivided power in itself, but it becomes a sign of divided desires when we use it to glorify ourselves and our concepts of value. This dividedness was seen in philosophy and its value judgments about the good, leading to Nihilism in the end and the notion of absolute resistance to the good, through which the goodness of beauty is negated. But beauty is left over as itself from the demise of philosophy. The philosophers have negated beauty in order to justify their love of judgment, but the beauty of nature is self-evident. Thus the word 'beauty' has *two* meanings for us now. It still signifies the great pleasures of a mild March day, bright skies and crocuses in the yard, a value as real to us as the very air that we breathe—but it has also become a sign of the dividedness of such grandiose identities as Idealism and the Transcendental Aesthetic."

"So the Nihilists are right about *beauty* as it is used in philosophy—usually it indicates hidden power agendas and divided values. But the pleasure it signifies also remains separate from the dividedness of those value judgments."

"This disparity reflects the difference between our value judgments about 'being' and life itself," Smith commented. "Life is a gracious value, absolutely desirable for its own sake, and the word 'being' derives its transcendent resonance from this gracious value; in fact Aristotle claimed that Supreme Being is nothing other than life. But our value judgments about being are divided in the same way that intellect is divided—between its capacity for resistance and the values found in existence."

"The descriptions of being seen in philosophy are *concepts* of what life is, which is not the same thing as life itself. They are pale pictures of life, like a painting of a beautiful spring day. There is a whole dimension of the original missing—its vividness, its ability to overwhelm the senses all at once as well as intellect."

"Yes, except that philosophy is even less capable of capturing the desirability of life than a painting because it is colorless. It does not have the luxury of appealing to the senses or the freedom of simply representing what the eye sees—freedom from the burden of having to justify one's identity. The descriptions of being seen in Plato and Aristotle are cauterized by intellect and its resistance to divided values and by the vanity of believing that we can use this resistance to obtain a transcendent identity. They are stick-figure versions of reality, and it is no longer possible for us to ignore their limitations."

"They do seem one-dimensional compared with life itself," I agreed. "Idealism negates the senses and sensuous pleasures, while Aristotle's method tends to lead to tedious and self-evident results, at least from my point of view. But was this the cheerful insight you had last night?"

"No—I had a sort of vision," he said, somewhat abashedly.

"A vision! Do tell."

"Well, it happened during a vast digression on some small and precious thing. I was just at the point of drifting off into an insensate torpor when my mind was filled with a vivid image of geraniums in a sealed room, a hothouse. I could almost taste them—you know the bitter aroma geraniums exude. And then in a flash that startled me out of my soporific daze I realized what it was. They were the florabundant words of the church, the institutional language that has become a barrier to any great value or power."

"Uh-oh," I said. "Now you're going to tell me religion is meaningless, too—in which case I may decide to follow the groundhog back into his hole."

"Too late," he replied good-naturedly. "It seems we are in the midst of a great change. There is a restlessness in the world today, a dissatisfaction with methods of judging value that lead to nothing but emptiness and despair. Kant and Hegel excised the gracious old teleology from the synthetic method, presenting us with an ethical universe devoid of transcendent resonance, as if sums and syllogisms could satisfy our thirst for life; and then the lovers of absolute values came along and rejected this synthesis through the nothingness of its concepts of being. But nothingness also cannot make us happy, since it is the same thing as our mortality."

"Nothingness can be used to negate our *concepts* of being, which are divided, but it cannot wipe away our consciousness of the value of life implicit in 'being.'"

"Nietzsche was right about those value judgments—they were annihilated by their own dividedness. But Nihilism is no less divided than any other identity supplied by intellect and judgment. The gloominess of modern culture reflects the difference between the great desirability of life and the concept of absolute resistance to the good. Nihilism was supposed to produce transcendent values by negating the 'pessimism' that came in the wake of the scientific synthesis, but in reality it led to a more virulent strain of pessimism by attempting to suppress consciousness of the value of life in living beings."

"It was impossible for Hegel to overcome the difference between nothingness and being because 'being' reflects more than just our thought-existence—it reflects life; and for the same reason it was impossible for Nietzsche to obtain a transcendent identity by embracing nothingness for its own sake, since nothingness reflects our mortality as well as the capacity of intellect for resistance to constructs of being."

"The superman negated 'being' by embracing nothingness, but this led to morbidity in his cultural identity and imposed a limit on his appeal. Just as Rationalism lost its power to deceive us into thinking that it could supply a transcendent identity when it decayed into the preening seen in Hume, so Nihilism has now degenerated into a supercilious love of irony and resistance to beauty and goodness—at which point it becomes impossible to conceal the smallness of its pleasures compared with the pink blush that steals upon the woods in March or the sweetness of the maple sap."

"Nihilism produces the bondage of having to resist those great pleasures as if they were nothing. In sum, it is impossible to find the freedom necessary to great pleasure in philosophy—either in the attempt to glorify the pleasures of nature through Transcendentalism, or in the attempt to annihilate their goodness through Nihilism and absolute resistance to the good. But you don't seem to think we can find the freedom we are looking for in the church, either," I said slyly.

"'The truth shall set you free'—but the church seeks institutional status in the world, and the only way to obtain such status is through the sword of judgment, which leads to same divided values that were seen in philosophy. It should not surprise us to find that some of religion's caretakers have active natures and a love of the sensuous universe. Like Aristotle, they are sanguine about existence and enjoy investigating the way things work—the highest expression of such a temperament being Thomas Aquinas."

"But others tend to be somewhat more negative about our prospects for making ourselves happy."

"That would seem to be the case," Smith replied with a smile. "An aversion to Thomas's rosy construct of being led the Reformers down the well-traveled path of pure resistance and nothingness. Such caretakers were not able to find a satisfactory identity in Thomism, which begins in sensuous existence and never seems to fully escape it, so they gravitated to the ideal of pure intellect seen in Plato and the belief that absolute resistance has the power to produce transcendent values."

"And this leads to the problem you see in institutional language. The verbiage of the caretakers has become divided in much the same way as Plato and Aristotle."

"The words found in institutional doctrine bear a strong *resemblance* to the word that resonates with the desirability of life—but something of the original power is lost as they are retrofitted onto our methods of judging value. The Schoolmen were prolific wordsmiths, flooding the world with increasingly oppressive syllogisms; the Reformers rejected this voluminous outpouring of words all in one middle stream, but they embraced an equally flagrant proliferation of words in the pulpit, which became the symbol of the power of judgment to cleanse theology through resistance."

"The pulpit was literally raised up to new heights in Christianity. Whatever its other merits, the Reformation involved a power-struggle between Scholastic theologians, who openly declared their love of Aristotle and his synthetic method, and lovers of absolute values, who were creatures of the age of pure reason; and perhaps, in another context, between a lingering culture of feudalism and the rise of the absolute rulers, who saw the Reformation as an opportunity to limit the far-flung influence of Rome."

"The Medieval religious sensibility glorified the sacrament because Aristotle's theory of value is based on the notion that the good can be found as itself in existent values. The antithetical age that followed glorified the pulpit and the capacity of intellect to produce pure value judgments about the nature of God and man. But factions within the church can only obtain power in the world by taking up the sword of judgment and forfeiting the graciousness of the value of life. The caretaker is a living being, after all, and nothing like the bloodless institution he is called upon to uphold through his capacity for judgment. Perhaps there is some serious problem in his family just at the moment that he is expected to climb up into the pulpit and impress us with the centrifuge of his reasoning; perhaps he is at low tide psychologically, or has money troubles, which seems altogether likely, considering what we pay the poor fellows."

"For that matter he may have been distracted by some pretty woman in the front pew," I said with a laugh.

"Not impossible," Smith agreed. "There is no reason to expect our caretakers to be more perfect than the fallen hero who was 'a man after God's own heart.' These are the foolish twists and turns experienced by actual human beings as they go through life with their manifold flaws and weaknesses—this is real human existence, as opposed to the stories we love to tell about life; stories designed to make us seem a good deal better than we actually are. But the caretaker cannot afford any appearance of weakness or foolishness if it is his responsibility to uphold an edifice of stone. He must attempt to conceal his humanity in a cloak of judgment—and this results in an obstacle between him and his listeners and their desire for life."

"Your point is that the sword of judgment he borrows from institutional doctrine comes between him and this gracious value, depriving his words of the natural communicating power of the word; making his words seem small and cramped, while graciousness is an expansive value. But what would you prefer?" I said teasingly. "Would you have the poor fellow look like a fool?"

"I would give him the *freedom* to look foolish, if I could—a freedom he cannot find as long as he clings to the institution and its value judgments—because the truth is that our predicament is rather foolish. We are mortal beings who are conscious of the value of life. Intellect can be used to resist this foolishness, as seen in the institutional church, a great and imposing edifice, but the identities rendered by intellect cannot give us what we desire because judgment is a dividing power; because life cannot be divided and still be life; because the gracious power that reveals itself in the desirability of life transcends mortal judgment. The caretaker must choose between the natural desire for status in the world, which is rooted in his nothingness and fear of the grave, and the gracious value of life; between the smugness and appearance of power provided by institutional doctrine and the fear and trembling that characterize a right understanding of the value of life and the difference between this value and our own existence; between the foolishness of never rising beyond the status of a pilgrim on the road to life and the vanity of wanting to appear to be a master of doctrine and authority in religion."

"Life is a gracious value, but not much graciousness is seen in the institution by its very nature, since it is built on judgment."

"The institution is perfectly capable of obtaining the power it seeks in the world through the sword of judgment, but then it cannot also reflect the graciousness of a God whose power is made strong in our weakness. Any attempt to dilute this paradox results in a loss of its resistance to our own limitations; its transcendent resonance. The natural desire to become strong in judgment also naturally makes us weak in graciousness—but if the church is weak in graciousness, then it is no different from the world."

"It loses its soulfulness and turns into mere religion. Meanwhile those who seek identity in the gracious value of life cannot *help* looking a little foolish to the world, since they must give up its love of judgment. It was considered foolishness to be hung up on a public road—and yet this foolishness is inseparable from the graciousness of the cross."

"This sign is nothing like the signs of power seen in the world," Smith noted. "In fact it is a subversive sign, since it indicates that the pride of the world and its value judgments are nothing. We use the signs of value seen in our rhetorical hothouses to conceal our mortality, our weakness, but those signs cannot escape the limitations of the hothouse itself, a thing made by men. Some caretakers are in love with resistance and its clarifying power; their sense of value tends to express itself in a love of form. Others prefer a more organic style and enjoy the varieties of value made possible by the senses. There is nothing wrong with such pleasures in themselves, but they deprive us of the power to reflect the value of life when they are used to hide our foolishness from others."

"We want to be seen to 'follow Paul or Apollo' because of the strength seen in their arguments—because strength conveys status in the world—but this same desire also makes it impossible for us to reflect the value of life."

"We cannot reflect this value through appearances of power because we ourselves are mortal. When I was a young man, I was quite smitten by the *Imitation of Christ*, that beautiful and entrancing old book. I loved Thomas's plain-speaking, the forthrightness of his style and absence of prevaricating rhetorical strategies. But I also loved his love of the notion of hermitage, or sanctuary. Those of us who feel harried by existence find it a little too easy to fall in love with his call to come out of the vile confusion of the world and seek our bliss in contemplation—but the problem with this pleasure is that the church has been divided over action and contemplation almost from the beginning."

"Thomas's hermitage seems sweet because it is a product of the mind and its resistance to the unhappiness of existence. We all go through times when we become weary of life and its complications, which is why there is a good deal of pleasure in the notion of coming out of the complexity of existence and purifying our minds; but the attempt to negate this fatiguing complexity requires a negation of life as we actually know it, which is a mixed value."

"The question is whether he really did find his bliss in that lonely forest cell, or was he telling us a story? Was he content to lead a cloistered life, or did his love of pure judgment lead to a different kind of restlessness, as seen in our modern Thomas? Now I am not trying to suggest that Thomas should not love contemplation. Far from it. We are who we are and cannot help loving what we love. But there is a clear divide in doctrine between lovers of action and contemplation. The problem is not that they love their own pleasures, but that they allow themselves to fall into the trap of seeking identity in those divided loves. They identify themselves as followers of the Thomas who loved contemplation or of the one who loved the notion of pure action, or of Calvin, or Luther, or some other rhetorical potentate; they begin to condemn those who do not join in their pleasures because they perceive them as a threat to their identity. And then it becomes impossible to reflect the value of life or the graciousness of the cross."

"In your view, the word overcomes the dividedness of the world through the gracious spirit of life; through the unity of the believers and the willingness to put aside all divided notions of value for the sake of that one shining goal. But it's interesting that you continue to describe these divisions as a manifestation of divided 'pleasures,' as if this were all that Thomas or Calvin had on his mind. I don't know that it is a matter of mere pleasure. I think it should be a matter of truth."

Smith started to respond but then suddenly withdrew and grew stony. The silence went on until it became uncomfortable. Apparently I had made some sort of faux pas but was not sure what it was. Finally I decided to try to draw him out on the "confirmation" he had joked about having that morning.

"So what happened when you were planting your moribund peas? Did you have another vision?" I said in a jocular tone, as if unaware of any tension in the air.

"Not really," he replied mildly, "although the experience was equally startling. There I was, shoveling the ground quite hard in my eagerness to break the frost under the leaves I had neglected to clear last fall, breathing in the brisk March air, when it suddenly occurred to me, as if it were not the most obvious thing in the world, that the sweet things of nature stimulate thought through pleasure. It is *desirability* that sets various thought processes in motion—not any power found in the mind per se."

"But this we already know from Locke."

"Not really. Locke was trying to debunk Descartes and the cogito. According to him, intellect is not a self-existent value; it is more like a blank slate upon which the sense realm makes her wanton impressions over time. Locke might have reformulated the cogito along the lines of 'I have concepts of value because I exist and experience sense impressions.' But this is nothing more than the age-old debate over pure judgment and synthetic judgment. Both Locke and Descartes believed that intellect was a transcendent power, and both gave intellect and its force of resistance precedence to desirability in our understanding of value and of being."

"The philosophers believed that intellect was 'the good,' and, therefore, that intellect had the power to provide the good of happiness. But you feel there is a power in consciousness that is different from intellect and is not divided as intellect is divided, between Locke and Descartes."

"The attempt to glorify intellect as the good leads to unhappiness because intellect is divided between its own capacity for resistance and the values found in existence. But we are familiar with another power at work in the pleasures of the garden that does not seem to lead to divided values—the power that makes itself known to us through the desirability of nature. A man working in his garden on a frosty morning may be moved by what he sees to think deep thoughts—to write a book of philosophy in his head and forget all about it over lunch—but it is not intellect or resistance that moves him to think those thoughts, and neither is it the garden per se. It is a power that remains separate as itself from both intellect and the sense realm."

"The first mover in our understanding of what is good is desirability, not intellect, as the philosophers claimed. It is the power in desirability—the power of love—that tells us if something is good; that is our primary arbiter of value."

"The mind is drawn to the great pleasures of nature through a power that is neither intellect nor nature but which is quite real in existence—an intermediary power between us and the garden, as it were. This power tells us unambiguously that the garden is good because nature provides great pleasure. Of course intellect is also good; in fact indispensable to great pleasure, since it is impossible to be conscious of the goodness of the garden without its reflective power. But we seem to be inclined to fall in love with intellect and its force of judgment and give it precedence to the power found in the desirability of the garden, which cannot be used to raise ourselves up at the expense of others."

"The philosophers spoiled the pleasures of the garden by equating intellect with the good," I suggested. "We are in love with intellect because of its comparative power, which can be used to make us feel more important than our fellow beings and ward off our feelings of nothingness; but this same force of judgment also deprives us of the transcendent identity we seek and causes misery by producing divided values."

"Different men find different pleasures in the garden, and thus any attempt to obtain a transcendent identity through judgment leads to divided results. The naturalist, for example, may feel a strong attachment to the names that men give to the things found in the garden, even a fascination. Now names obtain power in an honorable way—through their capacity to reflect the desirability of the thing signified, our sense of its value. Love is the logos of the names that we give to the things we see in the garden; and in that sense the knowledge of names can embellish a generous attachment."

"The very fact that the name is common, that it is shared, makes it somewhat generous; but there is no generosity in attempting to use our knowledge of names to make ourselves seem more knowledgeable than our fellow beings."

"The vanity of trying to distinguish ourselves on the basis of names leads to highly divided values and deprives us of the very identity we seek. What difference does it make, after all, to know that men call a certain bird a red-tailed hawk?" Smith said, as one of these majestic creatures circled overhead and into the woods. "The name we give has nothing to do with the bird itself; it is merely a sign of our attachment to the hawk, our sense of its value. The appeal of the name is rooted entirely in desirability and no other power—but this power cannot be used to judge others without producing highly divided results."

"Linking knowledge of the name to identity leads to bondage to the limitations of the name as a name."

"The ontological limitations of knowing names seem quite obvious since the name is not the thing itself; since it merely signifies the thing. But the garden offers opportunities for far more intoxicating identities as well—for instance through empiricism and causal reasoning. The sensuous universe is beautifully harmonized, which suggests the existence of certain natural laws; and the attempt to identify those laws can provide a good deal of pleasure by linking the mind's capacity for judgment to a transcendent value reflected in the goodness of existence."

"Science begins to blend into philosophy through cause and effect reasoning, which appears to put us in touch with transcendent forces and first causes."

"Such knowledge is a sore temptation to vanity. It is quite possible for a Locke or Newton to be in love with the functionality of nature and to be inspired by that love to try to understand how nature works without taking up the sword of judgment. But they also seem to have been quite taken with their theories of value and eager to obtain precedence for those theories in the world; and as soon as we take up science as a sword of judgment, we become slaves to divided identities—because the difference between sense and intellect cannot be overcome."

"Newton and Locke both clearly regarded their descriptions of value as rebuttals to Descartes, just as they themselves were rebutted in time by Einstein and 'thought experiments' and by Darwin and Freud."

"The same divide seen in Greek philosophy between pure judgment, with its power to annihilate unsatisfying constructs of value and generate unifying theories, and synthetic judgment, with its power to indicate ways of overcoming the nothingness that results from pure judgment, is also evident in science. The divide between empirical and theoretical methods cannot be overcome because intellect and its force of resistance is not the same thing as sense. It is impossible to obtain the identity seen in Descartes or Newton without following one of two highly divergent paths—either the path that attempts to blend intellect and sense, as seen in Locke and Newton, or the path of resistance and the unifying power of theory seen in Descartes, Einstein and Darwin."

"They were not just scientists; they also sought the identity of philosophers who had something important to say about happiness. Thus they wound up being divided in the same way as Plato and Aristotle."

"That philosophic desire is the basis of modern science," Smith replied. "Galileo's discoveries carry little philosophic baggage; he simply wrote down what he saw and assembled the physical evidence in the most logical fashion. But Descartes was not a scientist purely for the sake of science. He saw science as a way of redeeming the world. He believed that science had the power to purge theology of the metaphysical accretions produced by Scholasticism and lead to the happiness and perfect knowledge of God that Scholasticism had failed to provide."

"Descartes saw science as a means of reading the mind of God, just as the Greek philosophers attempted to use intellect and judgment to obtain knowledge of 'the good.'"

"The modern age is the age of science. The two greatest philosophers of the age before Nietzsche both regarded themselves as scientists—Descartes and Kant; and the explicit premise of their philosophy was that it is possible to go beyond the dividedness of the Greek philosophers and obtain happiness by using science to unlock the mysteries of the universe. Science was supposed to furnish a direct line to the mind of transcendent being. Galileo, Descartes, Newton and Locke were all Christians. But their science led to precisely the same divide as traditional philosophy by equating divine being with intellect and its force of resistance."

"They tried to substitute the topic of science and nature for the traditional topics of beauty and the good because they believed that nature was 'very good'; because they believed nature had been created by God. But this change actually worked against them in the end by depriving philosophy of the graciousness of the good."

"Modern philosophers were seduced by the magnitude of Galileo's discoveries into setting aside the pursuit of the good for the sake of science. They began by thinking that science would lead them to knowledge of the good, since nature was 'very good,' but they drifted farther and farther away from the notion of 'the good' as it became clear that Descartes and Newton were divided in the same way as the ancient philosophers. This is why Kant did not directly invoke the good; instead he made a point of setting it aside, as if it were an obstacle to good science."

"And then the Nihilists annihilated the good because they did not feel that it was necessary any longer to philosophy or to science. Science rose to such dizzying heights in the modern age that scientists began to think they could do without the good. But the loss of the good leads to the marginalization of philosophy in the end because the whole purpose of philosophy is to obtain the good of happiness."

"The irony of what Descartes wrought is that science can only make itself seem strong in natural judgment by alienating itself from the good, a transcendent value—by embracing naturalism—and naturalism cannot lead to the happiness that all men desire. Hence science has never seemed stronger than in our own time—and never has philosophy seemed less satisfying or less useful. Never has science enjoyed the degree of precedence it obtained through Darwin, the ultimate expression of naturalism, but Darwinism also bars the door to the garden, where modern science began its pursuit of happiness."

"Naturalism precludes any thought of the good; this gloomy conclusion is reflected in the writings of Gould and Dawkins and other proponents of the theory. And yet the goodness of the garden is still there in all its glory, as you discovered this morning."

"We may have reached the end of the age of science," Smith observed. "For four hundred years we deluded ourselves with the notion that it is possible to go beyond the dividedness of philosophy by using science to obtain the good of happiness. Science was unable to provide knowledge of this transcendent value because its notions of being were divided between theory and quantitation. Then science turned to the path of pure naturalism and attempted to find happiness by excluding the good from its value judgments. But this tactic leads to a dead end because pure naturalism cannot offer any hope to the human race—and philosophy without hope is nothing."

"Pure naturalism leads to the conclusion that all of existence is a manifestation of the survival of the fittest—a cold-blooded theory of value in which there is no loveliness, nothing soulful, nothing gracious or generous. And the limitations of this theory of value are exposed by the loveliness of the garden."

"Science has reached a pinnacle of power, but it has also reached a tipping point and is on the verge of losing its exalted status. This great change is latent in the pleasures of the garden where science began. Naturalism involves a conscious attempt to expunge any thought of the good from consciousness, the transcendent being; and naturalism obtained power because it was clear that the concepts of transcendent being seen in Kant and Descartes were hopelessly divided. But it is impossible to annihilate the goodness of the garden for its own sake—its capacity to provide delight—and this goodness indicates the limit of naturalism and its capacity to provide a satisfactory identity."

"The goodness of the garden is *left over* from naturalism and its devastating effects. Philosophy failed to identify 'the good,' and naturalism annihilated philosophy and its pursuit of the good in the end, but the goodness of the garden reemerges in a new way to expose the limitations of naturalism and its inability to account for natural values. And in that case all we have to do to escape from the devastation we brought upon ourselves through our infatuation with science is to return to the garden."

"In one sense, this is quite literally true," Smith replied chuckling. "The great pleasures of nature are still there, still waiting to welcome us back to our right minds even after we have succeeded in making ourselves miserable, like the prodigal son after dining with swine. But it is important to remember that the pleasures of the garden do not depend upon intellect and cannot be restored through intellect or judgment. Some power greater than judgment must restore those pleasures if we are to go beyond the living hell we have created for ourselves in the modern age."

"There is a way to restore those pleasures—by giving up intellect and its signs of power and seeking identity in the sign of life."

"This great value reveals the fatal limitations of naturalism. If life could come from that which is not life, then the naturalists might be right: perhaps there is no such thing as transcendent being; perhaps existence really is meaningless—a dark struggle to survive. But it seems increasingly clear that life resists the vanity of those who want to limit it to purely natural causes. Even the basic building blocks of life are bewilderingly complex and are highly unlikely to have come into existence by their own means."

"The more we know about life, the more mysterious it seems. And the inadequacy of naturalism to account for this great and mysterious value points beyond our current unhappiness—if we are willing to give up intellect and its divided signs."

"It seems we must go *through* the garden of philosophy and its signs of value in order to find what we are looking for. We cannot tarry there any longer because our love of judgment brings us nothing but misery. Plato and Aristotle tried to glorify intellect and its capacity to obtain knowledge of the good of happiness but were divided between intellect and sense. The modern philosophers tried to do the same thing through science, but were divided between being and nothingness. The followers of Nietzsche thought they could transcend the dividedness of philosophy by annihilating 'the good,' but their love of naturalism led to the exclusion of all great and gracious values from philosophy."

"They were not exactly the giants of objectivity that they claimed to be. Their partisanship is revealed as they continue to cling to naturalism, since the evidence indicates that naturalism cannot account for the existence of life."

"Naturalism is no more objective than Transcendentalism or Rationalism. It is based on intellect and its capacity for judgment—and all value judgments rendered by intellect are subjective and reveal the divided pleasures of the signifier. As soon as it becomes evident that naturalism is a manifestation of the will to power and not science per se, it loses its appearance of power and its stranglehold over the imagination. And at that point it becomes possible once again to see the pleasures of the garden in a more gracious light than anything afforded by Darwinism."

"At that point it becomes possible to use those pleasures in a more constructive way, to move beyond the devastation we brought upon ourselves and restore ourselves to our right minds."

"All of the signs of value produced by intellect are divided because intellect is a dividing power. This is why it is impossible to find what we are looking for in philosophy and the belief that we are capable of obtaining knowledge of what is good through judgment. But the very fact that the pleasures of the garden are still there for us to enjoy, even when we have ruined ourselves though our love of judgment, indicates the existence of a power that is greater than judgment; a gracious power that is capable of giving us the happiness we desire and exceeds the limitations of intellect."

"The way back to the simple joys that the garden can give is through a different kind of sign from the ones seen in philosophy and now in naturalism."

"It is impossible to return to the garden through philosophy. Those green and gracious pleasures have been annihilated in order to gratify the superman and his vanity. But they are still abundantly available to those who are willing to give up the pride of intellect and allow their identity to be informed by the sign of love. No one can cling to this sign and also cling to the vanity of the signs of value seen in philosophy. The power of love cannot be seen and cannot be used to obtain status or power in the world. But this is the only power that can relieve us of the burden we now feel."

"This gracious power is the only power that can restore the happiness of the garden in full measure."

"My experience this morning led me to believe that there are two kingdoms—a kingdom of graciousness and a kingdom of judgment. I was living in the latter kingdom in all of my early morning gloom, when for some reason unknown to me I suddenly burst through my own limitations and was overwhelmed by the graciousness of the values that were evident all around me. To me, this indicates that we ourselves are the main impediment to the happiness we desire. We are miserable because we insist on living in the psychological realm of judgment; because we want to feel that we are powerful and capable of justifying our existence. This is impossible because we are mortal beings and cannot give ourselves the thing we desire most, which is life. But just beyond the iron ring of judgment there is another realm waiting to welcome us—the gracious realm of life; a realm in which there is perfect freedom and delight."

"'The kingdom of God is at hand.'"

"All we have to do, apparently, is to reach out and grasp it. But we cannot grasp that other, unworldly kingdom as long as we continue to cling to the kingdom of death. If we insist on holding onto judgment, then we cannot avoid being unhappy, since judgment cannot give us what we are seeking—a desirable identity. Our love of judgment leads to Nihilism and despair. But such great values as hope and delight become possible again if we are willing to let go of judgment, let go of our excessive love of intellect, and seek happiness by the light of the gracious value of life."

"In other words, when we relinquish our divided loves for the sake of love itself."

Smith did not reply. I was starting to feel a definite chill as some clouds moved in, so I carried the tea-things inside and put them in the sink and left him to his garden and the blustery March winds that tell no lies.

Chapter 4

Exquisite Stranger

"Eliot was right—April is certainly the cruelest month," I said to Smith on a cloudy and brutish Good Friday afternoon.

"I see you choose to put the best construction on his native morbidity," he replied cheerfully. "Like many an Idealist, Eliot would rather not see the rekindling of life in nature, which establishes a perilous discord to the identity sought in resistance to embodied pleasures. Sensuous being once again raises her preposterous head, and the frozen perfection of the ideal suffers a thaw. But of course he might just as well have said that the cruelty of April is too kind."

"I don't know how you can find any *kindness* in such miserable weather. One minute we are spoon-fed a minuscule portion of sun—hardly enough to burnish the forsythia and solitary crocus—and then we are subjected to snow showers and bitter winds. The world would be a much happier place, I am quite sure, if spring did not come until it were certain of its own intentions and ceased this reprehensible teasing."

"April's snow showers seem painful only because they refuse to flatter us and our love of judgment," Smith opined in the same bantering tone. "No one can use fickle April to establish identity in the world because her pleasures are highly changeable. She is neither the negation of the unhappiness of mortal life suggested to the imagination by February, nor the lush affirmation of being that intellect finds in lovely June. No sign of undivided value can be found in her fickleness; thus our methods of obtaining happiness through intellect and its capacity for judgment come crashing to the ground."

"For our own good, you mean," I groaned, popping the tops off some ginger beer I happened to have brought along for the occasion. "The last time I was here you were trying to convince me that philosophy is rooted in the pseudo-paradisical garden of divided pleasures. Does this imply that all philosophies are of equal value?"

"They delude us into thinking our own pleasures must be more important than someone else's—and therefore they are equally vain," he replied chuckling. "The philosophers claimed to be able to use the power of intellect to identify 'the good,' an undivided value, but intellect itself is divided between its own capacity for resistance and existent values. Intellect and sense are both highly desirable; thus the value judgments about the good seen in philosophy are divided between the concepts of pure intellect and a synthesis of intellect and sense."

"Philosophy purports to be the pursuit of truth; but the truth, in your view, is that Plato and Aristotle had different intellectual pleasures and were divided by the vanity of wanting to equate those pleasures with the good."

"It seems obvious to us now that they were merely telling stories about the good. A good tale requires a hero who is justified and a villain who is repudiated, which is why they attempted to glorify their concepts of value through mutual vilification and caricature of each other's methods. But they cannot make us happy by discounting each other's pleasures if there is value in resistance as well as existence."

"Their descriptions of the good were *divided* between these values, and we have become too conscious of this dividedness to ignore it any longer."

"According to Nietzsche, their methods of describing the good were little more than manifestations of the will to power. And there would seem to be some validity to the accusation. Descartes claimed to be seeking knowledge of transcendent being, which is a gracious value, and yet he openly stated his intention of overthrowing Scholasticism; and Kant, who aspired to the loftiest heights of reasonableness and claimed to hate the spirit of disputation in philosophy, was not quite able hide his disdain for Rationalism."

"The sword they used may have been bloodless, but they were not above the love of conquering," I conceded.

"They tried to dominate each other by using the power of judgment to glorify their own methods of describing the good. And then Nietzsche tried to turn this love of domination against them by stripping away any pretense of 'the good' and embracing the will to dominate for its own sake. But just as it was impossible to obtain a transcendent identity by using the dividing power of intellect to make value judgments about the good, so it is impossible to overcome the dividedness of philosophy by attempting to negate the good and embrace the will to power—because the goodness of life cannot be negated."

"It is quite possible to negate the descriptions of 'the good' seen in philosophy, since they are divided between sense and intellect, but it is impossible to negate the value of life in living beings."

"The Transcendentalists left themselves open to Nihilism by setting aside the transcendent. They tried to avoid any appearance of teleology in their 'scientific synthesis' by describing a perfectly naturalistic construct of intellect and sense that did not rely on the power of a transcendent intellect. Since Rationalism had produced a certain nothingness in science by equating intellect and its capacity to doubt with transcendent value, the Transcendentalists proposed setting aside the transcendent and attempting to describe a synthesis of being and nothingness itself—of Empiricism and its concepts of being and Rationalism with its capacity for resistance to the limitations of those concepts. But setting aside the transcendent takes nothingness out of the mind of God, where it has immortal significance, and puts it in the human mind."

"At which point the mortality of our concepts of being is exposed," I concluded.

"Nothingness can be thought of as a useful limit to those concepts only as long as it is linked directly to the transcendent, an immortal value. In that case, our sense of the nothingness of those concepts can be said to stand in for the resistance of the transcendent to the limitations of our own understanding, which raises the possibility of identifying some middle term between this resistance and what we think about being. But setting aside the transcendent turns nothingness into an annihilating power, since nothingness in mortal beings reflects their own mortality."

"They themselves are mortal, and therefore any construct they describe of 'being' or immortal value may just be nothing."

"Hegel tried to demonstrate that it was possible to contain the deconstructive potential of nothingness through a scientific method without directly invoking transcendent being; but this effort had the counterproductive effect of raising nothingness up to parity with being. The more he tried to conquer nothingness and tame it so that it could be incorporated into a construct of being, the more conscious he made us of the power of nothingness and its resistance to any such construct."

"His attempt at describing a construct of nothingness and being led to such ponderous results that it became an easy target for Nietzsche and the idea of embracing nothingness for its own sake."

"Nietzsche found a rationale for Nihilism in the concept of natural selection, which seemed to do away with the need to invoke transcendent being at all. The philosophers based their pursuit of happiness on the concept that the goodness of existent values reflects the qualitative power of a transcendent intellect, but Darwin tried to show that the beauty of the species and even life itself had come into being without the guiding hand of a creator. And then Nietzsche took up the nothingness of natural selection—the absence of transcendent being—to suggest that happiness could be found in annihilating any thought of 'being.'"

"If belief in transcendent being leads to the divided values seen in philosophy, then perhaps it is possible to find happiness by negating being and embracing the transcendent principle suggested by natural selection—the will to power."

"Nihilism annihilated the transcendent being that ruled philosophy from Plato to Hegel—the being that was said to be intellect in its essence. But it led to its own form of dualism because the word 'being' intimates life. The superman must attempt to negate the value of life in order to embrace the deconstructive power of nothingness and justify his claim that it is possible to find transcendent value in existence for its own sake. According to Nietzsche, the superman must negate the 'will to live' as well as any thought of the 'right to life' before he can go beyond the dividedness of philosophy and its concepts of being. But those concepts are not the same thing as life itself—and it is impossible to negate the gracious value of life and obtain any undivided value."

"Plato equated 'being' with intellect in order to glorify his method of obtaining happiness, and this led to a divide between intellect and sense. Nietzsche tried to undo this dualism by negating 'being' and embracing nothingness and pure sensuous existence. But nothingness obtains its force of resistance to being through death itself—a value that is somewhat limited in desirability."

"A rather wormy value," Smith agreed. "Nihilism was supposed to have the power to make us happy, but it cannot negate the graciousness intimated in 'the good' without producing a brutish story about existence. The will to power is based on the survival of the fittest. Darwin seems to have had Adam Smith in mind—he thought there was some sort of cosmic shortage of supply in nature, leading to a murderous form of demand. This story about the parsimony of nature has nothing to do with what we see with our own eyes, however. Grass and wildflowers rapidly overtake the bare ground; maple trees send out thousands of petals that spring up all over our gardens and lawns; the birds seem to find everything they need on berry bushes and thistles."

"Nature would seem to have more to do with *abundance* than with shortage and meanness—which calls the transcendent potential of the will to power into question. If there is no need to dominate others in order to survive, then domination cannot be used to indicate transcendent value."

"In order for the superman to obtain a transcendent identity, the will to dominate must be the only real value in existence; the graciousness that the Romantics saw in nature must be overthrown by characterizing existence as a desperate struggle to survive. But no such desperation is seen in the robin as he pulls a worm from the ground, or at least the effort is not so all-consuming that it prevents him from sitting on a branch and singing for hours on end. No such desperation is seen in the wild rose, the ferns in our woods, the squirrel enjoying his seeds and nuts, the ladyslipper we find on secluded forest trails. Now it is true, of course, that we should expect to struggle if we desire to be known as supermen, since there seem to be many in the world who want to compete with us for this empty-headed prize. But the idea that we have to embrace the will to dominate simply to survive—simply to have good food to eat and clothes to wear or the pleasures of a spring day—this is empty prattling and has nothing to do with real life."

"It's a little too heroic, a little too self-congratulatory to ring true. It is not necessary to struggle very greatly in order to survive or to enjoy moments of delight; therefore the notion that struggle is the essence of existence cannot furnish a transcendent identity."

"The very meanness implicit in the will to dominate imposes limitations on the identity of the superman. He is compelled to negate the good and all gracious values in order to obtain the identity of domination. He must eschew such trifles as kindness and pity, according to Nietzsche, if he wants to be known as a superman, and become a man of steel—hard, unfeeling, willing to be brutal and to use any means in his power to obtain his goal. But then the end does not justify the means. The very coldness and brutality of the superman make it impossible for him to obtain the transcendent identity he desires."

"This steely coldness also seems to be coupled with an unlikely sentimental streak," I noted. "Nietzsche's enthusiasm for the will to power seems nostalgic in the age of modern warfare. He glorified the battlefield as the authentic venue of the overman and his struggle to obtain a transcendent identity—he was probably thinking of Achilles and Siegfried and other larger-than-life heroes who dominated their chronicles through individual valor. But those creaking old tales have nothing to do with the anonymous mass slaughter seen at places like Verdun."

"Identities that are rooted in a love of pure resistance often lend themselves to sentimentality," Smith agreed. "They begin by insisting that all existent values must be negated in order to obtain happiness, and then they overcompensate by making unrealistic promises about the potential benefits of this negation. Plato was the prototype—the philosopher somehow rises above the limitations of sense and the heaviness of existence and enters into the airy regions of pure ideas. He becomes a thing of incomparable lightness through the power of intellect even though he himself still has a solid body."

"Which is pure nonsense; no such thing is possible. And the same sort of sentimentality is very much evident in our own age and its love of resistance. Modern man is said to be consumed with the lust for money and commodities, but supposedly he can be transformed into a wholly new creature by simply abolishing private property and handing the means of production over to the enlightened few."

"Or, in the case of Nietzsche, all he needs to do to overcome the 'pessimism' and deep unhappiness of human history and turn himself into Dionysus is to negate being and the good. But this sentimental streak points to the central weakness of all methods of obtaining identity that are rooted in the love of resistance. The force of resistance to the unhappiness of existence found in intellect is nothing more than a negation. Plato can make extravagant promises about the bliss that awaits those who have the courage to negate the value of existent beauty for the sake of his luminous Ideas—but then he cannot provide any concrete idea of what the value of those Ideas actually is. The happiness promised in his method is nothing more than a negation, and this makes it intrinsically sentimental, since he has us wishing for a happiness that is impossible."

"It is impossible to overcome the negative effects of absolute resistance to existent values and describe anything that represents the transcendent beauty he attributed to intellect, which is why he became enamored of the idea that there is redemptive value in form for its own sake. And in the same way, it is impossible to go 'beyond good and evil' and obtain any transcendently desirable value."

"There is *nothing* beyond good and evil," Smith averred, "nothing but nothingness and despair. The negation of the good does not lead to a transcendent existence; it leads to the bitter grave. Nihilism was supposed to make us feel like supermen by negating the difference between our existence and the good, but in fact it made us more conscious of our limitations. As long as we sought identity in knowledge of the good, those limitations were not so obvious to us; our devotion to the good had the effect of concealing our nakedness from ourselves. But as soon as we agreed to negate the good, that nakedness was revealed—because we ourselves are mortal."

"We lost the covering that transcendent being provided in philosophy by negating the good. And this would account for the bitterness of the modern age."

"The superman was able to dominate the world of philosophy by embracing nothingness and its resistance to the dividedness of Transcendentalism and its concept of being, but he cannot obtain the transcendent identity he desires through Nihilism if he himself is mortal, since anyone can see that a grave is a small and trivial thing. The annihilation of being cannot lead to a happy Dionysian indifference to the dividedness of philosophy because living beings are naturally conscious of the value of life."

"They are aware of its goodness. They desire it and cannot be happy with nothingness."

"The superman is not being honest with himself when he claims to be scornful of the will to live. He wants to be known as a transcendent being—Nihilism was supposed to produce 'new gods and new ideals'—but his desire for such an identity is firmly rooted in the value of life. It is the nothingness of the grave and nothing else that makes men restive and causes them to compare themselves with their fellow beings; that causes them to want to be known as supermen. But then the superman cannot obtain the transcendent identity he longs for by negating the value of life."

"The grave is the greatest leveler of all. Nihilism has undone itself by attempting to negate the value of life."

"We cannot help being conscious of this great and gracious value when we experience the eternal return of spring. The philosophers made themselves famous by equating the good with intellect and promising that intellect had the power to make us happy by providing knowledge of 'being.' Whether they saw being as pure intellect, as Plato did, or tried to describe it as a construct of intellect and matter, in either case intellect was assumed to be the essence of being. But there is another value implied in being that has nothing to do with intellect and remains perfectly fresh and untouched by the power-struggles seen in philosophy—which is life itself."

"An integral value," I punned. "This value is not the same thing as 'being' as the philosophers described it; thus it is left over from the negation of being seen in Nihilism."

"Life is an exquisite stranger to the limitations of our concepts of being. Philosophy has exhausted its possibilities through the vanity of its love of judgment. No one believes anymore that Plato or Aristotle or Descartes or Kant found the secret of happiness. The limitations of their methods of describing being have become far too obvious for us to continue to delude ourselves any longer with the notion that they can provide a desirable identity or knowledge of transcendent value. And we now know that it is also impossible to find what we are looking in Nihilism and the foolish attempt to annihilate being and cozy up to the grave. But the annihilation of being has the unintended effect of making it easier for us to see the value of life—a value that is not the same thing as 'being' and does not exhibit any of the dividedness seen in philosophy."

"Ah—I think I see what you're driving at. The impediment of 'being' has been removed by the catastrophic demise of philosophy. It is no longer possible to find the transcendent value we long for in philosophy and its concepts of being—the strangeness that is absolutely necessary to transcendent value—but such a value can still be found in life, which is a complete stranger to our limitations."

"Life is an absolutely desirable value for its own sake. This value is implied in 'being'; but as soon as we equate being with intellect we find that our concepts of value are divided and limited by the nature of intellect itself. By the light of intellect, the good is divided between Plato and Aristotle because intellect is a force of division. But no such dividedness is found in the power that makes itself known through the desirability of life. There is value in present being—in the mortal life we now know—and yet life as itself is absolutely different from present being. Plato with his love of pure resistance and Aristotle with his love of existent values are hopelessly divided by the light of intellect—but not by the light of life, which transcends their dividedness."

"So the philosophers stumbled because they were in love with intellect and its power to make value judgments. This power leads to divided values, which cannot satisfy a desire for life. And in your view, there is a way to go beyond the limitations of philosophy—by rediscovering the value of life for its own sake; by disengaging this great value, as seen in the pleasures of spring, from the pollution that attached itself to our concepts of 'being.' But this troubles me somehow. Are you suggesting that we must discard intellect in order to embrace the value of life?"

"Life does not negate intellect," Smith replied. "All it negates is the desire to use intellect to glorify some mortals at the expense of their fellow beings—Plato at the expense of Aristotle or Kant at the expense of Descartes. They were the greatest philosophers the world has ever seen, but they were divided. It should be quite clear, then, by the light of life, that it is impossible to obtain the knowledge of transcendent value they were seeking through philosophy. Life does not preclude this entirely sensible conclusion—it does not negate the use of intellect and its ability to make value judgments—but it does prohibit us from using intellect to make ourselves seem like immortal beings."

"It prohibits us from using the negative power of judgment to obtain the transcendent identity we naturally long for, since our mortality is quite evident."

"Actually it is the philosophers who have now negated the value of intellect— through their excessive love of intellect," Smith pointed out. "They began by equating intellect with the good and claiming that it had the power to make us happy by providing knowledge of being. When it became obvious that intellect did not have any such power, they became rather spiteful toward philosophy and attempted to become supermen by embracing absolute resistance to any notion of 'the good.' But then the identity of the superman requires us to annihilate our ability to think about the goodness of being."

"That goodness actually exists, and we cannot help being conscious of it. Therefore intellect must be negated in order to make ourselves into overmen."

"By the light of life, existence is a mixed value, made up of the goodness of life itself and the evil of our mortality. The only way to go 'beyond good and evil,' then, is to attempt to blot out any consciousness of what is good. This is why Nihilism leads to a type of benightedness or willing dullness. The effect was not quite so evident in the first generation of supermen because their resistance was rooted in Transcendentalism, a construct of being; but after they succeeded in negating that construct, modern discourse deteriorated into a celebration of nothingness for its own sake and a forgetting of history. Thus Wittgenstein is lionized as a foe of transcendent being without any apparent awareness that he was an ardent Idealist; thus the word *synthesis* finds its way back into the lexicon to indicate interdisciplinary synergies, which is a Platonic concept; thus English professors forsake literature to write with winking smugness about topics that Socrates and Descartes would have considered far too obvious to merit serious attention, such as the labored attempts at deconstructing the signs of capitalist culture."

"There really is no exit from Nihilism—not because hell is other people, but because Nihilism requires absolute resistance to any thought of the goodness of being; and this imposes severe limitations on its discourse."

"Nihilism produces a vicious circle through its love of nothingness and the vanity of believing that absolute resistance to the good has the power to produce a transcendent identity. The statement 'April is the cruelest month' is rooted in the clever idea that we would somehow be better off if the awakening of life did not come and rouse us from the static oblivion represented to the imagination by winter and its frozen resistance to the unhappiness of existence. But the cleverness of the concept undoes itself, since no sane person wants the world to remain frozen and lifeless as long as there is the possibility of spring—even though the transition may cause us some pain."

"It is the pain we are trying to avoid," I suggested.

"Indeed. Mortal life lies somewhere between the painlessness of oblivion and the absolute desirability of life—which is this realm of suffering, where pleasure and pain are experienced together as a mixed value. The purpose of philosophy was to overcome this suffering and obtain happiness through its methods of thinking about being. Since those methods led to divided results, the Nihilists decided to attempt to annihilate suffering by blocking out any consciousness of the goodness of being. But Nihilism led to greater suffering in the end by forcing us to suppress our consciousness of the value of life."

"The philosophers tacitly admitted, by embracing Nihilism, that they were powerless to provide an undivided description of being; but neither is it possible to obtain happiness through the desperate stratagem of attempting to negate life as if it had no value."

"We suffer because we are mortal. The shame of this limitation makes us impatient to attempt to justify our existence before the candle of life is snuffed out by eternal night. All of philosophy is a manifestation of this impatience and the belief that it is possible to obtain happiness through the power of judgment. But no such impatience is seen in the power that manifests itself in April and the return of spring. The life-giving power that produces the great delights of the season does not seem to be in a hurry to justify itself. It is patient; it unfolds its pleasures leaf after leaf."

"It seems we cannot find happiness by running away from suffering, since we are mortal—by attempting to run away from our mortality—but perhaps we can find what we are looking for by resisting the desire to find instant gratification through intellect and its dividing power and allowing the suffering we sometimes experience in April to move us forward to some more productive place in the psyche."

"April indicates the most desirable identity of all—of coming out of death and into life. But such an identity is likely to cause some pain through its resistance to our mortality. A living identity requires us to give up our excessive love of intellect and the vanity of thinking that judgment has the power to justify our existence. This is painful because judgment is a power we ourselves have; because we are vain and do not want to let go of the idea that we can obtain happiness by our own means. But the dividing power of judgment cannot avail us if the thing we desire most is life."

"You're suggesting we should actively embrace our suffering; we should look beyond the quick fix offered by intellect and its force of judgment and seek a more lasting solution to our problem."

"Intellect and its value judgments cannot satisfy immortal longings, but the pleasures of April indicate the existence of a power that is capable of restoring life and overcoming the grave. This mysterious power is dynamic and forward-moving. The power that is disclosed in the pleasures of spring is constantly renewing and transforming the face of existence. It is nothing like the static value judgments seen in philosophy, which are rooted in a desire for status in the world. The Idealists sought the status of having obtained knowledge of being through the concept of pure mind, pure resistance to the mutability of existence, but this is a static value and cannot satisfy a desire for life. Similarly the lovers of constructive methods tried to make themselves seem like philosophers by claiming that being is a ratio of intellectual and material causes—in short, that being is fixed by the nature of the antitheses. But present being is precisely what we are trying to supersede in our pursuit of happiness."

"The problem with the static value judgments seen in philosophy is that we are living beings before we are intellectual beings, and life is a dynamic value."

"Life moves forward, leaving all static value judgments behind. We can seek identity in our value judgments, but this identity cannot make us happy because they are nothing like the thing we desire most, which is life. In fact our love of static judgments reflects our mortality and not any immortal value. We are afraid of the grave and think we can resist it through intellect and its qualitative force of resistance; that we can use this resistance to make a heroic stand against death and obtain an immortal identity."

"But the problem with such heroism is that the dividing power of judgment deprives us of the very thing we desire—a transcendent identity."

"Philosophy is dead. It has negated itself and its pursuit of the good of happiness through Nihilism, or absolute resistance to 'the good.' And so we find ourselves squinting into the dark tomb of philosophy at the end of the age, trying to find a desirable identity in a bitter draught of nothingness. But the good news is that there is no stone at the mouth of the tomb.

Life is a value that exceeds philosophy and its self-constricting concepts of 'being.' We have brought a great conflagration on ourselves through our vanity and love of judgment; we have made ourselves miserable by attempting to embrace the grave in order to go beyond the limitations of philosophy. The Modern age is the age of gloominess and despair—and yet there are still yellow daffodils by the barn in the soote season; marsh marigolds and violets still spring up from the frozen ground to invade the wasteland of the mind."

"The only thing preventing us from enjoying them, it seems, is our unwillingness to let go of our pride and excessive love of intellect."

Chapter 5

Asymmetry, Mathesis, 'The Good'

STILL, SOMETIMES I can't help wondering if we are not tottering on the brink of some new barbarism. Maybe that sounds hackneyed, but the political and social upheavals that precipitated the "dark ages" no longer seem quite so remote to me as I race on to middle age, at least as far as art and culture are concerned. Just as good old Ambrose found himself staring into the abyss at the demise of a relatively peaceful empire, and was moved to cry out *veni*, so there are many today who wonder if we are once again facing a world without order. Humanism, that old crutch, seems to be splintering—and maybe it's just as well. But it is disconcerting to think of it all happening so soon.

In any case, I seem to enjoy worrying about such things, which is probably why I found myself feeling a bit unhinged a while back by a certain best-seller that happened to come my way. It struck me as a frank invitation to chaos and was still weighing heavily on my mind when I went to visit Smith one sparkling May evening.

"Doctor Moore!" he bellowed cheerfully, coming into the parlor to greet me as I eased my way through the porch door. "How are you on this glorious spring night?"

"Well enough, I suppose," I replied wanly. "Somewhat battered by modernity, but well enough for all that."

"What has modernity battered you with now?"

"Oh, the usual. My sister gave me a strange book for my birthday—all about asymmetry and string theory and other such charming esoterica—just the sort of thing that makes me wonder if we were not better off before modern science came along to confound our moral compass and throw our intellectual underpinnings into a mad eclipse."

"What!" Smith said teasingly. "Better off with ignorance?"

"'The center cannot hold,'" I said, sinking into an old overstuffed recliner. "Or at least not if we insist upon destroying it."

"How now—what makes us any different?"

"Good question. Man has more power now than he's ever had—and therefore one would think he has more reason to be happy. But this does not seem to be the case. It seems the more powerful he becomes, the more he sees himself as a miserable creature, grinding on without any view to future good. The warm spring breezes are blowing and the bloom is in the meadows, just as in every age and for everyone, but you would never know it from our heroic culture-mongers, who revel in everything that is ugly and repulsive in existence while they pursue their ideal of perpetual revolution, a bloody purge to last until only virtuous people like themselves are left."

"Nihilism's ongoing reaction to 'pessimism,'" Smith observed with a sigh. "But do you suppose it has ever seemed any less grim?"

"Perhaps not—but at least we were able to *pretend* there was some hope for the world. There was a time when we were able to placate our natural self-destructive tendencies by creating solid, productive intellectual systems that seemed much more in tune with the captivating splendor of the month of May than chaos theory or string theory or whatever it is that currently reigns supreme. But such comforting illusions seem impossible now. First we rushed out like lemmings to embrace a materialism utterly destructive to the old eternal forms; then evolution crept in, a veritable earthquake in the stillness of the academy; then brash relativity, a celestial skepticism where nothing is real but thinking makes it so; and now *asymmetry*, of all things!—a universe out of kilter at its very core. We've grown too smart for our own good; there's no room left for civilization."

"But the universe has not changed at all in its essentials, in spite of our twists and turns," Smith noted. "It is just the same as it always was—still beautiful, still confoundingly right and good in and of itself. Only our relationship to the universe has changed, our concept of who we are and our existence."

"That's just the problem," I said. "I don't know if I'm ready for our modern concept of existence. I seem to have been made for a somewhat less jaded age."

"Such as?" Smith said with raised eyebrows.

"Oh, the grand old days of Plato, for instance. The universe seemed perfectly ordered to those poor, benighted souls. Pythagoras thrilled us by talking about the mysterious properties of numbers; Euclidean geometry was downright genial. We have studied the nature of things, it seemed to say in a smiling way, and are pleased to announce that the relationships we anticipated are real, and they are fixed. Oh, sure—there's the occasional irrational number to annoy us—disturb our pleasant dreams—whatever.

But there was also a certain reasonableness and optimism to such philosophizing. The world had not yet opened Pandora's box, and probably knew better than to try."

"And yet Plato's cosmology was false."

"Gloriously false! But I, for one, would rather live by a civilized falsehood than sink into asymmetry and brute chaos, the dogmas de jour. It seems we agree these days that Plato and Aristotle and Newton and Descartes were simply telling 'stories' that were used to prop up the prevailing cultural identity—but then why are we so credulous when it comes to our *own* storytelling? Every cosmology ever invented has been overthrown in the end, and the modern age also seems overdue for a comeuppance, with its 'big bang' theory and black holes and alternate universes and multiplying dimensions and other such arcane hallucinations. If we agree that our cosmologies are nothing more than stories—nothing more than a means of placating a desire for closure and facilitating a good night's rest—then why not delude ourselves with something a little more edifying than asymmetry? In short, why not let our stories reflect something of the goodness of nature as we actually find it, instead of making the whole thing seem ugly and chaotic?"

"I think I see your point," he said. "The cosmology that reflects the modern Zeitgeist cannot reflect the beauty and order of nature because it is opposed to any notion of 'the good.' This makes it somewhat suspect, since those qualities are self-evident. But it seems a little late in the day for restoring Idealism."

"I don't see why. Relativity indicates that physical reality is nothing but a distorting mirror—which is exactly the same thing Plato said. Only Plato was wiser than we are, in my view. He saw that beauty cannot come from nothing, and therefore he claimed that beauty reflects the existence of a transcendent being that imposes its gracious qualities on existence. Frankly, this seems a little more cogent than anything we find in modern theoretical science, which would have us believe that the beauty of nature came into existence of its own accord; is nothing more than an astounding accident."

"The followers of Darwin strained out a gnat and swallowed a camel. It seems foolish to insist that the overwhelming beauty of nature came into being of its own accord, especially since human beings cannot make anything as beautiful as what is seen in nature even by conscious effort. One of the main limitations of materialism is that it cannot account for the existence of beauty, just as Plato indicated—but Idealism also cannot account for beauty. According to Plato, the beauty of nature comes into being when the divine intellect imposes its forms of value on matter. In his view, 'the good' was intellect, and the sensuous universe was beautiful because it reflected the capacity of intellect for resistance to formlessness."

"This accounts for the attempt to link form to intellect through geometry and rational numbers. They thought they could demonstrate that beauty is rational in nature."

"Yes, but they failed miserably. The underlying reason for the excitement generated by geometry is the notion that intellect has the power to disclose the essence of the beautiful forms seen in nature through rational numbers. In that case, men could use intellect to draw themselves up to God and obtain knowledge of the goodness seen in beautiful things. But intellect does not have any such power. Nature is infinitely more beautiful than the shapes described in geometry. Any of a billion trees in the forest is more pleasing than the golden rectangle, a mere illusion of perfection, forever approaching to pure rational form without ever quite getting there. The roses in the spring garden, the clouds in the deep blue sky, the waves upon the sand—all are asymmetrical according to the rigid rules of geometry; and yet all overwhelmingly beautiful."

"So the assault on classical geometry is justified, in your view. Analytical methods do not have the power to disclose the nature of the good. But doesn't it ever occur to you that we might just fall into the abyss under the weight of such knowledge and lose all sense of orientation and relationship? That the good itself might be lost?"

"Our belief that the Highest Good is intellect has had a great fall and cannot be put back together again," Smith agreed. "Any attempt to describe the goodness of beauty in rational terms reflects the concept that the good is intellect in its essence, the qualitative force of resistance found in the mind; but this resistance leads to divided theories of value because it is not the same thing as sense. It was not some fad that caused us to give up Idealism and the notion that pure intellect has the power to provide knowledge of the gracious value known as 'the good,' the value we see reflected in the goodness of nature. We gave it up because we realized that intellect cannot account for that goodness."

"The attempt to use intellect to obtain knowledge of 'the good' led to divided value judgments. But chaos and asymmetry seem to indicate that there is no transcendent power at all at work in the universe—no good and therefore no goodness. Which still leaves the problem of beauty and how it could have come into being."

"Such concepts are incompatible with the belief that the creative power seen in natural beauty is *intellect*—but they do not mean there is no such power. In fact just the opposite is true. The philosophers tried to describe the beauty of nature as a product of intellect in order to justify their belief that intellect is the good, and then the naturalists rejected 'the good' and tried to account for beauty through nature itself. But it seems that asymmetry overthrows both points of view. It is impossible to account for the goodness of natural beauty through intellect if the substrate of that goodness cannot be conformed to intellect and its forms of value—and equally impossible to embrace naturalism, since there is no evidence of a natural tendency in matter to produce beauty."

"Lucretius was wrong if asymmetry is right. Nondirected processes cannot lead to beautiful results, no matter how much time is added to the equation. A transcendent being of some type would seem to be absolutely necessary in order to bring the beauty of nature into being if the basic substances of nature are asymmetrical and chaotic. But your point is that this being cannot be 'the good' of the philosophers, since intellect cannot be used to calculate the appeal of beauty with any degree of certainty."

"The philosophers thought God was intellect because they were intellectual beings. They were in love with the qualitative power of intellect and with their theories of value. But perhaps God is not intellect in his essence. Perhaps it is time to entertain the weird notion that the text actually knows what it is talking about and was not lying when it stated 'God is love'—that the text reflects a deeper wisdom than can be found in Plato and Aristotle. In that case, the appearance of such oddities as asymmetry should not trouble us. Such things can be regarded as an opportunity for growth rather than an impediment, since they force us to stretch our minds and give up the tired, old assumptions about God that dominated Western culture for over two thousand years."

"You're suggesting that this is difficult to do."

"*Deus caritas est* indicates something very different from the concepts of transcendent being seen in philosophy. In order to begin to conceive of God in this way, intellect must give up the crown it has always worn in philosophy. And this is difficult because we are mortal beings and love to use the power of intellect to distinguish ourselves and justify our concepts of value. The philosophers were delighted to find that analysis of certain abstract figures was capable of producing rational results. This suggested to them that existence was intellectual in essence; that it was possible to obtain knowledge of the transcendent power that brought the universe into being through intellect and its force of judgment. But the problems they encountered as they attempted to demonstrate the rationality of even simple figures suggest that intellect is very limited in its power to account for the goodness of natural beauty."

"The problem of irrational numbers cannot be fully overcome without resorting to flat lines and negating the dynamic qualities of existence."

"Plato launched the age of philosophy by claiming that the goodness of beauty was a product of intellect and intellect could be used to obtain knowledge of 'the good,' but the value judgments rendered by intellect do not have the power to reflect the great desirability of nature. We know that even a lowly circle is beyond the pale of geometry—but the power of intellect to describe the goodness of beauty decreases almost to nothing when the circle is changed into the whorl of a cedar or the radiations caused by an acorn falling into a still mountain pond. These are gracious values, expansive values, compared to which the brilliant rationalizations of the *Timaeus* seem empty and cold."

"Sophocles' rationalizing is a relatively small value compared with the beauty of nature," I admitted grudgingly. "On the other hand, it was far more gracious than what is typically seen in the age of asymmetry and doctrinaire iconoclasm. The dinner guests in the *Republic* were not embarrassed by the thought of attempting to describe a good man because they actually believed in the existence of the good. They felt that a good person should be just, a value of some weight, and they agreed to use the state as a metaphor of justice, which led to a discussion of such edifying topics as rational behavior and good government. As soon as we negate the good, however, it seems all we have left to talk about is sex and power."

"But there does not seem to be a great deal of *graciousness* in Plato's theory of value—his concept of what is 'good,'" Smith countered. "Just as a few rigid geometrical shapes can make us feel good about ourselves by appearing to justify our love of analytical reasoning, so an attempt is made in Plato's Republic to obtain happiness by imposing rigid forms of behavior on existence and calling them 'justice.' Men and women become the common conjugal property of the state, for instance, so that the philosopher-prince can breed them optimally, the 'good with the good and the bad with the bad,' thus keeping some in perpetual servitude where they can perform odious labors but cannot rise up and threaten the dominance of 'the good.'"

"Plato's concept of justice may not be quite as gracious as his gorgeous rhetoric makes it sound," I conceded with a feeble smile.

"Justice is one of the most gracious values known to man, and Plato is perfectly correct to make it the measure of goodness in his idyllic state. But his concept of justice has nothing to do with the gracious behaviors encompassed in *deus caritas est*—such as helping those in need, defending the powerless and oppressed, protecting the strangers in our midst. Instead, it seems that 'justice' in the Republic entails such noble schemes as taking our children away from us at an early age and herding them into state institutions where they can be reliably instructed in good order. But what if we happen to love having children around the house more than we love Plato and his totalitarian enthusiasm for order? What if we enjoy hearing their cheerful little voices and feeling the strength of their attachments, which are far more edifying than anything found in his philosophy?"

"Such natural pleasures are negated by Plato's love of form; and to tell you the truth, I do not have any great desire to live in his Republic. But isn't there some danger in dismissing him too lightly? Can we reject Idealism out of hand without rejecting the values that Plato made famous—truth, beauty and the good? In fact isn't that just what we have done in the modern age?"

"Those values do not depend upon Idealism," Smith rejoined. "Plato's concepts of value reflected his infatuation with intellect and its qualitative force of resistance, its capacity to judge what is 'good.' Intellect cannot reflect the graciousness of the good, since it is a dividing power; but there is another qualitative power in consciousness that truly is gracious, a power that makes itself known through the *desirability* of nature. This power is not the same thing as the divided loves seen in philosophy. It is 'love itself.' Naturally 'love itself' is a gracious power by its very nature, but it is also gracious in the sense that it is far more expansive than anything seen in Plato or Aristotle, since sense and intellect are both highly desirable—both are good. It is a power that can supply the absolutely desirable content to justice that cannot be found in Plato because it takes justice out of the realm of pure form and empty abstractions and connects it to the value of life. And it also restores the great values of truth, beauty and the good—the good, because the power in desirability is love itself; beauty, because beauty is highly desirable; and truth, because the desirability of life plainly tells us what is right or wrong."

"The challenge you are proposing, then, is to change our time-honored view of the nature of transcendent being from intellect to 'love itself'; to take what is stated in the text literally and give up our obsession with intellect in order to free ourselves from the crushing burden of Nihilism."

"Putting aside intellect and its dividing power is painful because it requires us to accept our nothingness, to give up the alluring illusion of power produced by the philosophers and their rhetoric. Intellect can make us seem strong in the world, which is why we love it so dearly, but 'love itself' works in just the opposite way. It resists the vanity of the world; it is made strong in our weakness. The divided value judgments seen in philosophy reflect divided loves—Plato's love of pure values and Aristotle's love of nature and synthetic judgments. Their theories of value obtained power in the world through the dividing power of intellect, and this dividedness cannot be overcome. The identities furnished by intellect are mortal identities; but if we are willing to give up our infatuation with intellect, we become capable of obtaining knowledge of an immortal power."

"It is just when we give up the sword of judgment and outward appearances of power that we obtain access to the gracious realm intimated in the good, a kingdom that cannot be seen. Hence the paradoxical notion that transcendent power is made strong in our weakness. As long as we cling to the sword of judgment, we are clinging to a dividing power; in fact to our own mortality. The only way to go beyond this dividedness is to make ourselves available to the power revealed in the desirability of life."

"This paradox can be seen in Plato himself," Smith claimed. "His most beloved passages are Diotima's hymn to beauty and Socrates comforting his friends. These passages are powerful, but they do not obtain their power through intellect and its sword of judgment. On the contrary; they indicate that we do not have the power to give ourselves the happiness we desire by mortal means. The hymn to beauty influenced such potentates as Augustine, Boethius, Castiglioni, and Spenser; but it is not the cold power of judgment that accounts for the enduring value of Diotima's hymn. It is the passion of her love, which reflects a consciousness of her inability to obtain what she desires."

"The very warmth of the hymn that is so inspiring to others is a sign of her weakness, of the limitations of intellect. Otherwise there would be no reason for her passion."

"No passion is seen in Plato's description of the Highest Good. Those who attain the good of pure reason go beyond passion and become coldly intellectual beings. This coldness is very evident in the *Timaeus*, by the way, when Socrates imagines that he is in actual possession of the truth. But Diotima is wiser than Socrates because she knows that she has not yet obtained the happiness she longs for. Her theory of value has not enabled her to transcend this transitory existence, and her willingness to let us see a little of her vulnerability is the cause of the passionate tone of the hymn."

"In Diotima, Plato gives himself the freedom to express some misgivings about the effectiveness of his method of obtaining knowledge of the good—possibly because she was a woman," I suggested.

"That seems likely. Diotima would not have been expected to reach the heights of perfection he attributes to Socrates. But of course the irony is that her passionate hymn to beauty is one of the most popular passages he ever wrote; far more famous than anything found in the *Timaeus*. What is seen in this hymn is an unconscious example of how it is possible to be made strong in our weakness through the power of love. Plato obtains a more desirable identity through the passionate love seen in Diotima than through the coldly dispassionate theories of value and descriptions of being seen in Socrates."

"Plato comes closer to the immortal identity he desires when he allows us to have a glimpse of his weakness than when he is trying to convince us that he has transcended the sorrows of the mortal realm and obtained perfect possession of the good."

"The shows of power provided by intellect are an illusion, since we are mortal beings, but Diotima's passionate hymn reflects the value of life and the difference between this gracious value and our divided existence. Diotima is longing for something she cannot have by her own means—the happiness intimated in the goodness of life—an immortal identity—and we are moved by the passionate tone of her hymn because we share this same longing. Hence it is not through the power of intellect that she obtains the immortality she desires; it is through the passionate love seen in her hymn, a love that reflects the desirability of life."

"And of course this paradox becomes quite explicit in the last act of Socrates' life, when he feels compelled to let go of judgment and comfort his friends. At that point there was absolutely nothing he could do—no argument he could make—to save himself from the foolishness that confronted him in the irrational wrath of the state. He was forced to face the limitations of reason, since reason cannot give life."

"This is the only time when we see Socrates at a competitive disadvantage. Plato had a story to tell about the greatness of Idealism, and his hero was Socrates, the coolly dispassionate master of reason; and yet Socrates is never more compelling than when his weakness is exposed for all to see. He cannot be a hero of rationality in the face of death; his philosophy cannot save him. But he finds a way to reach beyond himself and his own limitations by appealing to the graciousness intimated in the value of life."

"This value is so great that it cannot let him die. Basically this is the reasoning he uses to comfort them. But it is not very good reasoning. Its power is not found in intellect or its sword of judgment. It is found in the value of life."

"Socrates had characterized the Highest Good as a supremely dispassionate power because he wanted to glorify intellect and its force of resistance. The Highest Good does not care about the problems of men; it is unmoved and unmoving forever. It cannot help him in the face of death, nor can he comfort his friends by invoking such a coldhearted monster. But when it was no longer possible to evade his nothingness through clever arguments, he suddenly became aware of a great value in consciousness that is not the same thing as intellect and its dividing power—the value of life for its own sake. This value is so great and so gracious that it makes death seem like a trifle, even an impossibility."

"It provides Socrates with a way out of the trap he set for himself by equating intellect with 'the good,' the highest value known to man. It is quite literally gracious in the sense that it is going to have to be willing to overlook the shortcomings of his philosophy in order to give him life. And his sense of this graciousness is reflected in the kindness he shows to his friends, attempting to comfort them when he himself is facing death."

"Plato and Aristotle have nothing to say to us in the face of death. They cannot give us the happiness or reassurance we desire because we are conscious of the value of life and the resistance of this value to the dividedness of their theories of being. But this same resistance also reflects a power that transcends the limitations of philosophy—a power revealed to us through the desirability of life. This power is not divided between resistance and existence. Life is an absolutely desirable value, but there is also great value in this mortal life. Therefore this power is capable of providing the knowledge of what is good that cannot be found in philosophy or its methods of judging value."

"It is capable of transcending the dividedness seen in philosophy, in your view. But there's one little problem here," I pointed out. "You have not dealt with the question you yourself raised—of how beauty could have come into being. Plato's description of the Highest Good accounts for the existence of beauty because intellect is a differential power; that is, the Highest Good is said to differentiate beauty through the forms of value it imposes on existence. But how can we account for this creative differential power if the nature of transcendent being is 'love itself'—a force of pure attraction?"

"That's just my point," Smith replied. "Love is not merely pure action; it is also a qualitative force of resistance. The power found in desirability resists the limitations of the value judgments seen in philosophy. It was the philosophers who tried to define love as nothing more than an attractive power—and that was because they were in love with intellect and its differential power. Plato wanted us to believe that the Highest Good is pure intellect and a force of absolute resistance to existent values, but then love comes into conflict with his theory of value because it continues to draw us powerfully to the values that already exist and which are said to be 'very good.'"

"The great goodness of nature resists Plato's attempt to characterize the Highest Good as a force of pure resistance."

"The natural beauty that already exists is incomparably more desirable than the empty figures and concepts of beauty seen in Idealism, which is why Plato found it necessary to discount the power in desirability in order to glorify Idealism. He tried to make love seem like an inferior power to intellect by claiming that it was nothing more than a force of attraction—that it had no capacity for differentiating good from evil or for providing happiness. But the power that makes itself known through the desirability of life is not merely a force of attraction, as Plato claimed. It is also a force of absolute resistance to everything that detracts from life—including his own theory of value."

"Actually there appears to be a differential side to love even in Plato, since love not only draws us to the beauty of nature but is also said to push us away from the limitations of existence to the contemplation of transcendent being."

"The truth is that Idealism is nothing without love because it bases its appeal on the good of happiness. We all want to be happy, and our desire for this good draws us to philosophy. Plato claimed it was possible to obtain this good through intellect and its differential power, at which point the philosopher is said to have transcended the foolish dependency of love—'No one desires what he already has.' But the problem with Plato's concept of transcendence is that 'the good' cannot be desirable without love."

"The good cannot be separated from the power in desirability without losing its goodness. If we really did transcend love, then the good would cease to seem good and would become an indifferent value."

"The power found in the desirability of life poses a problem for philosophers because it resists the vanity of their methods and their belief that intellect can provide them with knowledge of transcendent being. It will not permit us to find happiness in the nothingness caused by Idealism because nature is very good—a far greater value than Idealism and the empty talk about 'the good' found in Plato. Nor will it permit us to be satisfied with the attempt to overcome the nothingness of Idealism by grounding our understanding of the good in existent values, since the value we desire most is life."

"Both concepts of value are basically wrong."

"They are both right and also wrong—if the good is life. Plato was right to claim that the good cannot be found as itself in existent values because there is an absolute difference between life and mortal life. The thing we desire most transcends our present existence. And yet Plato was also wrong to claim that the good is a negation of present being because the life found in the mortal realm is nothing other than life."

"It is still life—still 'good' for its own sake and far beyond the thinking of men. Thus it is impossible to obtain knowledge of transcendent value by negating it."

"For this reason Aristotle was right to resist Idealism and to claim that valuable knowledge can be obtained from the goodness of existent values. If nature is 'very good,' and the product of transcendent being, then nature does indeed have important information to impart about the eternal qualities of that being as well as how to lead a good life—and indeed, from my point of view it seems like insanity to claim otherwise, since everyone knows that attempting to fly without wings is hazardous to one's health. And yet all of the great goodness found in nature does not add up to knowledge of what is good if the good is life—because nature is a mortal value."

"So 'the good' as it is understood by intellect is divided between pure negation and pure action, while 'love itself' does not appear to have this limitation. But is it a *formative* power? In what sense can it be said to account for the existence of beauty?"

"In the sense that desirability can be regarded as the ultimate form of everything that is desirable," Smith replied. "The philosophers claimed that intellect was the source of everything beautiful and good—that the differential power of intellect was responsible for the existence of natural beauty, a highly differentiated value. In reality, Plato's forms have no substantive value whatsoever apart from the beauty that already exists. There is no power in intellect per se that can account for beauty because intellect for its own sake is nothing more than resistance. But intellect is not the only differential power known to man. A great artist does not have to make conscious value judgments or employ a method of thinking in order to create something beautiful. He has a higher muse to follow than intellect, which is the power found in desirability itself."

"Love is a formative power in the sense that it informs our understanding of what is desirable."

Asymmetry, Mathesis, 'The Good'

"Beethoven did not use theory or logic to write his music. He did not have to stop and analyze what he was doing because desirability dictated to him what the next note or chord should be—and what it should not be. Desirability is the power that draws us to music, and it is also the power that draws highly desirable music from composers. In a great melody, the note that follows the one that has just been sounded is not called out of nothingness by intellect or any theory of value; desirability is the power that brings the next new note into being."

"This would explain the strange phenomenon of improvisation, which can produce desirable results with little or no premeditation at all."

"Desirability has the power to lead musicians out of nothingness and into a desirable state of being. And this same power can also explain how nature can be overwhelmingly beautiful when its underlying substances appear to be chaotic and to exhibit no intrinsic tendency to form. Chaos and asymmetry seem troubling as long as we continue to have one foot in the old realm of intellect and judgment. They undermine philosophy and the belief that the good is intellect by indicating that the universe is not rooted in rational values. But they have no bearing on the power found in desirability because this power does not depend upon intellect to produce desirable results."

"In this sense, then, Nihilism is not something to be feared. In fact what you're saying is that the death of intellect and its methods of describing the good provides us with a golden opportunity to reorient our fundamental understanding of reality."

"The modern age began with Descartes and the attempt to obtain an understanding of transcendent being by using the power of intellect to analyze nature. Our thirst for such knowledge led us to develop increasingly sophisticated instruments that enabled us to peer more deeply into the essence of things—but what we found there does not seem to justify our faith in intellect and its power to make us happy. On the contrary; it seems we are becoming aware of a realm of reality that appears, from the outside, to be pure chaos. And yet nature itself is not chaotic. Far from it. The trees still turn green in May; the earth does not veer from her narrowly defined course; spring nights continue to astonish us with their loveliness."

"We were looking for *rational* order, and when we did not find it we described what we saw as 'chaos'; but this may be nothing more than a sign of the limitations of our methods of judging value, because the moment we take our eyes away from the microscope we do not see chaos at all."

"We assumed that the power that brings the great values found in nature into being was intellect because we were in love with our ability to think. This assumption is shattered by chaos and asymmetry—and yet nature is good, highly desirable. Perhaps, then, we are just now beginning to approach the outer limit of a creative power that is so far beyond the thinking of men that it has the appearance, from the outside, of pure chaos, and yet is somehow capable of producing the highly desirable results seen in nature."

"This is a postmodern form of Origen's defense," I suggested. "Our concepts of 'the good' have self-destructed, but the goodness and beauty of nature have not changed at all; hence there is nothing to fear from chaos and asymmetry."

"Such things may be regarded as birth pangs. They are manifestations of a process of deconstruction that has now become self-conscious and can certainly be dangerous to the social order if it is combined with the will to power. But they may also be signs of a new way of thinking about value. It seems that the old order must be utterly destroyed before we become willing to give up the vanity of our love of intellect. The process of annihilation is not without danger—but there can also be great benefits in the death of philosophy to those who have eyes to see them."

"Our faith in the power of intellect has to be annihilated before we become willing to look at reality in a new way."

"If 'God is love,' and existence is ordered according to divine love and not intellect, then love for its own sake has the power to overcome the limitations of intellect and provide knowledge of what is good. For example, the statement 'all things work together for good to those who love God' can be understood through the power of love—but not through intellect and its dividing power. And if it was the *graciousness* of the good that overcame the grave and gives life—if 'mercy triumphs over judgment'—then the qualitative power of love provides an opportunity to obtain a desirable identity; an identity that is rooted in life instead of judgment."

"But the problem with grasping this power is that we have to let go of judgment. We have to let go of the very thing that provides us with identity and an appearance of power in the world and is the basis of all philosophy and theories of value."

"A revolution must take place—but not a revolution in the world, which can accomplish little to our purpose. I am talking about a revolution within. We must overthrow reason and the exalted throne she inhabits in our imagination. We must give up the purely delusory notion that it is possible to obtain happiness and a transcendent identity through intellect and its power to compare ourselves with other mortals. Only then does it become possible to explore the possibilities of 'love itself' and go beyond the misery we cause for ourselves when we cling to judgment."

"This would be the true perpetual revolution, since human vanity can never be fully overthrown," I noted with a laugh.

"Unfortunately that seems to be the case. We are what we are—mortal beings with a desire for life. 'God has put eternity into the hearts of men,' but men are mortal and cannot satisfy their thirst for this great and gracious value by their own means. It is possible to go beyond their limitations by enthroning 'love itself' in their hearts instead of the vanity seen in philosophy and its methods of judging value, but vanity is a mighty usurper and constantly strives to regain its power."

Smith grew pensive. I ran outside to fetch the bottle of champagne I'd left in an ice bucket on the porch for celebrating his birthday. While I was out there I paused for a moment to admire the stars, thick in the fragrant May sky.

Chapter 6

Sanctus

THEN AGAIN, what exactly is this deep wisdom that is said to be obtained from love for its own sake, if love is the power in desirability? Is it anything more than knowledge of a pleasurable way of living? And in that case, how can it satisfy any higher longing? The standard of desirability found in life may indeed resist the dividedness of intellect—but what form or shape does it give to the existence we now know? Aren't we attracted to wrongdoing? Can desirability be said to resist it? What is the mode of understanding provided by 'love itself' that is capable of bursting through the limitations of philosophy?

I decided to press Smith on these foolish questions when I went to visit him one fabulous June evening not long after graduation. It was not difficult to find an opening. At the time, the popular media happened to be fawning over an egregious new book by one of our colleagues that dismissed all traditional valuations with the whiff of cultural imperialism. This furrow is well-plowed, but the colorful personality of the author, coupled with the almost cult-like status he had obtained in elite circles, seemed to provide a useful illustration of the problem I saw in making love the standard of transcendent value.

"You missed our old friend H—— on TV last night," I said as we sat down at the kitchen table over a glass of Pim's and tonic.

"And what did H—— have to say for himself?" Smith replied as he dipped a piece of cheddar cheese into some maple mustard my wife had made.

"Oh, it was all about this new tome of his, which, as you probably know, is being greeted like a second *Kapital*. Apparently the rain forests are not impaired when radicals pontificate in prose, for few writers are as profligate with the pen as the good Professor, the belle don sans merci, who spares no verbiage in his furious assault upon the establishment—apparently without any awareness that the establishment is now virtually the same thing as himself. Meanwhile I am told that he has embarked upon his second subtropical fling since September, wife and five children notwithstanding."

"Uh-oh," said Smith, visibly shrinking.

"Oh, I know—I *am* rather small-minded about these things. But it shows a certain lack of delicacy, it seems to me, to be larding one's political tracts with grandiose proclamations about the 'morality' of the world's various economic and social systems at the very same time that one is attempting to impregnate the entire adjunct faculty. Like Stern or Dickens, his behavior seems somewhat out of sync with the tender and compassionate feelings he loves to exhibit in prose. Nor does he feel at all constrained from judging others according to the absolutism of the social gospel. Those who dare to disagree with the party line are subjected to withering personal attacks, and would probably have their ears cut off too, if it could be done with a telegenic smile. At the very least he should be encouraged to remove the bulging logos from his own eye before attacking the rhetorical sliver in everyone else's. This latest manifesto is water-high with sniffling judgments."

"Unfortunately H—— has a certain protean quality about him," Smith observed with a smile. "Resistance only seems to whet his appetite."

"But this is one instance where your concept of 'love itself' does not seem to provide an adequate response to the sheer perfidy of the human race," I noted. "I can only assume that H—— agrees with you about the transcendent power of love, given his history. Unfortunately the liberal theologians seem to forget that God is not only love; God is *holy*. In fact God is 'holy, holy, holy.'"

"So then holiness is *different* from love."

"That would certainly seem to be the case. Holiness is said to be like a refining fire—which does not sound very loving to me, unless the flesh can cozy up to an open flame. We don't like to talk about such things these days because we are reluctant to hurt anyone's feelings, but I do not know if it is a good idea to water down holiness in order to accommodate the world. Our conduct must be plumb with eternal truth; there can be no deviation from the rule, it seems to me, or the rule loses all verticality and we find ourselves wallowing in the warm mud of relativism."

"But there is nothing relativistic about Professor H.," Smith observed blandly. "He seems quite certain of the righteousness of his Nihilism."

"Surely there's a difference between holiness and Nihilism!" I cackled.

"Perhaps, but holiness can also be said to resemble Nihilism—when it is rooted in a love of absolute values. The combination of depravity and arrogance seen in Nihilism is so offensive to every notion of what is right and good that one may feel moved to oppose it with the absolute form of resistance implied in 'holiness'—but we forget that Nietzsche was also fond of that word. Dionysus is said to obtain a new standard of holiness through absolute resistance to philosophy's preoccupation with the good."

"But then are you suggesting that holiness is *not* an absolute value?"

"Not at all. But holiness cannot be an absolute value unless it is absolutely desirable—in which case it cannot be the same thing as the absolute values identified by intellect through its capacity for resistance to existent valuations."

"Granted, intellect produces divided value judgments. But what gives you the idea that holiness should be 'absolutely desirable'?"

"I was under the impression that holiness is good."

"Of course!"

"Can anything be 'good' if it is not desirable?"

"I suppose if it is good, then this implies that it must be desirable."

"Then holiness must be absolutely desirable, since we both agree it is an absolute value. In short, holiness should be perfectly sweet—but it seems to me that we have deprived holiness of much or all of its sweetness by attempting to divide it between pure intellect and synthetic constructs of value."

"There's just one problem with this clever demonstration. How can something seem 'sweet' and also exhibit a force of absolute resistance to the depravity of our own existence?"

"This is possible—if our concept of holiness is rooted in the gracious value of life, which is perfectly sweet. But the descriptions of holiness seen in institutional doctrine are rooted in judgment, which leads to bitter results through its dividing power. The popular notion of holiness as a force of pure wrath and negation came into being as a way of dethroning Scholasticism. It was a reaction to Thomas's characterization of holiness as a purely active love, which in turn was a reaction to the Platonism that had crept into the church through Augustine. Thomas saw that methods of judging value which are rooted in pure intellect result in nothingness by negating embodied values, but the only way to overcome the negative force of pure intellect is to characterize holiness as pure action."

"His concept of holiness is modeled on Aristotle's attempt to describe 'the good' in terms of the good things found in existence, and therefore it has the same limitations as Aristotle—it blurs the distinction between holiness and existence."

"Like Aristotle, Thomas assumed that God is intellect in his essence, but intellect intimates the possibility of holiness—an absolute value—

through its capacity to totalize its own qualitative force of resistance. Plato and his admirers were enthusiastic about the notion of 'pure intellect,' which they equated with the holiness of the Highest Good, the difference between this value and the unhappiness of present existence. But the problem with equating holiness with the capacity of intellect for pure resistance is that it results in the negation of all existent values."

"It turns holiness into nothingness by negating human existence."

"Pure resistance is pure negation. But if we assume that 'the good' is intellect, then the only way to overcome this negation is to negate it and turn the holiness of the good into pure reciprocal action. Thus intellect has two ways of characterizing holiness according to its own lights—either as pure negation or as pure action. But pure negation results in nothingness, while pure action deprives the transcendent of its force of resistance and draws it into existence."

"If our standard of holiness is life, then it is impossible to obtain holiness by pure action, since it is quite clear that all men are mortal."

"There is a vast difference between the holiness of God and what is seen in even the greatest saints," Smith agreed. "Paul had no confusion at all on this matter, as seen in his description of himself as the 'worst of sinners' and his statement that he was unable to do the good that he wanted to do. If that is the case, then it is impossible for mortals to obtain the holiness of God. Thomas's doctrine reflects the same limitations as that of his beloved 'Philosopher.' He accepted the premise that the good is intellect, which leads to the absurd notion that it is possible to obtain sanctity through pure action. A reversal was inevitable, especially when his followers began to distort his doctrine and turn it into something he never intended."

"But in your view the cure was no better than the disease. Calvin equated holiness with absolute resistance to existent values, which results in pure negation."

"The negative power of intellect intimates the *possibility* of the sweetness implied in holiness by negating present existence, which is, at best, bittersweet; but then it burns up both that which is bitter in existence and also that which is sweet. The finite is incapable of the infinite, according to Calvin—but then it is impossible to taste the sweetness of holiness in this present life. Holiness becomes relegated to the realm of pure form, just as in Plato's *Republic*; to resistance to dancing, for instance, or to spirituous beverages, or, most famously, to the glorification of study and prayer, as if those who were seen to do such things were somehow holier than their fellow beings."

"Holiness in this view exhibits the same limitations as Idealism. It tends to emphasize form and to be somewhat lacking in content. It tends to be rather shallow."

"The followers of Calvin put a great deal of emphasis on 'holiness,' but they cannot describe what holiness actually *is*. They have no concrete concept of holiness beyond certain shallow behaviors that are used to indicate the differential power of form. And the reason for this is that they conceive of holiness as a force of absolute resistance to the unhappiness of existence. In their minds, the shortest route to happiness is simply to negate all existent values and cling to form for identity and a sense of purpose."

"This goes along with your notion that a preference for negation or action is actually existential. You believe that unhappiness causes the lovers of resistance to have an overly negative view of existent values and to view pure negation as a way of relieving their burdens, their pain."

"I am not saying that the lovers of resistance should not love what they love. They are, for whatever reason, naturally inclined to favor resistance. But the problem is that mortals are also naturally inclined to use intellect and its capacity for resistance to compare themselves with others. We favor what we favor and think that it makes us more important than those who favor other things. But then our love of pure resistance divides us from those who have other notions of value—in which case it becomes impossible for us to reflect the sanctity of life."

"You are not condemning the lovers of resistance for being who they are, but you feel they should not be quite so eager to judge people who have other concepts of value."

"It is strange that those who gravitate to negation are inclined to characterize the holiness of God as a force of absolute resistance to existent values when the text that they themselves cite as the sole authority for their doctrine says 'God is love.' This discrepancy arises because they are seeking knowledge of God in intellect, which misleads them into thinking they can identify transcendent values through resistance. This is why those who follow the path of resistance often wind up in the awkward position of having to attempt to discount the power of love, like Plato. The problem with love is that it continually draws us back to the goodness of existent values and resists the characterization of holiness as pure resistance; therefore they find it necessary to devalue love to some degree in order to support a purely negative concept of holiness."

"But love is not discounted," I protested. "Holiness and love are described as complementary *attributes* in the divine nature—a very different thing from Plato. And this would seem to make sense. If God were nothing but wrath, then there would be no room for love, since our lack of holiness is obvious; but if God were merely love, there would be no room for wrath, because holiness cannot tolerate anything that is not holy."

"But in that case how does God know his own mind?" Smith countered. "If holiness and love really are dialectical attributes in the divine nature, then they would either cancel each other out or become competing interests in existence, like Thetis and Apollo. Some power greater than either one would be necessary in order to keep these conflicting attributes in good order."

"In other words, the very description of holiness and love as dialectical attributes indicates a belief that God is a dialectical power."

"What is it, precisely, that takes priority to love in the nature of God, if love is merely one of God's 'attributes'? Thomas and Calvin were both influenced by the premise that the transcendent is intellect in its essence and that intellect is therefore capable of providing knowledge of transcendent being. But this flattering notion comes from Plato and the Greeks—not from the text, which does not give any indication that intellect is the essence of God. In fact the excessive love of intellect was said to have been the cause of the fall of man and the beginning of his unhappiness."

"But I thought the Reformers claimed that the essence of God was unknowable."

"To say that the essence is unknowable is the same thing as saying that it is pure resistance. We know beyond a shadow of a doubt that Thomas thought intellect was the essence of God because he openly stated this opinion. As far as Thomas was concerned, intellect and 'the light' were one and the same thing. And you are right about Calvin—he was a good deal coyer about the divine essence than Thomas because he wanted to separate himself from the attachment to Greek philosophy seen in Scholasticism. But he too believed that intellect was the essence of God. He talked about obtaining knowledge of God through study, which indicates that such knowledge is intellectual in nature. Indeed, the very existence of his doctrine indicates a belief that it is possible to obtain knowledge of God through intellect and its dividing power. And a telling sign of this underlying belief is his equation of holiness with divine wrath, since the most immediate way for intellect to intimate purity is through the concept of absolute resistance to the unhappiness of existent values."

"The equation of holiness with absolute resistance indicates a belief that the good is intellect or resistance in its essence. But you do agree that holiness is something absolutely different from human existence—that it resists our own limitations?"

"Of course."

"And you have no problem with the descriptions of divine wrath seen in the text?"

"Not at all. It would seem very strange to me if my own abject failures were not the cause of wrath in a holy God."

"But then how can holiness be 'sweet'? How can it exhibit wrathful resistance to the foulness of human existence and at the same time have any sweetness in it?"

"This would be impossible if the transcendent were intellect in its essence, as we are sorely tempted to believe because of our love of judgment and its power to make ourselves and our theories of value seem important. In that case holiness would have to be exactly what Thomas or Calvin said it was—pure action or pure negation. But we are familiar with another standard of holiness that has nothing to do with intellect and its dividing power. It is said that 'in him was life, and this life was the light of men.' According to this view, holiness is found in the gracious value of life, not in intellect or its concepts of value. And this gracious value does not divide holiness between pure negation and pure action. Life as itself is absolutely different from mortal life—there is no mortality in it—and yet mortal life is still life. It is still a thing of great value."

"The holiness of life for its own sake is not the same thing as mortal life, and yet it can be tasted in mortal life because mortals are living beings. Thus it is possible to conceive of holiness as something that is absolutely sweet by thinking of life as our highest value, as the good and the light of men, instead of intellect."

"Intellect seemed sweet to the philosophers because they were able to use it to chase away their feelings of nothingness by comparing themselves with others; to glorify themselves and their concepts of value through its capacity for judgment. This sweetness was an illusion, however, because judgment is a dividing power and cannot produce any undivided value judgment about what is 'good.'"

"Intellect divides holiness between pure action and pure negation, and therefore it cannot give us the one thing we desire most—an immortal identity."

"We are mortal beings who are conscious of the value of life. This value is quite literally our 'light' in the sense that it transcends our mortal darkness. All of philosophy involves an attempt to find our way back to this light; all philosophers used the power of judgment in an attempt to obtain an immortal identity. But just as light appears to be both particle and wave and cannot be divided between theoretical and quantitative methods, so life cannot be divided and still be life."

"It is impossible to obtain knowledge of this transcendent value through intellect for the very reason that intellect is a dividing power."

"Intellect can plainly tell us what is good—what seems desirable—but our own intellect cannot identify 'the good,' a transcendent value, because we ourselves are divided beings with divided desires. All we know by the light of intellect is that we are natural followers of Plato or Aristotle—natural lovers of pure resistance or of the goodness of nature and the notion that this goodness has something important to tell us about 'the good.' And anyone who thinks this is not the case is simply deceiving himself, since the fault line between Plato and Aristotle runs right down to the present day."

"Our concepts of holiness are divided by the nature of our divided loves, by the uniqueness of our being. According to you, it is possible to go beyond this dividedness by seeking knowledge of what is good in 'love itself,' the power that reveals itself through the desirability of life, a power that is different from the divided loves seen in philosophy. But then are you suggesting that love *is* holiness—that not only is holiness not different from love but they are somehow one and the same thing?"

"This notion seems strange to the mind steeped in philosophy because the philosophers were in love with intellect and its differential power and were thus inclined to discount love as a force of mere attraction. They did not attribute any holiness or differential power at all to love—any capacity for resistance. If love were nothing more than human love, then perhaps this would be the case; but we have a higher understanding of love than is seen in philosophy. According to the text, 'the cross tells us what love truly is'—in which case it is quite clear that love is not merely a force of attraction, as the philosophers claimed. It is also a force of pure negation."

"The love seen on the cross is a *judgment* on the world and its vanity."

"The holiness of the cross is perfectly sweet because it is both pure action and pure negation. Its purpose was redemption, and in this sense it is an act of pure love. But at the same time it also exhibits a force of pure resistance to the world and its depravity, since we ourselves are the cause of his suffering. This sweetness, then, reflects the value of life. There is a force of pure resistance to existent values in life because life is absolutely different from mortal life, and yet mortal life is worth redeeming for its own sake."

"Mortal life is not absolutely without value; otherwise there would be no sense in redeeming it."

"I understand the reluctance in some quarters to embracing love as the essence of God," Smith commented. "There is a fear that this valuation negates the resistance of the holiness of God to existence. But just the opposite is true—the love seen on the cross negates human vanity and the desire to make ourselves seem equal to God. There is an absolute difference between the purity of this love and mortal, selfish loves; between the self-aggrandizing behaviors seen in the world and a love that is willing to empty itself completely of all pride and self-interest."

"Thus there would appear to be a rule of some kind in love. It is not merely a force of attraction but also draws a line between the kind of love seen on the cross and mortal loves."

"We are told that all of the law and all the prophets are summed up in the command to love. If that is the case, then love is a force of negation as well as action, since law is a negative power. Love is a fully differential power, contrary to what the philosophers claimed. The love seen on the cross indicates pure resistance to the selfishness of human existence. It provides a rule for what is good—the way to obtain life is to lay down the pride of this mortal life. And this rule is established by the light of life."

"The sanctity of life is a light to mortal minds, furnishing an understanding of what is good through its resistance to all self-seeking motivations."

"The greatest commandment is designed to preserve our own lives. To love God more than we love ourselves or the world is to orient our thinking in a way that leads to health and happiness. The second commandment reflects the sanctity of the lives of our fellow beings. To love our neighbors as ourselves is to give up the natural desire to attempt to obtain happiness at their expense—the desire that is at the root of all the transgressions listed in the second set of commandments."

"But here's my problem. Thomas also equated holiness with love."

"Not really. Thomas's concept of a purely active love is not the same thing as the love seen on the cross, which is both pure action and pure negation. He did not view love as the essence of God any more than Calvin. A purely active love is said to be the result of the reciprocal action of grace and human existence—a construct of value rooted ultimately in intellect, not love for its own sake. Thomas may have *seemed* more amenable to the notion that love is the essence of God than Calvin, but this was an accident of his method of describing value. Synthetic philosophers base their concept of what is good on the notion that the transcendent willingly overcomes the difference between itself and matter in order to bring the goodness of the sensuous universe into existence. But this requires them to identify some power that can move intellect to give up its force of resistance—and many of them described this power as love."

"Which was natural for Thomas, since love is so prominent in the text."

"Thomas made an ingenious adaptation of Aristotle to Christianity. We are enjoined by the text to seek goodness by being active in charity, and Aristotle's ratio of intellect and matter leads to the characterization of the good as Pure Act. Thomas combined the definition of goodness in the text and Aristotle's concept of value into the concept of a purely active love. But while it is true that love is seen as pure action in the parable of the sheep and goats, it is also seen as pure negation in the law, since 'no one is righteous, not even one,' and also on the cross, which indicates that it is impossible for men to draw close to a holy God by their own natural means."

"It is not possible to compare ourselves to others on the basis of a purely active love, since we are all mortal. Thomas's concept of a purely active love is not the same thing as 'love itself,' which resists the vanity of wanting to make ourselves seem holy."

"The power revealed through the desirability of life is a force of pure action as well as pure negation. It is not divided like intellect and its theories of value between resistance and existence. Married love can be holy by the standard of desirability found in life, first because marriage facilitates procreation, but also because it has the potential to give life to the other by building her up and making her happy. And yet this same standard of holiness is also experienced in actual human existence as a force of fiery resistance, since there is no such thing as a marriage without selfishness."

"Love exhibits pure resistance in married love, but this resistance is different from what we see in Plato and his dialectic of intellectual and physical procreation."

"Plato tried to devalue sensuous existence because he wanted us to believe that the good was pure intellect. He was not so bold or foolish as to deny the importance of procreation, which is necessary to the perpetuation of life; but he claimed to have discovered a value that transcends mere physical procreation—something called 'intellectual procreation,' which supposedly produces pure values through the capacity of intellect for resistance to divided values. But intellectual procreation is an oxymoron, since it is impossible for pure intellect to overcome its own force of resistance."

"Plato's concept of holiness is actually the opposite of procreation because pure intellect is the negation of all existent values."

"There is something inherently morbid about Idealism. According to Hegel, an enthusiasm for pure resistance is a manifestation of the 'unhappy consciousness'—and there may be some truth to this. The antithetical impulse, it seems, is often a manifestation of such strong discontent that it leads to a desire for annihilation. Socrates' comment about the desirability of death is a well-known example. This morbid strain is not so visible in Descartes, perhaps because of his strong faith, but it surfaces again in the superman and his purported love of battle, as well as in those postmodern followers of Nietzsche who interpret Dionysian existence as self-destructive recklessness."

"The love of pure resistance leads to rather negative results," I conceded. "But the synthetic method also cannot produce any undivided value judgments about what is good if you are right in characterizing the good as life."

"Aristotle described Supreme Being as 'nothing other than life,' but this had more to do with a desire to glorify his concept of the good at the expense of his teacher than with the sanctity of life for its own sake. Just as the Idealists were in love with the word 'soul' and its power to intimate individuality and difference, so synthetic philosophers loved to use the word 'spirit' to make their method seem more lively than the inanition that results from Idealism. But they characterized spirit as the pure reciprocal action of divine intellect and matter that they claimed to see in existence—in which case spirit cannot be the same thing as life."

"'Spirit,' as described in synthetic philosophy, is not the Spiritus Sanctus—the spirit of life. It is a product of intellect and ratiocination."

"It mimics the liveliness of the spirit of life through the concept of the pure reciprocal action of intellectual and material causes. But mimicry is not mimesis. To return to the example of marriage, we are told that two become one flesh and leave behind their dividedness. This led the Schoolmen to conclude that marriage has sacramental significance. But no one should delude himself into thinking that human marriage can become holy if even the *thought* of dalliance is condemned."

"This standard of holiness reflects the desirability of life, since such thoughts detract from the value of the other—and it is not a standard that mortal beings should presume to have obtained. But then who in the world can be holy?"

"The desirability of life sets a far higher standard of holiness than anything seen in synthetic or pure doctrine," Smith said with a sigh. "If we measure ourselves by the concept that holiness is pure resistance, then we may be able to delude ourselves into thinking we are holy, since it is not difficult to negate existence as if it had no value, or to exhibit puritanical attitudes. And it is also possible to deceive ourselves into thinking we are holy if we measure holiness by the concept of a purely active love, since it is not difficult to devote ourselves to charity. But no one can claim to be holier than anyone else by the measure of life, since all men are equally mortal."

"But doesn't this lead us back into the jaws of our conundrum? If our standard of holiness is life, and if 'no one is holy' and the heart is 'deceitful above all things,' then holiness is, in reality, a force of pure resistance to human existence."

"It is true that no one can pretend to be holy by the standard of life, and it is also true that too little holiness is found in human existence. But this does not mean that holiness is a force of absolute resistance to existence, or that we are incapable of tasting its sweetness. Holiness did not remain far off from human existence when the 'word became flesh' but was actually manifested in existence; and in him we also saw that holiness can be perfectly sweet—for instance, in the story about woman at the well. This story is useful for our purposes because he had a choice to make between the standard of holiness established by the desirability of life and a concept of holiness that was rooted in judgment. Was he going to allow himself to look foolish to the existing order by talking to the woman and offering her his living water—or would he seek an appearance of holiness in the convention of shunning?"

"Clearly there was a conflict between his concept of what constitutes holy behavior and the notions of holiness held by the priestly class."

"Religion is based on outward appearances—religion that seeks to distinguish itself in the world and obtain an appearance of holiness. But the problem with outward appearances is that they can be deceiving, as is clearly the case with shunning. This practice came into existence to protect the men of Israel from their weakness—the weakness of Samson, the strongest man—not to glorify their capacity for holiness. When they reached the Promised Land, it soon became evident that their most dangerous enemy was not the Philistines or foreign armies, which they seemed to have little trouble defeating. It was their own attraction to Pagan women."

"It seems they had a tendency to fall in love with them; to marry them and adopt their gods, as Samson did. And this was more of a threat to them than foreign armies because it undermined the integrity of Israel as a covenant nation."

"Shunning reflects the need to resist this attraction in order to preserve their very existence. It seems the only way for them to resist their natural desires was to put up a barrier of pure shame between themselves and women who were considered 'unclean.' Shunning became encoded in the national consciousness as a sign of holiness in order to prevent the unholiness to which the nation was highly prone. But over time this original significance was lost, and shunning came to represent holiness itself."

"The outward shell of shunning, which is actually a sign of weakness, rightly considered, became transformed through vanity into a sign of moral strength and a means of comparing oneself with others."

"The same thing is seen in all of the ceremonial law. Circumcision, for example, is a sign of repentance; of being willing to sacrifice the pride of the flesh for the sake of a God who is spirit. The actual significance of circumcision, then, is that men are naturally concupiscent and need to make this outward sign in order to remind themselves of what is right and good. Circumcision, as an outward sign or seal, signifies the weakness of men; but over time it came to mean almost the opposite."

"It came to indicate holiness itself, or difference. This is what he meant when he told the Pharisees that they were clinging to the dividing power of the law without understanding its significance."

"The law is 'spiritual' because it is rooted in the value of life, not in judgment for its own sake. The story about the woman at the well provides a stark contrast between the holiness of his behavior, which reflects this gracious value, and self-limiting notions of holiness such as shunning, which reflect the love of judgment. The purpose of such concepts is to distinguish some men at the expense of others and identify them as people who are especially holy; but the holiness revealed through the desirability of life resists the vanity of such value judgments because no life is more valuable than any other."

"To shun the woman at the well is to fail to come to terms with one's own mortal limitations."

"The holiness of his behavior was rooted and grounded in love, not in intellect or its concepts of value. He felt compassion for the woman at the well. He wanted to offer her his living water and relieve her of the type of labor in which she was engaged, which cannot satisfy the soul. Now first of all, note that this love of his does include a force of pure action or attraction. Clearly he had affectionate feelings toward her, in spite of her manifold weaknesses. His compassion for her was not merely some sort of 'metaphor'—a purely outward behavior or form of value—as some of our clever theologians would have us believe. He saw real value in her existence."

"Holiness as it is seen in him is not a force of pure resistance to existent values. It is not rooted in intellect or its concepts of value. He was not merely play-acting with her but actually seems to have enjoyed the conversation."

"There is something beautiful about breaking down the walls that exist between mortals and having pleasant conversations with people we do not know, conversations in which our objective is to be pleasing and not to distinguish ourselves. Such conversations reflect the gracious value of life. There is value in present existence if the good is life because the life seen in the woman at the well was nothing other than life. Mortal life falls short of the sanctity of life itself—but this does not mean that mortals are not to be cherished. In fact if mortal life is without value then his whole mission was madness and story of the text an empty show."

"There can be little doubt that he cherished many of the people he encountered along the way. His love for them was holy, and it included an active side. But in what sense is it differential?"

"His behavior exhibits the differential dimension that is necessary to holiness on many levels. First of all, his treatment of her reflects the moral law and the clarity it provides about sexuality. The moral law is rooted in the value of life—it prohibits behaviors that are harmful to health and happiness and seeks to protect the weak and powerless. To be holy in a sexual sense is to reflect the power revealed in the desirability of life, which is 'love itself.' And this type of holiness is reflected in the fact that he did not flatter her but found a gentle way to let her know that he was aware of her colorful history."

"He was not flirting with her, nor were there any antinomian tendencies on display in his willingness to speak to her."

"He did not come to destroy the law but to uphold its spirituality against the false concepts of holiness seen in the Pharisees, who used the law to glorify themselves. If the law reflects the holiness of life, then it cannot be used to flatter any mortal. But the differential character of his holiness is also seen in his unwillingness to shun the woman at the well. The fact that he spoke to her at all reflects the difference between holiness that is rooted in the sanctity of life and concepts of holiness produced by judgment, since it resists the notion that holiness can be found in shunning our fellow beings."

"There is a marked difference between holiness as it is seen in him and the supposed holiness of the Pharisees. Your point is well-taken; love is not merely a force of attraction but also a differential power."

"His behavior toward the woman at the well was perfectly holy—and yet it was also perfectly sweet. It was sweet because of his kindness. It was sweet because of his humility and willingness to give up his cultural identity and speak to her as an equal. It was sweet because of the possibility of redemption—redemption stories make us happy because they reflect the great desirability of life. And it was sweet because he was brave. We know he ran afoul of the ruling authorities by standing up for love and the spiritual content of the law against their abusive vanity; we know his willingness to talk to her was just the sort of thing that got him into trouble and led ultimately to his demise."

"Which brings us back to Professor H., I suppose," I groaned. "In order to reflect the sweetness of the holiness seen with the woman at the well, it is necessary to follow his example and embrace our nothingness."

"Holiness in this sense is hard—something painful and far off—and yet his story suggests that it is the only path to follow if we desire happiness; the only path that leads to an identity that reflects the desirability of life. The question confronting us every waking hour of the day is whether to seek identity in outward appearances of holiness—in the power of judgment to establish differences among men—or whether to root it in the hidden power that reveals itself through the gracious value of life. Appearances of power cost us nothing. A sanctioned behavior such as shunning comes at no cost to the Pharisees and in fact endears them to the world. But the sign of love indicates that we must give up the world in order to seek identity in the gracious value of life."

"The Pharisees were able to gain the whole world through shunning, but not without losing their souls, since shunning required them to devalue life. Meanwhile his resistance to outward appearances of holiness put him at odds with the world and got him into hot water with the Pharisees—but it led to a far greater identity in the end."

"There is a difficult choice to be made between the vanity of the world, which can bring instant gratification but cannot make us happy, and the possibility of obtaining true happiness in the soulfulness of 'love itself.' Every fiber of our being clamors for the dark pleasure of putting Professor H. in his place, not only because we find his theory of value repellant, but also, frankly, because of the celebrity he enjoys in the world, which makes us feel undervalued. By nature we want to resist these bitter feelings of nothingness, and we find that a remedy is close at hand in the power of judgment, since there is no question that we can inflict damage on him by taking up the sword and denouncing him. We know we can obtain a ready-made audience for such a denunciation; there is a place of honor in the public square for culture warriors. We may even be able to talk ourselves into believing that it is holy to denounce him and expose his foibles, since there is an obvious difference between true holiness and his sanctimony. But it is impossible to find the happiness we are looking for in judging him if *life* is the measure of holiness. We are mortal, and any judgment we use to cut others also cuts ourselves."

"I may feel an urge to expose his moral shortcomings, but it is perhaps fortunate that others cannot see into my mind and my own lack of holiness," I admitted. "The old saw is still in force."

"Holiness that is rooted in the desirability of life is characterized outwardly by two traits—humility and gentleness. Not that either trait is seen in me or my behavior—I make no claim to be holy. But I have just enough sense to value these traits and to understand their hidden significance when I see them in a story like the woman at the well. We can attempt, like Hamlet, to take up the sword against our sea of troubles, whether real or imagined; but the sword of judgment cannot give us the happiness we desire because we ourselves are not holy. There may be a brief and fleeting pleasure in denouncing H. and having our philippic talked about in those circles where we know in advance that it will be welcomed, but we also know from long and weary experience that this initial thrill of conquest will be followed by unhappiness and a long train of bitter consequences, since it is unlikely that H. will lie down like a lamb for the slaughter, or that his followers will not rise up to defend him and denounce us in kind."

"You are reminding me that there is a practical benefit to such qualities as humility and gentleness. We may think we are solving our problems by wading into the culture wars with our swords flashing when in fact we are making things far more complicated for ourselves—very much like Hamlet."

"The decision is difficult because it is linked to identity. We are afraid of our nothingness and crave with all of our being to be known. The thought of embracing graciousness and giving up the sword made Hamlet feel that he was forsaking being—that to be humble and gentle was not 'to be,' to have a forceful identity in the world. But to seek being in the world through the sword of judgment is to lose the immortal identity we desire and make ourselves seem like the world. Hamlet ceased to be Hamlet—the Hamlet who had 'that within which passes show'—and began to resemble

Claudius and his murderous plotting. He no longer knew himself because he had given up the graciousness that he loved for the sake of making his grievance known to the world."

"This type of identity cannot satisfy us because we are conscious of the value of life, which transcends the world and its little struggles to be known. Hamlet attempts to obtain 'being' in the world—the type of being that is readily apparent to us all, which is tempting because it can be seen. But we are told that there is another means of obtaining being and identity; indeed, that a unique identity is reserved for those who give up the world and cling to the graciousness exhibited with the woman at the well."

"This identity cannot make itself known in a forceful way to the world because it is hidden from the vanity of the world; because it comes into being through resistance to the limitations of mortal life and our concepts of value. Life is not the same thing as mortal life, and therefore the identity that is obtained by seeking to reflect the desirability of life cannot be known until it is disclosed. And yet such an identity is not without its consolations, even in the present tense. It may be undervalued, but it is not unknown. I know people who are gracious, who are truly humble and gentle, and there can be no doubt that this is an identity worth having."

"But then the identity sought in humility and gentleness requires faith in a transcendent power and not our own; a power that is love in its essence."

"Hamlet believed in this power—but not strongly enough to give up the sword. And this fact of his existence (as well as our own) points to two completely different and irreconcilable conceptions of moral strength, or virtue, and indeed of reality itself. In order to give up the sword and seek identity in the graciousness of love, Hamlet must be strong in his belief in the sovereignty of love in the universe, his belief that love is a transcendent power—*deus caritas est*. And much more strength is required to hold on to this belief in the face of the trials and temptations of existence than to take up the sword because its value cannot be outwardly seen; is hidden from the vanity of the world."

"The strength seen in the journey to the cross, where he 'turns his face like flint.' So love, then, is not merely a force of attraction but also has differential power. The holiness attributable to love can be found in such traits as gentleness and humility—which are holy specifically because of their resistance to the world. And this difference has immediate practical implications as well as long-term implications for identity."

"If 'God is love,' then 'all things work together for good to those who love God.' What we see on the outside is not the sum of reality. The triumph of the will in the world is a delusion if there are unseen forces ruling existence by the power of love. Those who appear to be great today and are lifted up by the world and its vanity will be cast down in the end, while those who remain humble and gentle for the sake of love will be lifted up. This is the secret wisdom imparted to us through the power that reveals itself in the desirability of life. But it is not always easy to allow ourselves to be guided by its light."

"We know these concepts very well on an intellectual level, but it can be difficult to internalize them and actually allow them to inform our identity; a process that requires us to let go of the world and its illusions."

"Everything in us screams to be known, and we have the tools to make ourselves known in a forceful way. That is our greatest temptation. But the only way to obtain the type of identity we desire—an identity that reflects the gracious value of life—is to cling to graciousness and give up the natural desire to judge others, the desire to overcome our nothingness through judgment. The only way to go beyond the well-known limitations of the past is to leave the past behind and learn to live in the present, exploring the possibilities of the will of 'love itself' and trusting in its redemptive power."

"There is indeed a rule in love," I concluded, "and in fact it turns out to be the most difficult, the most demanding rule of all."

"Love is the most difficult rule because it compels us to give up our excessive self-love and seek identity and contentment in a power not found in ourselves. It compels us to take up the cross, in which there is no outward sign of happiness, apparently nothing but suffering and foolishness, and put aside the meretricious signs of value seen in the world. And yet there is no way to obtain the great sweetness of the cross and the unselfish love that it exhibits without taking it up; no way to obtain the gracious identity we desire without letting go of our natural urge to judge others. Thus the desirability of life establishes a far higher standard of holiness than anything seen in our concepts of value."

Chapter 7

Seasons of Creativity

It was a surly July afternoon, heat thunder roiling in the hills. I remember glancing furtively up and down the empty, unlighted hallway as I locked my office, like a character in a spy movie—and then laughing out loud when I realized I had cast myself as the hero. Of course there never had been any conspiracy in the department, despite the lurid rumors. The alleged instigators, not a Brutus among them, were too busy stabbing each other in the back to engage in any concerted effort. Still, the thought of having to answer to the campus thought police at this late stage in my career was unsettling. Also I was feeling anxious about a favorite poetry class that had been on the decline, attendance-wise, in recent years—much to the delight of one of my more vocal colleagues, who thought all such courses irrelevant or worse. (This was the same bright young fellow who did not seem to be resisting the mantle of leadership that was being thrust upon him by shadowy forces on behalf of "rethinking" the department and its objectives.)

As much as I like to be useful, I don't enjoy being made the whipping boy of traditionalism. But since there did not appear to be any conspirators on hand to thrash, I decided to head over to Smith's house and try to blot out the petty insults of life with a mint julep or two. I found him out back in his terraced vegetable garden, tinkering with some tomato plants in spite of the heat and muttering to himself.

"Looks great," I called out with forced cheerfulness, trudging down the dusty tractor road with a bottle of rather nice bourbon in my hand.

"Oh—it's you," he said without looking up. "Yes, the soil's quite rich here. I hardly have to lift a finger."

"You're lucky. Mine is mostly sand. But I suppose that's comforting, in a way," I said, making a doleful attempt at badinage. "At least I don't have to worry about sending out soil samples every year to no avail—unlike the poor fellow next door."

"Come, now. An idealist like you would probably refuse to make use of good soil even if he had it," Smith said with a chuckle.

"Only a fool would deliberately *choose* bad soil," I replied, feeling stung.

"In that case it is fortunate I did not have an opportunity to make a fool of myself. The soil here is the best in the valley, and it seems there is nothing I can do about it," he said in a softer tone. "But I'm surprised to see you. Why aren't you up at Moosehead, dangling flies in front of somnambulant trout?"

"Too much to do. I refuse to stray too far from the library until I've made a palpable beginning on that blasted book of mine. I just recently realized, to my horror, that it's been five years already, counting the early inquiries."

"Horace recommends a decade, I believe."

"Horace's idea was to put a manuscript in a drawer somewhere and come back to it with a fresh eye. But I haven't *got* a manuscript. Meanwhile I continue to lag behind those ambitious young colleagues of mine who seem to be able to whip up their frothy soufflés at will."

"Are you worried about that?" Smith said, glancing up at me. I started to reply, but the words caught in my throat with a swirl of summer dust. He straightened up and squinted inquisitively at the object in my hand. "Interesting bottle."

"Juleps," I explained.

"Good," he said, painfully peeling a pair of yellow leather gardening gloves from arthritic fingers. "Haven't had one in years."

A few minutes later Smith was standing at the kitchen sink, cracking ice in a linen towel, and I was mixing spearmint he had picked near the back door with some sugar and water. He was silent and thoughtful, and I was half hoping the subject had been forgotten when he surprised me by taking it up again.

"Of course your concept is excellent, as I have told you many times before," he said encouragingly, and somewhat out of the blue.

"Perhaps—but it might be nice if I could get something down on paper," I replied. "At this point I seem to be unable to write down anything I don't want to tear up the next morning. I feel like I have fallen into some sort of creative black hole; the old ways of doing things don't seem to be working anymore."

"Maybe you've outgrown them," he suggested.

"How so?"

"The problem may be with method itself. Method can provide an *appearance* of creative power, but it is limited by the difference between resistance and existence. Hegel seems almost endlessly creative as he imposes the synthetic juggernaut on every subject under the sun, but the more we see of him the more we realize his creativity is limited to the repetition of a single tedious refrain. Similarly, one has the impression *Das Kapital* could go on forever if the great idealist did not have to lay down his pen occasionally to eat and sleep—but the method always follows the same rigid path."

"Where can we look for creativity if not in Hegel and Marx?" I said with a laugh.

"The highest standard of creativity is life. The philosophers tacitly acknowledged this when they devoted their methods to describing 'being,' but they confused this value with their own thought-existence—with intellect and its concepts of existence—and life is a far greater value than intellect. You feel you have lost creative power because you cannot be satisfied with your writing, but this may simply mean that you are grappling with the creativity seen in life—that the resistance found in this value is making you aware of the insufficiency of method and driving you to greener pastures."

"Very comforting. But I can't help thinking it would be better to finish this masterpiece while I'm still alive."

"The value I am talking about is not a force of absolute resistance to existence," Smith replied with a smile. "We are living beings, after all, and there is no reason why our writing cannot reflect our consciousness of the value of life. But it is impossible to reflect this value through any method of making value judgments because judgment is a dividing power. It is the graciousness of the value of life that causes us to want to make our concepts of value known. The difference between this great value and our nothingness spurs us to attempt to establish a forceful identity in the world before our miserable existence is blotted out by eternal night—and method seems especially congenial to this purpose because it is limited by the difference between sense and intellect. But for the same reason the seeming power of method is an illusion."

"You're suggesting that the very limitedness of our methods of judging value is what makes them seem appealing, since it facilitates finite conclusions about value."

"Method enables us to hurry to a conclusion, and well-supported conclusions can be used to obtain an appearance of power; but no identity that is rooted in judgment can make us happy because we are conscious of the value of life. It seems we are becoming especially sensitive to this problem at the end of the age of philosophy. We are too familiar with the limitations of our methods of judging value to flatter ourselves with the idea that they can satisfy our deepest desires. At one time this seemed possible; at one time we felt quite certain we could obtain knowledge of transcendent being through such methods as Rationalism or Transcendentalism. But Nihilism indicates that we have lost faith in our own methods of describing transcendent being."

"We would not have been so eager to annihilate philosophy and its concepts of value if it had not been perfectly obvious to us that those concepts are hopelessly divided and cannot give us the happiness we desire—which is the purpose of philosophy in the first place."

"Nihilism indicates a collective awareness that it is not possible to satisfy our thirst for the good of happiness through philosophy. It bars the door forever to such identities as Rationalism or Transcendentalism, which were rooted in intellect and its sword of judgment. No dividing power can provide knowledge of what is 'good'; therefore we must throw in with Nietzsche and attempt to satisfy ourselves with the empty vanity of the superman if we want to continue to cling to intellect for identity. And yet intellect is not the only means we have of obtaining knowledge of value. Consider these tomatoes of mine. We know perfectly well when a tomato is ripe—we taste it to see if it is sweet."

"The ripe tomato provides a standard of goodness which has nothing to do with philosophy or its methods of describing what is good."

"The sweet goodness of the tomato is becoming useful to us at the end of the age because of its resistance to the bitterness of the superman. According to him, the good does not exist. He must cling to this tenuous conclusion because it has now become the only way for intellect to intimate transcendent value—through the notion that it is possible to go beyond the limitations of philosophy and its value judgments about the good by negating the good itself. But the negative ideal of absolute resistance to the good leads to a conspicuous absence of sweetness in the modern identity. There is no room for sweetness in the will to power; thus the great sweetness seen in such antithetical philosophers as Plato and Descartes cannot be found in any degree in Nietzsche or his followers."

"Foucault cannot begin to understand Velasquez and his affection for the Infanta because there is nothing in his frame of reference except naked power; no room for any appreciation of the natural sweetness of children."

"Nihilism results in the annihilation of the sweetness that Velasquez wanted to reflect. This natural sweetness cannot be annihilated, however, which is why Nihilism cannot provide a transcendent identity. Foucault may not have been capable of experiencing the great pleasures of family life himself, but this does not mean that they are an illusion. Nihilism cannot blot out the goodness of family pleasures for the sake of the totalitarian value of the will to power because those pleasures are real; in fact are far greater than anything found in philosophy."

"The sweetness of those pleasures forms a natural force of resistance to Nihilism and a limitation on its capacity to provide a desirable identity."

"The notion of 'sweetness' has disappeared from the modern palette. The superman cannot afford to be sweet when he seeks identity in his ability to dominate his fellow beings; when all of one's thought-existence is believed to be purely the product of evolutionary urges reflecting the will to power. Find me a poem or novel or musical composition or work of art or architecture in the Modernist vein that celebrates the great quality of sweetness known to us in family pleasures and nature—indeed, see if you can find the word 'sweet' in the self-absorbed scribbling of the avant-garde."

"Sweetness must be put out of mind because it is redolent of the good. The absence of sweetness in Modern culture reflects the vanity of the overman as well as the limitations of his method of judging value. But what does all of this have to do with my poor book?"

"Perhaps it is a lack of sweetness that is troubling you," Smith replied with a shrug. "The problem confronting the writer today as he sits down at his keyboard is his consciousness of the desirability of sweetness. He knows this great quality from nature, from the blossom of the tea rose or a ripe tomato or a perfect summer day or even a simple glass of water. He knows it from family life and friendship. He knows it from life itself, since there is nothing that seems more desirable to him than a transcendent identity. This same consciousness prevents him from finding what he is looking for in the superman, an identity in which any trace of sweetness or any gracious value has been annihilated for the sake of the will to power. But it also prevents him from being satisfied with anything in his own writing that is not sweet; anything, for instance, that is infected with the bitterness of philosophy and its divided concepts of value."

"He is aware of the great desirability of sweetness, and this awareness makes itself known in a negative way as resistance to divided values in his writing."

"It is the sweetness of life that we are seeking in philosophy and its value judgments about being. No one can reflect this gracious value through the dividing power of intellect. Life cannot be divided and still be life, and it is impossible to use intellect and its dividing power to forge an imposing identity without following the divided paths of pure intellect and constructs of intellect and sense. But it seems there is one more path for writers to follow, even after exhausting philosophy and its methods—the path of desirability itself; the path that reveals itself through resistance to the lack of sweetness in their own writing; through resistance to all divided values."

"This is beginning to sound like just the sort of thing I'm trying to get away from," I said with a laugh. "Are you talking about resistance to closure?"

"Not in the sense of your cliché-loving friends down at the school," he replied. "There is a force of resistance in consciousness that is far greater than anything seen in their philosophy. The modern ideal of absolute resistance to the good is a trifling resistance and no less divided than the Transcendentalism it was designed to dominate. The fact that philosophy is incapable of furnishing an undivided value judgment about 'the good' does not mean that there is no goodness in life, nothing greatly pleasing or sweet; and the attempt to obtain a transcendent identity by annihilating that goodness is counterproductive when the sweetness of a ripe tomato is perfectly obvious."

"Nihilism was supposed to destroy all limitations on value by negating the concept of the good and the difference between good and evil, but it produced its own form of closure by insisting upon resistance to any thought of what is good."

"This can be seen in the fierce resistance now manifesting itself to the concept of design. Why should there be such resistance, from a purely objective point of view? Evidences of design are abundant in nature, from the complexity of the cell to the beauty of the forests to the delicate balance that prevails in the cosmos, which is necessary to life. There is no rational reason to prefer Darwin over design; his origins story is equally incredible. But the Nihilists are compelled to annihilate any notion of design in nature because of their fealty to Nietzsche and the fanciful concept that it is possible to obtain a 'transvaluation of value' by negating the good."

"Their worldview requires absolute resistance to any hint of the existence of a designer, but then it does not reflect a true resistance to closure. It becomes a new form of closure in which 'the good' is excluded from all discussions of value."

"The superman embraced the ideology of absolute resistance to the good because he thought it would set him free from the limitations of philosophy, but in reality it resulted in the same slavery as the Transcendentalism it supplanted. Nihilism is a totalitarian value—a show of absolute resistance to the good is necessary these days for tenure and publication—but it cannot provide the identity or sweetness we desire. The limitations of Nihilism were hidden at first in its own fiery force of resistance, but the superman cannot remain nothing and also be something; cannot hide behind Nihilism forever and also make his value known. At some point it becomes necessary for him to reenter being in order to validate his claim to domination; and as soon as he does, we become conscious of the limitations of his love of nothingness."

"His love of resistance has the same limitations as Plato and Descartes. It cannot lead to any substantive value. I must say, however, that my esteemed colleagues do not seem to be aware of those limitations. If anything, Nietzsche is more popular than ever."

"Indeed he is, for the very reason that Nihilism has become the prevailing cultural identity with all of its potentialities realized and creativity exhausted, as seen in the lockstep uniformity of our literary journals. It is not difficult to put on the rigid forms of expression facilitated by the ideal of absolute resistance to the good, especially since Marx and Freud and Foucault have shown the way. Nihilism is in its institutional phase. It has become the opposite of what Nietzsche envisaged—a way for the herd to rise up without talent or imagination. Anyone can become a superman by grasping a few simple concepts and applying them in a conventional way. But the Zeitgeist is a fickle muse, and most of yesterday's bestsellers can be found languishing on the shelves of dusty second-hand bookstores—if at all."

"The Spirit of life resists the spirit of the age. But I must say, it's easy for *you* to be enthusiastic about this resistance. You're out of the fray."

"Ah—but I experienced something similar when I was just about your age," Smith replied.

"You did?"

He nodded. "I began to hate my own writing. Eventually I realized that this resistance was good for me—but I assure you it was a very painful time."

The drinks were frosting up nicely, so we trooped out to the Adirondac chairs at the edge of the garden and sat down to watch the black thunderheads roll in.

"Now what's all this about hating your own writing?" I said as soon as we were comfortably ensconced.

"Disappointed love turns rapidly to hate," he replied with a chuckle. "It is one thing to be disgusted with inadequate research or poor structure. I did not happen to be guilty of such obvious transgressions, as far as I could tell—and yet my dissatisfaction with my own writing began to border on loathing. I think I understand now what it was all about. My infatuation with my writing was in the process of being broken to pieces by the force of resistance found in desirability itself. I can assure you, however, that it was a very trying time. I was often tempted to give up the fight."

"But you did not give up."

"I could no more give up writing than breathing. I never lost the desire to express my sense of what is valuable and true. What I lost, perhaps, through sheer foolishness, was the heroic identity of writer, a worldly value that produces hidden obstacles to creativity—obstacles that are hidden to the writer himself. Vanity deceives us into thinking of ourselves as masters of being, forging on by the power of method to a new understanding of value; but then we find ourselves angling for the reversals and epiphanies that lead to comedy or tragedy in the imagination—to a happiness we are not quite able to believe or a self-pity that exaggerates our plight."

"There is an inherent logic in narrative that makes our stories want to go in certain ways. And the problem is that real life is nothing like those stories."

"This inherent logic is shaped by our desire for a transcendent identity. We want to appear to have gone beyond our fellow beings in some way, and this vanity becomes encoded directly into our narratives. But the problem with such storytelling is that it cannot give us the thing we desire most—cannot furnish a desirable identity. We ourselves are mortal beings, and any method of storytelling that we might adopt reflects our own mortality and the limitations of our concepts of value."

"This is an uncertainty problem," I suggested. "The position of the observer affects his measurement in ways that are not immediately apparent to him."

"The gracious value of life transcends the thinking of men and the desire for closure seen in their stories about value. It is well-known, for instance, that the human body is organized to protect itself from traumatic injury, and that this life-preserving system is complex. But what is perhaps not fully appreciated is how complicated the system really is. In fact it is so complicated and so folded in upon itself that at some point it begins to look almost circular. And at that point any attempt to impose a narrative voice reflects a selection bias of some kind."

"The mechanism in the body for preserving life resists the starting point of all stories; the beginning that is necessary to a middle and an end."

"These aspects of storytelling reflect a need to interpret life in such a way as to bring honor to the narrator—to put life, which transcends human understanding, into a mortal framework. The blood-clotting cascade resists our limited modes of understanding through its evanescent complexity. And this complexity is multiplied many times over when one leaves off the relatively solid ground of sense and attempts to describe being. At one time it was possible for Plato and Aristotle to prop themselves up as masters of being by telling stories about the nature of 'the good'; but it is perfectly obvious to us today that their descriptions of transcendent being were divided between sense and intellect and cannot satisfy any great desire."

"The problem, in your view, is that they were trying to glorify themselves and their concepts of value—and it is impossible to glorify ourselves and also reflect the great desirability known to us through the value of life."

"We fall in love with divided methods of describing being because we are mortal beings; because our mortality makes us feel that we must hurry and build our citadels of reason while there is still time. Meanwhile no rushing or straining is seen in a tomato and its great sweetness. The sweetness of the ripe tomato has nothing to do with men or their impatient methods. Tomatoes obtain their great value through the growing season, which is linked to life itself. The tomato is not perfectly sweet until it is ripe; this is the irreducible reality of the season of desirability."

"The growing season indicates a force of resistance in nature to our desire to hasten creativity through any method—a resistance that is as real to us as the sweetness of the tomato and the great pleasure it provides. But I don't know how comfortable I am with making *pleasure* the beacon of creativity. Shouldn't we be setting our sights on something higher than pleasure if we want to be useful?"

"You sound just like the philosophers," Smith said with a chuckle. "They were scornful of what they called 'pleasure' because they were infatuated with intellect and its force of resistance. There can be great pleasure in such things as a summer evening or fireflies or a piece of good cheddar cheese or the monarch butterfly that lights on our daylilies, but the philosophers made a show of contempt for such pleasures because they provide no opportunity for storytelling. They wanted to be known as heroes of being who had overcome the mutability of existence through some method of judging value. They wanted us to believe they had obtained knowledge of the good through intellect and its heroic capacity for resistance to the unhappiness of existence—the same force of resistance that led to the divided value judgments seen in philosophy, since intellect cannot overcome the difference between itself and sense."

"Their love of intellect led them to dismiss mere sensuous pleasures as if they were nothing. But then are you a follower of Epicurus?"

"I will say this—the simple pleasures of a summer day seem far more desirable to me now than anything I see in philosophy. But no, I would not call myself an Epicure. I enjoy the fact that Epicurus struck a blow at the vanity of the philosophers and the seeming heroism of their ethereal concepts of the good by appealing to the greatness of sensuous pleasures. But the identity sought by Epicurus is also a divided value because it attempts to *exclude* intellect and its force of resistance."

"He went to the opposite extreme and glorified sense at the expense of intellect."

"Epicurus was rightly dismissive of the philosophers and their pretensions of having obtained knowledge of transcendent being—but he was no less vain. Any attempt to describe the good through intellect leads to the divided value judgments seen in philosophy. Epicurus thought he could avoid this dividedness by putting aside any thought of the good and concentrating his energies on obtaining an equilibrium of pure sense—but then the natural limitation of such a philosophy is that it cannot satisfy a desire for intellectual pleasures. Epicurism produces value judgments that are hopelessly dull. It is not good to eat too much or too little;—how surprising! Any cornfield savant could do as well."

"Intellect supplies a highly desirable force of resistance to the limitations of sensuous existence, but Epicurus had to discount this resistance in order to make us think we could be happy with pure sense."

"His concept of happiness is limited to the satisfaction of physical appetites in such a way as to maintain the comfort of the stomach and bowels. But then it cannot reflect the great pleasures of the stars on a hot summer night, or the upland meadow just before mowing, or the goldfinch that finds its way to the thistle; pleasures that exist outside our bodies and give us joy by lifting our thoughts to the loftiest spheres of being."

"The pleasure provided by such things is so great that it intimates transcendent value—and the only way to become good epicures and truly immerse ourselves in pure sensuality is to negate it or block it out of our minds. Thus Epicurism is no less divided than the divided value judgments about 'the good' that it condemned."

"Intellect and sense both provide great pleasure, but the capacity for resistance that makes intellect pleasurable is not the same thing as sense; therefore a chasm appears between these two values as soon as we attempt to use intellect to justify ourselves and our pleasures, our concepts of value. Aristotle and Plato cannot obtain the transcendent status they desired by discounting sensuous pleasures, nor can Epicurus make us happy by clinging to sensuous pleasures in resistance to that dividedness, since we are fully aware of the pleasures of intellect and the difference between them and sense."

"The word 'pleasure,' then, has a special significance for you. It does not merely indicate the sensual enjoyment we can obtain from a sweet tomato on a hot summer day. It also includes the pleasures of the mind."

"Let us not deceive ourselves—every value judgment we make is based upon pleasure. The notion of pure intellect can provide great pleasure by intimating a transcendent realm of being, a pleasure that may be especially attractive to those who feel alienated from existence and who love absolute judgments. Similarly the constructs of value seen in Aristotle reflect a strong attachment to nature as well as to ratiocination, which is a distinct intellectual pleasure unto itself. To claim that philosophy and its concepts of what is good are not rooted in pleasure is nonsense, since 'the good' indicates that state of being which is more desirable than any other."

"The mistranslation of 'Jesu meine freude' strikes inadvertently upon an important truth in order to meet metrical needs. It is not pleasure for its own sake that is the cause of our unhappiness but rather the kind of divisive pleasures seen in philosophy."

"It was the perverse pleasure of thinking intellect had the power to make us equal to God that is said to have been the cause of all unhappiness," Smith noted. "The human race has proven to be very resourceful when it comes to perverting pleasure and turning it to destructive ends—but that does not mean that pleasure for its own sake is in any sense evil. Indeed, paradise is perfect pleasure. To embrace the disdain for pleasure seen in philosophy is to embrace the vanity of the philosophers and their belief that they were capable of obtaining a transcendent identity through resistance. But we would not attempt to negate the value of pleasure if we did not find pleasure in such a negation."

"The attempt to negate pleasure in philosophy indicates the pleasure of excessive self-love; the pleasure of Narcissus. And in this sense the very foolishness of pleasure can be seen as a force of resistance to the limitations of philosophy."

"It resists the foolish pride of those who think they can obtain knowledge of the good through intellect. The sweetness of a ripe tomato provides great pleasure, and this pleasure stands as a legitimate sign of goodness against the dry and sterile descriptions of 'the good' seen in philosophy. This reality was obscured in the past by the supposed devotion of philosophy to the good, but it has become perfectly obvious through Nihilism. The simple sweetness of nature is infinitely preferable to the morbid puritanism of the superman and his ideal of absolute resistance to the good."

"So the contrast that comes into view through the demise of philosophy is between the rather foolish pleasure of a sweet tomato and the bitter vanity of the overman."

"Philosophers did not care for the foolishness of mere pleasure. They wanted to seem like great men, so they took up the sword of judgment and negated pleasure as if it were nothing. But the nothingness of mere pleasure has now become a force of resistance to the vanity of philosophy. It is possible to go beyond the limitations that are all too evident in the superman by laying aside his blind infatuation with himself and seeking identity in the foolishness of the growing season. It is possible to find freedom from the limitations of the prevailing culture and its 'discourse' by embracing the season of desirability, which cannot be rushed by any means and brings forth its fruit in due season."

"But how can we incorporate the goodness of the growing season into our writing if it is a force of resistance to our own methods?"

"The growing season reflects the value of life. No one can obtain knowledge of this gracious value through judgment because judgment is not a gracious power. The truth is that we are under judgment. We are not 'good'; we are mortal, and it is impossible to go beyond our natural limitations through any power we ourselves have. But at the same time we are also living beings and intimately familiar with the sweetness of life. We know we cannot obtain this sweetness by our own power—but we can certainly *cling* to it. We can grab hold of it through our livingness and refuse to let go in the darkest nights and arid times of life, even when it seems that all of our efforts are futile."

"Hmm. If I understand your trope correctly, the end result is that we are lamed."

"Indeed," he said with a chuckle. "We are a disfigured generation, having fallen from the heady optimism of Descartes and Kant into the swill-pit of Nihilism. We have been deprived of our figures of value—but this is not necessarily a bad thing. To be disfigured is to obtain a golden opportunity to know and accept one's limitations; and perhaps at that point it becomes possible to let go of our infatuation with method and its empty appearances of power and allow our understanding of value to be informed by the power found in the desirability of life, a gracious power that is unlike intellect and judgment."

"You believe it is still possible to produce good fruit in spite of the loss of 'the good'—if we are willing to give up vanity and our infatuation with our methods."

"I have faith in you and believe you will continue to do great things. But since you are tenured and have more freedom than some of your unfortunate colleagues, I would counsel you to allow yourself to forget about what others think. The desire for status is a snare. It is rooted in resistance to the grave—and resistance cannot overcome resistance. Hegel was able to obtain precedence because he lived in a time that was looking for a way to resist the limitations of Rationalism. He was a powerful storyteller with an uncanny grasp of the revolutionary moment, but it is impossible to obtain knowledge of any transcendent value through resistance to the limitations of the preceding age."

"His resistance to the nothingness of Rationalism enabled him to obtain status through the concept of a synthesis of nothingness and being—but then the limitations of his own identity gave rise to new form of resistance."

"Anyone who is familiar with the historical context can only marvel at the ingenuity of his description of this synthesis. I remember the first time I read the Prelude—I actually had to lay the book down from time to time and walk around the house in order to calm myself. But Hegel could not go beyond his resistance to the limitations of Rationalism by clinging to resistance itself. He could not obtain a transcendent description of being by resisting the nothingness that resulted from Rationalism because this resistance simply makes the power of nothingness more evident."

"The more he resists nothingness, the more aware we become of its power—which is why Nietzsche was able to obtain status through nothingness itself and its resistance to any concept of being."

"Nietzsche lived in a time that was already growing tired of Hegel and his omnivorous middle terms, which seemed to produce a 'herd mentality' and crowd out any possibility of transcendence. He claimed it was possible to overcome the limitations of our concepts of being through absolute resistance to their very dividedness. His method was rooted in resistance for its own sake and not for the sake of the good. But then the limitations of resistance became self-evident, since it is impossible to obtain the good of happiness promised in philosophy by negating the good itself."

"Nihilism has to negate the goodness of a ripe tomato in order to cling to its ideal of absolute resistance to the good, which seems fairly counterproductive in the end."

"The philosophers attempted to obtain status or 'being' in the world by resisting the foolishness of becoming—the uncertainty of the season of desirability. According to Plato, we are unhappy with present existence because the soul has been yoked to matter and longs to escape confinement in a body. He dismissed this mixed state of existence as mere becoming, the striving of the soul for the perfection it lacks, but claimed it was possible to go beyond becoming and obtain knowledge of being by negating sensuous being for the sake of pure intellect."

"Plato was dismissive of mere becoming because he wanted to appear to have obtained knowledge of being; he wanted to be known as a philosopher."

"Aristotle was equally dismissive of becoming. In his view it was Idealism that was nothing more than becoming, since it is impossible for thinking things to turn themselves into pure thought. He tried to go beyond the uncertainty of becoming by describing a synthesis of intellectual and material causes where the force of resistance found in intellect is resolved into the goodness that actually exists. But the problem with this description of being is that existence is mortal—and we are conscious of the value of life."

"We cannot be content with the pure resistance to becoming described by Plato because we know that it cannot lead to the solid value that we sense in being, but neither can we be happy with Aristotle's concept of becoming as something that has or can be resolved in present being. It is not our mortal existence that we desire; it is life."

"To admit that we are merely becoming is to confess that we have not yet arrived at our goal; that we are pilgrims and not masters of being. Thus a state of becoming is foolishness to the world, which bases its value judgments on appearances of power. But becoming also reflects the resistance of the sweetness of life to our own limitations. The creativity of philosophy was largely exhausted as soon as Plato and Aristotle had articulated their theories of value. Others stated the case in different ways, but the results were always the same. The only way to find the creativity we desire, then, is through the resistance of becoming to the vanity of wanting to be known as masters of being. We must be willing to seem foolish if we want to reflect the sweetness of life because life is a value that transcends our own existence."

"In your view, the resistance of becoming to 'being' can provide the creativity that is no longer seen in philosophy. But then are you siding with the Nihilists? Are you saying we should reject being for the sake of pure becoming?"

"Nihilism is not pure becoming. It has come into being, and we have seen its limitations. Nor should we saddle ourselves with the vanity of the superman and attempt to negate the value of being. Philosophy divides being from becoming because intellect is a dividing power—but these values become synergistic if we make life our standard of desirability instead of intellect. There is great value in present being because we are living beings—mortal life is not nothing—and yet there is also great value in becoming, since the sweetness of life that we desire is beyond the grasp of mortal beings."

"So the message here is that we have to be willing to stretch ourselves if we aspire to any kind of creativity. We have to be willing to suffer."

"We can suppress our consciousness of the value of life and use the power of judgment to gain a foothold in the world—but then we deprive ourselves of the possibility of going beyond the limitations of judgment. Think of Beethoven and all the agonizing indicated by those manuscripts. Clearly the creative process was painful for him, but perhaps the only way to rise to the great joy and sweetness seen in Beethoven is to be willing to experience some growing pains and even to appear to be foolish."

"This requires two things, then," I suggested. "First, we must be willing to look foolish and uncertain in order to go beyond the limitations of our natural vanity. And second, we must embrace the counterintuitive discipline of counting our creative sufferings as joy, since suffering is a sign of our consciousness of the value of life."

Smith did not reply. Lightening flashed in the distance and the dark wind shook the maple leaves and made them silver. I was contemplating a mad dash for my car, having left my window open, when he surprised me by taking up the thread again.

"It seems that any attempt to impose our will on the growing season results in slavery and a loss of pleasure. Perhaps I feel a need to meet the standards of perfection peddled in those glossy gardening magazines you see in the supermarket. Such tomes tell us we must learn the best techniques for preparing the soil before we plant any tomatoes. They make us think we must know something about the countless varieties of tomato that are available. We must also pay attention to aesthetics and make ourselves worthy of a visit from the gardening club. But these techniques give us little control over the prime object of the garden—which is the pleasure of a ripe tomato."

"There are factors that cannot be controlled in a garden, factors that are beyond any degree of technical perfection. Tomatoes require hot days and balmy nights in order to ripen properly, and not every New England summer is obliging."

"Now of course we can attempt to overcome these wearisome limitations by removing our tomatoes from the realm of nature—by negating natural law and putting them in a hothouse. Such a heroic gesture does not come cheap. Greenhouses must be paid for and maintained. They also cause their own distinctive problems; the plants have to be watered and pests and diseases controlled with extra care. And even then we are not guaranteed a perfectly desirable tomato. We may discover, very foolishly, that our hothouse tomatoes do not seem as delicious as those dumped carelessly on our doorstep by the farmer down the road, who seems to do little more than stick his plants in the dirt with some manure and run a hoe between them from time to time."

"By removing them from the realm of nature we deprive them of the sweetness that nature naturally gives. But then are we talking about some sort of 'organic art'?"

"Not at all," he replied. "There is no middle term between a perfectly desirable tomato and one that falls short of our expectations. This value cannot be constructed; it must come into existence by means that remain veiled to intellect and method. The purveyors of organic art negated the state of pure becoming that seemed to them to have resulted from Rationalism in order to glorify their construct of being; but the growing season indicates that there is value in being as well as in becoming. My tomato plants have value just as they are—the plant must grow from seed and be a fruitless vine before it can bring forth anything of great value. But they are also becoming something more valuable than they are now until their fruit is ripe and ready to be picked."

"To put the sickle in before the grain is ripe is to deprive it of the fullness of the growing season."

"We sow the seeds, but we are not the ones who make them grow; in the same way, it is a delusion to equate our methods of judging value with the creativity that is necessary in order to obtain a desirable identity and satisfy our desire for knowledge. Intellect divides value between being and becoming because intellect is a force of division and cannot be used to glorify the thinking of men without arriving at some definite judgment. But it seems we must 'hold onto the one without letting go of the other' if we want to reflect the desirability of life. We must be willing to appear to be nothing in order to obtain the identity we desire."

At that point the rain started pelting down; but it was so oppressively hot and the storm so rancorously wonderful that I forgot about my car, and the two of us sat there transfixed for quite some time as lightening crashed into the surrounding hills.

Chapter 8

The Law of Desire

SMITH WAS looking a bit ragged when I dropped in on him on a hot August afternoon, like a camera lens vaguely out of focus. He retrieved a couple of ales from the rusty green refrigerator in the mud room, kept there, apparently, for just that purpose, and we walked out back and sat in the shade of a hemlock tree, facing his garden and the thick woods beyond. His brooding silence gave me an opportunity to ponder the stonework of the patio—cement slabs of irregular shapes and sizes with soil trapped between to permit or promote the growth of crabgrass and other assorted weeds.

"Another ant marches to his death," Smith announced with a dark chuckle, gazing down in the direction of his left foot.

This statement startled me somewhat, as it seemed to follow eerily upon my own macabre ruminations. "Must be on a foraging expedition," I said, spotting the tiny, solitary black spot rushing willy-nilly toward a well-worn boot.

"The poor, little creature has no inkling that such godlike beings as you and I sit here monitoring his small insective progress. And yet note how positively he rushes forward into destruction."

"It appears to be *pleasure* that is leading the poor creature astray," I said slyly. "Ants are wholly driven by appetite and are incapable of using reason to ponder the consequences of their actions."

Smith nodded. "Undoubtedly there is some miserable speck of nutrition down there that he simply must have. Reason sounds no doubtful discord, casts no cloud upon ambition, and therefore he is perfectly free to march into destruction with his minuscule dignity intact."

"That isn't quite what I had in mind," I said with laugh. "The power to reason might save him from destruction, as it might have saved Thoreau's bellicose ants. What makes us different from ants is not desire—which, at least in this case, appears to lead to death and destruction—but reason, which is capable of recognizing deleterious desires and steering the will in a more salubrious direction."

"Unfortunately the fruits of reason do not support such optimism," Smith replied. "The philosophers were our most reasonable men, and yet nothing could be more destructive than their reasoning, since it led to Nihilism. Descartes inaugurated the modern age by launching a devastating attack on Scholasticism through the sword of pure judgment; then Kant took up synthetic logic to 'annihilate the idea'; and finally Nietzsche embraced the 'will to dominate' as the remedy for the dividedness of philosophy—a form of discourse that seems no more enlightened or gracious than ant warfare."

"Now wait a minute," I said. "You have to admit the philosophers were somewhat more gracious than Thoreau's ants."

"The old philosophers wanted to *seem* gracious—but this was because they saw themselves as masters of the good. The image of Socrates reasoning good-humoredly at dinner parties or Aristotle patiently writing and thinking things over in his study are appealing because they indicate a gracious force of resistance to the meanness of existence. Such an identity is highly desirable, but the truth is that Plato and Aristotle were no less eager to dominate each other than Thoreau's ants."

"They wanted to seem gracious because graciousness is characteristic of the good—graciousness is the quality of the good that exceeds our limitations—but they also wanted to seem to have surpassed each other through the power of judgment."

"Intellect is good, a thing of great value, but the graciousness implicit in 'the good' cannot be found in intellect or its force of judgment. This is shown by the fact that all graciousness disappears from philosophy when we agree to negate the good. The philosophers were not able to obtain knowledge of the good through intellect and its value judgments because intellect is not the same thing as sense and leads to divided descriptions of value. When this dividedness became impossible to ignore, the Nihilists decided to negate the good and seek transcendence in the will to dominate—but of course this theory of value does not leave any room for graciousness at all."

"The graciousness that made the concept of 'the good' seem so appealing to philosophers is not found in intellect itself, which they equated with the good."

"From the human point of view, the good—that which is absolutely desirable—is not intellect, which leads to small and divided valuations; it is life, a gracious and expansive value, a value that truly transcends our limitations. This value was enshrined by the philosophers in their reverential attitude toward 'being,' but their value judgments about being fell far short of the gracious value of life. The philosophers *seemed* more gracious than Thoreau's ants, on account of their soothing rhetoric about the good, but Nietzsche pointed out that they were just like them in one sense. They all longed to dominate each other and obtain precedence in the world of philosophy, and most of their fine talk was little more than a covering for this vain desire."

"They talked about 'the good,' but their theories of value were based on the power of judgment, a harsh and dividing power."

"Judgment is rooted in the restricting power of law and not any gracious value. Plato based the enterprise of philosophy on the law of resistance to existence found in human unhappiness. He claimed that unhappiness is a sign of the existence of the good, a transcendent state of being; we would not be unhappy, according to Plato, unless we were conscious of a state of being that transcends the limitations of existence. But it is impossible to use this law of resistance to obtain 'the good,' an undivided value."

"Resistance cannot overcome its own dividing power, its own innate restrictiveness, and produce the expansive value implicit in the good."

"The philosophers may have seemed larger than life, but in one sense they were not much different from our little ant—they were following the inexorable law of desire, which leads to divided ends in mortal beings. Socrates was in love with resistance and its capacity to negate mixed constructs of value, to purify philosophy. This purifying power led him to believe that pure resistance had the power to produce knowledge of transcendent being. And at first glimpse, this may appear to be the case; it is true that we are unhappy, and that unhappiness indicates resistance to the limitations of existence, and it is also true that totalizing this resistance leads to absolute values—that pure intellect intimates the purity or goodness implicit in 'the good.'"

"But pure resistance is not an undivided value," I said, finishing the thought. "Socrates was attracted by the seeming purity of pure intellect, but this purity cannot be the same thing as the good because it is pure negation."

"All theories of value rooted in pure resistance lead to nothingness by negating existent values; thus the law of unhappiness to which Plato appealed in order to justify his theory of value cannot be used to obtain the transcendent identity he desired. And it is equally impossible to obtain happiness through 'natural law.' Aristotle thought he could overcome the problem of nothingness by making an appeal to the goodness of nature and the laws that are evident in its functionality. No life can occur on Venus or Mars because they are too hot or too cold; a middle term is necessary for sustaining life—and this middle term can be identified as a natural law."

"Aristotle claimed that the good is a middle term between intellectual and material causes. Nature is indeed good, but it is not 'the good' as measured by the goodness of life because nature is mortal."

"Aristotle was no less in the thrall of desire than Plato. He was in love with the goodness of nature and wanted to preserve it against the attacks of the Idealists. He positioned himself as a model of moderation by claiming to have found a way to avoid the extreme results of Idealism—the nothingness that comes from negating existent values—as well as the pedestrian results of observational science. But he could not obtain the transcendent identity he desired by defining the goodness of 'being' in terms of the goodness of existent values when mortal life is the very thing that makes us unhappy."

"Both Plato and Aristotle tried to use the dividing power of law to overcome their dividedness and obtain knowledge of what is good—which is impossible. A dividing power cannot lead to undivided results. Law cannot provide the gracious quality that makes the notion of 'the good' seem so appealing."

"Life is a gracious value because it is free from our mortal limitations. Plato and Aristotle both thought that they were pursuing this freedom through intellect and its force of resistance, through its capacity to provide value judgments about being, but the love of intellect leads to slavery because resistance is a dividing power. Plato hated the unedifying drudgery—as he saw it—of attempting to make up constructs of intellect and sense. Any such endeavor leads to convoluted results for the simple reason that intellect is not the same thing as sense. And indeed, he succeeded in freeing himself from the entanglements of constructive methods by using the law of resistance found in his unhappiness with those valuations to negate the value of matter and glorify intellect for its own sake. But pure intellect also is not free. It is limited by its own force of resistance to the goodness of existent values."

"In fact the love of pure intellect seems to lead to totalitarianism and an enthusiasm for rigid forms of value—the very opposite of freedom."

"The law of resistance that Plato identified seems attractive to us at first glance because we can plainly see its power. There can be no question that the human race is generally afflicted with unhappiness. But this same law also indicates the difference between human existence and the happiness we seek. That is, the very power of the law reflects the reality of that unhappiness. Therefore this law cannot obtain the transcendent value that Plato sought to obtain through pure resistance without making our unhappiness or dividedness worse."

"We are divided beings with divided desires, and the law identified by Plato reflects this dividedness. In his case, he was in love with the idea that pure resistance can lead to a transcendent state of existence, but the dividedness of his concept of value is seen in the fact that pure resistance results in nothingness."

"Plato did not obtain the freedom he was seeking by invoking the law of pure resistance, the freedom from mortal limitations intimated in the word *being*; instead he became enslaved to the limitations of intellect itself and its difference from sense. The same loss of freedom is also seen in Aristotle and his invocation of natural law. He was trying to escape from the nothingness caused by Idealism. His notion was that it was possible to overcome this nothingness by rooting our concept of the good in the goodness of existent values. This led to the attempt to validate the goodness of nature as a ratio of the good of pure intellect—as he saw it—and of matter; of intellectual and material causes. But of course nature is a mortal value."

"The goodness and freedom we sense in being cannot be found in nature. We long to be free from our mortality, but death is a fact of natural law."

"Aristotle claimed to be able to provide the freedom that the human spirit longs for through his method—specifically freedom from the nothingness of pure intellect and the totalitarianism of Plato's Republic. But his middle terms are fixed by the nature of the antitheses. The law of the golden mean or middle way results in middling values. It does not provide freedom from the limitations of that which exists; it chains us inexorably to the reality of those limitations."

"Aristotle's method appears to be more expansive than Idealism because it provides more than one option to the philosopher—more than one predicate—but this too is an illusion, since the philosopher is not really free to choose pure intellect or pure sense and still be in conformity with Aristotle's notion of what is good."

"Aristotle's love of the dividing power of law produced its own form of slavery by eliminating the possibility of resisting the limitations of existent values. This can be seen in every attempt to put his theory of value into practice—not only in his own ethics and aesthetics, but also in later manifestations of the method seen in Thomas and Hegel. Any attempt to describe a ratio of intellect and sense leads directly to muddles and entanglements because intellect is different from sense. And these entanglements deprive the philosopher of the delicious freedom he senses in being."

"To put it simply, Aristotle's concept of value deprives us of freedom by limiting our pursuit of happiness to the goodness of that which already exists. The only way it can overcome the nothingness of Idealism is by eliminating the possibility of going beyond the limitations of existence."

"Both methods use law to seek freedom from the limitations of prevailing theories of value—to obtain the graciousness implicit in the good—but this same dividing power chains them to their own natural dividedness. Law obtains power through the difference between what is absolutely desirable and present existence, but then law cannot be used to obtain the good of happiness that we desire. This became obvious after we decided to negate the good and seek happiness in law for its own sake. The Nihilists tried to obtain a transcendent identity without making any appeal to the notion of the good or transcendent being—through the law of the will to power, which they claimed to see in evolution and nature for its own sake. But then the identity of the superman requires the explicit repudiation of the good and all gracious values."

"The most desperate slavery of all," I said with a laugh. "Never have the limitations of our infatuation with law been more evident than in Nihilism."

"The superman is the perfect embodiment of those limitations. The fact is that we are mortal beings. Law obtains power through the unhappiness caused by our consciousness of the difference between life and our own existence. Without that unhappiness, we would not be aware of the force of law. The supermen thought they could overcome unhappiness by extinguishing the light of life and embracing their own mortality. But then it became impossible for them to obtain the transcendent identity they desired."

"The attempt to extinguish the gracious light of life did not lead to happiness in the modern age," I concurred. "All the overman succeeded in doing was to expose the difference between that light and his own miserable existence."

"'The law is spiritual' because it reflects the desirability of life; but then any attempt to glorify ourselves through the power of law simply reveals our own dividedness. The words 'thou shalt not kill' obtain power through consciousness of a gracious value that exceeds our own existence; through a dim awareness that life is precious and should not be destroyed. And it would not be difficult to obtain the sanctity indicated by this law if all we had to do was to refrain from literally committing murder. But it

The Law of Desire

seems that life establishes a far higher level of perfection than the human spirit can bear, since we are condemned by this law if we are even angry with our brother."

"It is impossible to use this law to obtain the transcendent identity we desire, since the very power of the law is found in its capacity to reflect our fatal limitations."

"The law would have no power over us if we were not conscious of the fact that we fall short of the gracious standard of value seen in life. The expansiveness of this value causes us to long for an immortal identity, but it is impossible to obtain such an identity through the same law that reveals our fatal limitations. 'The law is spiritual' when it shows us the futility of obtaining what we desire by comparing ourselves with others; but then this is precisely why the love of law and judgment seen in philosophy leads to highly divided identities and not to the happiness that was promised."

"We are so vain that we cannot help using intellect and its differential power to glorify ourselves and our theories of value—but then our value judgments cannot reflect the gracious power known to us through the value of life."

"We have proven ourselves to be not unlike this little ant," Smith observed. "We marched merrily off to Nihilism and self-annihilation because we were too proud to let go of our vanity and love of judgment. Our frame of reference is bounded by our mortality. It is not the gracious value of life that is foremost in the consciousness of mortals; it is our limitations and the limitations of our fellow mortals. And so we deceived ourselves into thinking we could obtain what we desire by comparing ourselves to others. We began to imagine that we were rather large and that our value judgments had immortal significance, when in reality those judgments reflected the difference between our divided desires and the gracious power that makes itself known through the value of life."

"We are conscious of this value and desire an identity that reflects its great desirability, but it is impossible to obtain such an identity through judgment. It is impossible to use the law and its restricting power to obtain the gracious identity we desire."

"This is illustrated in an interesting way in Thoreau himself and the existential horror he experienced when he discovered the carnage of the ants. Thoreau did not go to the woods to chronicle the brutality of nature; he went because he was in love with nature and thought it was possible to use this love to obtain a transcendent identity. He was a follower of Kant's constructive method, and all such methods attempt to overcome the nothingness of pure resistance by grounding their concepts of value in the goodness of existent values. Now some who became associated with the term *Transcendentalism* clearly did not understand it, such as Emerson, who declared himself to be a Platonist, and whose unhappy meeting with Wordsworth one wishes one had had the good fortune to have witnessed. Nor is it clear just how much Thoreau knew about Kant—whether he thought of his philosophy as 'constructive' or even realized what this term implied. But one aspect of Romanticism that was strongly reflected in his sojourn to the woods was his love of nature and its great pleasures, which were used by the Transcendentalists to discredit the formalism of the preceding age—to make themselves seem important."

"Like many poetic young men of his day, Thoreau believed he could find what he was looking for in the beauty and sublimity of nature; the same belief evident in Wordsworth and Beethoven, the leading lights of the age. And this belief was represented in narrative fashion through his pilgrimage to the woods."

"Kant was a follower of Aristotle and the belief that it is possible to obtain knowledge of transcendent value through the goodness of the values that already exist; specifically through the resistance of the goodness of nature to the nothingness caused by Rationalism. Hume had destroyed the usefulness of nature to philosophy by claiming that the scientist cannot draw any definitive conclusions from the causes and effects he thinks he sees in nature, but his skepticism of Newton led to the same nothingness as Idealism, since it is impossible to obtain any substantive value judgments at all about what is good through pure skepticism."

"The nothingness caused by Rationalism and its attachment to the cogito was becoming quite obvious by Kant's time, and he resisted this nothingness by appealing to the goodness of existent values."

"For Thoreau, the act of going to the woods represented his desire to leave behind the totalitarian social values of the town for the sake of the variety and freshness of nature. He sought identity in the resistance of nature's pleasures to the love of form and order represented by the town—the same seemingly expansive identity that informed the cultural identity of his day. He began his pilgrimage in something like a dream state, as seen in the idyllic description of a day spent floating in a boat and admiring the pond's intoxicating pleasures; but Thoreau was not content merely to drift. He wanted to obtain the identity of a philosopher of nature, and this desire caused him to attempt to go beyond his poetic attachment to the woods and examine them more closely."

"At which point he had the misfortune of stumbling on the ant war," I said with a laugh. "An ant is a magnificent little creature, but the

The Law of Desire

Transcendentalists were looking for something more than excellence in the woods—they were looking for a gracious identity, an identity that was more expansive than Rationalism. And while the woods are highly desirable, the ant war does impose rather definite limits on the graciousness of the identity that can be obtained through their pleasures."

"Thoreau experienced a shock to his system as he recognized what was really going on with the ants. He was an ardent lover of the woods—seeking a desirable identity in the desirability of the woods—who had the extreme misfortune of stumbling upon an example of sheer brutality and waste of life in those same woods. He experienced the ant war as the annihilation of the very identity he was attempting to acquire, and this annihilating effect can be seen in the strangely clinical pose he assumed as he described his fatal encounter with the ants."

"He could not be honest and pretend not to have seen what he saw—but neither could he pretend to love what he saw in the ant war. He goes walking again, as it were; walking away from his own construct of value and its limitations."

"His love of walking was used elsewhere as a sign of his resistance to the limitations of the town. In this case he does not literally go walking—he stays to watch the war to its bitter end, apparently at some psychic cost to himself. But the pose he adopts is a form of walking because he abandons the persona of uncritical lover of the woods. And this illustrates our point nicely—resistance does not have the power to overcome resistance. Thoreau can walk away from any identity that seems inadequate to him, but it is not possible to keep walking away and also get to where he wants to go."

"The interesting thing about this pose is that literary poses are, of course, quite common, especially among the better writers," I noted. "Thoreau's near-contemporary begins the greatest of all American novels by saying 'Call me Ishmael.' Apparently he was struggling with a little theoretical problem. He was strongly attracted to the Nihilism that was gathering force in his day, to its resistance to the great white whale of Being, as we see from Bartleby and other stories. But it seems to have occurred to him that the desire to annihilate being does not necessarily lead to any positive result in its own right; that in some sense this was an unhealthy obsession, a self-destructive pursuit. And the pose he struck gave him the liberty to explore these misgivings with poetic power."

"The pose liberated him from the confines of the narrative voice and the need to justify oneself," Smith suggested. "This need, which is predominant in the human spirit, imposes legalism on the narrative voice—and one way to break its bondage is by striking a narrative pose."

"I found another such pose recently in a place where I was definitely not expecting it—*Mont St Michel and Chartes*. I had not read the book since college and had forgotten about Adams' strange desire to portray himself as a cultural naïf. There is something odd about a world-famous critic and progeny of presidents making himself out to be nothing more than an unthinking summer tourist; but then it occurred to me that he must have experienced something in the old churches that made him want to break the mold of conventional narrative and seek freedom in such a pose."

"This is the opposite of what happened to Thoreau—he was more affected by what he found there than he thought he would be. And it caused him to want to go beyond the conventions of criticism and the narrative strategies it provides."

"I have the sneaking suspicion that he started the tour with the same bemused detachment seen in the autobiography—the world-weariness that was popular at the time and skepticism of the clichés of Medieval devotion. Adams was not your typical pilgrim. Much of his appeal comes from the freshness intimated by the New World and its resistance to everything that seemed old and worn-out in the one that was left behind. Also he describes himself as a child of the Enlightenment who had 'lost the instinct for religion.' But he seems to have been quite moved by what he saw in the old churches. Apparently it occurred to him that he was not just looking at a bloated value called 'religious art,' ripe for colonial debunking; he was looking at a culture and identity built upon devotion to craft, which is a different thing entirely."

"This devotion happened to be very much at odds with his own persona of impatient iconoclasm, just as the ant war rudely interrupted Thoreau's dreamy bliss."

"The old cathedrals are a glass into a living value—life expressing itself through art. One finds oneself in touch with yearnings that can be communicated across the ages, first because the yearning for self-expression is universal; and, in Adams' case, because the art of the cathedrals exposes the shallowness of American capitalism, which negates the devotion necessary to craft by turning it into a commodity. Adams was confronted with a new idea—with the fetching notion of art and craft as culture, as a way of living and obtaining happiness, which cannot be found in the impatient commercialism of the new world. And the pose of naiveté provided him with an opportunity to put aside his habitual brashness and become a true pilgrim, paying homage to a culture so very different from his own."

"There is another lesson to be learned from his pose as well," Smith said. "It seems he had to set aside the pride of judgment and the world of art in order to express his feelings adequately. This reflects an important difference between 'craft' and 'art.' Those who obtain the identity of Artist are the pride of the world. We all long for an immortal identity, and their fame makes them seem immortal, and so they become our gods. But what Adams was looking at in the old cathedrals was something entirely different—the humbler value of craft. Men who are craftsmen do not aspire, in general, to be 'artists.' They are not seeking fame and glory in the world because craft cannot give them these things. But for this very reason craft can provide freedom from the legalism of the world. Craft can reflect the value of life in a way that is not always seen in art."

"Craft indicates devotion to something that is not the same thing as oneself—a devotion that is not always evident in those who aspire to be known as artists. In the case of the anonymous craftsmen who built the old churches, that devotion was at least partly to their blessed savior and the Virgin they adored for her meekness and mildness. And it was probably also a devotion to craft itself—to the great and honorable labor of craft; to the capacity of craft to bring one's highest feelings and aspirations into visible form."

"The pride of the identity of 'artist' precipitates legalism because the artist feels compelled to justify the prominence he seeks in the world. Meanwhile the humility of craft provides freedom from judgment. What the craftsmen gains by giving up the pridefulness of art is a holistic way of living—there is no disjunction between who he really is and what he seems to be—as well as wisdom, since the truth is that even artists are insignificant when weighed in the scales of eternity. And something similar is seen in Adams' pose. He gives up the vanity seen in those who make themselves arbiters of art but gains a soulfulness that cannot be found in the gods of criticism."

"The foolish pose seen in Adams is powerful in a way that the world is not necessarily equipped to see," I suggested.

"Its power is hidden from the world," Smith agreed. "Soulfulness is a quality that can be obtained only by divesting oneself of the cold power of judgment. It is necessary to have 'eyes to see' the power of this quality because it is not like the shows of power seen in the world. But this also makes it precious. The more Adams allows himself to look foolish in order to express feelings that cannot be expressed by more conventional forms of criticism, the more we appreciate the humility of the gesture."

"It is a *gracious* gesture in the sense that Adams negates himself in order to provide greater pleasure to his readers."

"Adams' pose indicates that reason cannot give us the gracious identity we desire. It is impossible to embrace judgment and also seem gracious—a reality of existence that reflects the difference between life and mortal life. The truth is we are no more likely to obtain the happiness we desire through reason and its dividing power than our little ant, since the same force of judgment that makes reason seem attractive also prevents us from obtaining an immortal identity."

"Now wait a minute," I said laughing. "I have to believe our ability to reason makes us *somewhat* more likely to find happiness than an ant. Reason gives us the power to make choices, and the choices we make go a long way toward determining whether we are happy."

"Give me an example," Smith said skeptically.

"All right. Every day on the way to work I come to a fork in the road down by the berry farm. This fork presents me with a simple, straightforward choice—I can take the bucolic route, which is soothing to the soul but not the swiftest or smoothest of roads, or I can take the ugly state highway that goes down by the river and mills."

"You mean we have *free will*."

"Of course! I am perfectly free to choose between the two roads. I know what each has to offer—all I have to do is decide which one to take; which one is most conducive to happiness, as it were."

"But then this concept of 'choice' suggests that you do not always take the bucolic route; otherwise there is no real choice at all."

"Well, no; not always," I admitted. "It's not always convenient."

"And yet you seem to feel that the bucolic route is more nourishing to the soul than the highway, like our friend Thoreau."

"True, but there may be mitigating circumstances. I may be late for work or low on gas. Or I may simply not be in the mood for taking the time for the country road."

"So then are you saying that you sometimes deliberately choose a route that you know cannot make you happy?"

"Sometimes I find it convenient or necessary to choose that route. I never claimed it was the route to happiness," I replied, smiling at this Socratic demonstration.

"My point is not that the bucolic route can make us happy; my point is that we cannot obtain happiness by glorifying reason and its power to choose. We are in love with reason because we believe it can make us happy, but let's look at this faith a little more closely. We like to go fast, and the highway is speedy—actually it provides an apt analogy to the longing for transcendence seen in Plato—but we know it cannot make us happy if we are also in love with the country road and its pleasures. But neither are we guaranteed to obtain happiness by following Thoreau down the road less traveled. The country road cannot give us what we want if we seek *identity* in its pleasures because it cannot live up to our expectations. It can provide great pleasure—but as soon as we link those pleasures to identity we also become more critical of its pleasures."

"We begin to notice oil from roadwork splattered on wildflowers; a deer that we see may have mange and not be the idyllic creature of the poetic imagination; the dead and fallen trees will stand out to us more than they usually do. The same woods that are lovely in their own right may begin to look drab and disordered when we make the mistake of linking identity to the woods because the identity we are looking for cannot be found in the woods, a mortal value."

"It is a strange fact of existence that we may be fully convinced of the superiority of one route or the other and still not be able to find the happiness we desire in its pleasures. But here is something even stranger—we may wind up taking one of these roads against our will and find we are happy nonetheless. Perhaps we have decided on a given morning to take the speedier route, but for whatever reason our mind wanders as we approach our fork in the road and we veer right and left—I have driven with you before—and suddenly find ourselves traveling on the route we did not choose. At first this may make us angry, but then something catches our eye. We spot a blue heron or red-winged blackbird, or find ourselves attracted to the profusion of lilies on Trapper's Pond."

"We are surprised by a happiness we did not anticipate and were not actively seeking. What you seem to be suggesting is that, at the moment where we forgot about human will and decision—at that very moment a will different from human will steered us onto the country road; a will that has the power to give us the happiness we seem to have some difficulty finding in our love of judgment and its dividing power."

"This other-will seems to be quite real in existence," Smith observed. "There can be no question, for instance, that nature is highly desirable—and one may be forgiven for wondering how something of such great value could have come into existence apart from the existence of a will that desires to produce great value. But there's more. If we reflect with any seriousness on our lives, we will discover that very little of what we value most is obtained through intellect and human will, as the philosophers claimed. Whether it is nature itself and its pleasures, or our ability to think, or our friends, our work, our mate, our children, where we live, how we behave, our craft, even what we believe—in everything that gives real contentment there is evidence of a will above and beyond the will of men and their divided paths of judgment."

"A will that often seems to be in direct conflict with human will and our desire to make ourselves seem important," I admitted. "We seek to obtain happiness through intellect and judgment and their power to equip the will, but they cannot give us the freedom we desire from our own mortal limitations."

"That would be like expecting a thorn bush to produce pears. The philosophers thought their ability to reason had the power to make them happier than our little ant, but we have no idea of how happy an ant might be. If it had more than an atomic pinprick of a brain, it might see the danger lurking ahead and find some way of clinging to existence. Then again, perhaps I am not a malevolent being after all. Perhaps I am a follower of Saint Francis and desire to succor the exquisite little creature."

"You might even be moved by the pleasure of kindness to feed him a piece of cheese," I said, tossing a crumb on the stone, "in which case the little ant would think itself very much in heaven."

"Our little ant is propelled to destruction by his idiot automatic nature, but we seem to be fatally propelled as well—by the vanity of thinking we can obtain happiness through law and the power of judgment to compare ourselves with others. In that sense the lowly ant is far happier than we are; at least he does not deliberately choose unhappiness for himself, as we have now done for the sake of the superman."

"We must give up our excessive love of judgment if we want to avoid the catastrophic loss of desirability that the philosophers brought upon themselves."

"We are not really free as we approach our fork in the road if we are depending on the power of judgment to distinguish us and make us happy. In that case we become the slave of mortal desires. It is necessary to choose one path over the other in order to make judgment seem powerful, but then the very dividedness of our reasoning deprives us of the happiness we desire. The only way to obtain the freedom we desire is to lay down our love of judgment and allow ourselves to be guided by a will that is different from our own—the will that makes itself known through the desirability of life. And the strange thing is that if we follow this gracious will we find that 'nothing is lost' in the end—since the country road and the speedy road both have their pleasures."

"Meanwhile our poor little ant continues to march to his doom," I noted, gesturing to said victim, which was now not an inch away from the thundering power of Smith's boot.

"Oh, I don't know," he replied. "I begin to feel almost benevolent. It can only be your sunny influence. Perhaps I will not crush him after all."

The ant seemed to sense the folly of its present course and turned away. We had a good laugh and then sat silently gazing into the woods. It was almost evening; the deep shadows of August lay soothingly on the grassy margins. The fireflies were long gone, but in their place was a chorus of katydids, those cheerful harbingers of fall.

"I have the sense, however, from your discussion of the limitations of law, that it's not really the dividedness of judgment per se that troubles you," I said after a long pause. "It is legalism. It is the bondage of the law."

"You're accusing me of being a little like Thoreau—and perhaps I am," he said with a laugh. "I am a Yankee, after all. But you are right: my story about the dividedness of the identities seen in philosophy is a parable and nothing more; a framework for fighting a two-front war and illustrating the difference between 'love itself' and the divided loves seen in philosophy. What I am really interested in is graciousness and its resistance to the limitations of judgment. The philosophers peddled the notion that those who did not put their faith in intellect had small minds, but it strikes me at my advanced age that the truth may lie elsewhere. It is the philosophers and their theories of value that seem small-minded to me now. What seems expansive is the quality of graciousness, the only true force of resistance left after the burning of Valhalla."

"And legalism can be especially annoying when it mimics graciousness—when it deprives the law of its spirituality by clinging to it," I said, trying to probe further into this resistance of his and its root cause.

"It is not that Plato and Aristotle did not love the good, but their concepts of what is good were divided by the vanity of clinging to judgment. And the same thing is seen in those who cling to law and judgment for identity. True graciousness is seen in the story about the woman at the well. It is seen in the story about the 'sinful woman' who came to wash her master's feet—in him, I mean. True graciousness is seen in the story about that same 'master' eating at the house of the tax collector, or forgiving his murderers from the cross. Graciousness is a large value, an expansive value; it exceeds the thinking and value judgments of men."

"But this graciousness is not necessarily what we see in the institutional church."

"It is difficult to be gracious when, at the very minimum, we divide ourselves between Catholic and Protestant," Smith observed. "A church may begin in graciousness, but the laws pile up annually into a funnel. And the sheep who subsequently find themselves laboring under the unhappiness of their own legalism, not knowing any other way, have no one to lead them out of their captivity. They hear about 'grace' from the would-be shepherds, a theological concept, a dividing line between Catholicism and Protestantism, a sword of judgment, but they do not hear about the reconciling power of graciousness. They hear about 'love' and the sacrifice that was made on the cross, but there is no one to tell them that those who love know God because God is love. There is no one who even understands the message. Instead there is an interminable stream of words that we now associate with religion, of value judgments and institutional rationalizations, while the quality of graciousness is swept away and forgotten."

"This is the graciousness of the early church, the sense of complete freedom rooted in loving-kindness. And your resistance to legalism reflects a desire to get away from the barnacles of judgment that have attached themselves to the ship over the years, the hard crust that the church has accumulated."

"I would encourage all those who cannot be satisfied with the church and its sterile version of religion to seek a higher calling. Feel free to put its theories of value and its legalism completely out of your minds and give your spirits to the liberating power found in the gracious value of life. Become a light of the resistance of this great value to the vanity and small value judgments seen in the world—not to glorify yourself, since glory in mortal men is nothing, but to glorify the God who in whom there is life; the God who is said to be tenderhearted, patient and kind; the God whose glory is declared in the heavens and not in the thinking of men; who pours out his life for the sake of those whom he loves. Let the force of resistance to the limitations of existence found in the graciousness of such a God become your guiding light and source of identity—because this is the only way out of the trap we have set for ourselves."

Chapter 9

Something of Substance

If it is not reason per se, but a certain resistance to the dividedness of reason found in the desirability of life, that indicates transcendent value, then it is necessary for us poor mortals to put our stock in a power not found in ourselves in order to pursue happiness and a desirable identity. This would seem to be the obvious conclusion of Smith's critique of philosophy and its divided concepts of value. And yet he had always exhibited a strange antipathy to the word *faith*. The mere mention of this word was enough to bring a shadow to his face, as if one had stumbled onto sacred ground. I began to hope I might flush him out of this unaccountable reticence after our conversation about the shortcomings of law, however. Emboldened by a glorious September afternoon and the hint of fall produced by a Canadian high, I plied him with some pale unblended scotch before setting the trap.

"Parson A—— certainly seems to be having fun with those articles of his in the *Minuteman*," I said, hoping to strike a nerve. A—— had recently been installed as senior pastor at the Corner Church with all of the fanfare that can be generated by impressive academic credentials and an impeccable CV and had immediately commenced a barrage of recondite encyclicals in the religion section of the local paper. "He seems especially fond of the word *faith*, which he throws around like a prose freshener every time he finds himself in a troublesome logical predicament."

"Why, any cold-blooded church mouse can find something to boast about in such a 'faith' as that," Smith growled, rising with unexpected ease to the bait.

"I take it you find his concept of faith less than gratifying."

He started to reply and then stopped himself. "No—I am no better. I do not claim to have anything intelligent to say about faith."

"But what is the reason for this unreasonable reluctance?" I said laughing. "It seems to me your whole way of thinking leads inevitably to the conclusion that faith is the only means we have of finding happiness, since reason is divided."

"My problem with our endless discussions about faith is that they are rooted in reason—in a foolish infatuation with intellect and its dividing power. Consequently the word 'faith' has suffered such a severe loss of value in our time that it almost seems necessary to wipe the slate clean and start over again. And even then we have not solved the problem, since discourse is rooted in the dividing power of intellect, which cannot provide the certainty of faith by its very nature."

"The very act of trying to describe faith somehow leads to a loss of certainty?"

"Yes, because we do not seem to be able to refrain from conflating faith with intellect. Faith is certainty of an undivided power, but we want to believe in the power of intellect and the superiority of our own value judgments; and intellect cannot provide the certainty of faith because it is divided between resistance and existence."

"Intellect and its dividing power cannot lead to certainty of any undivided value."

"The doctrines obtained through intellect do indeed show faith—in the power of intellect. No one buys a chicken to see if it lays eggs or builds a house to find out if it will keep him dry; in the same way, no one reasons about the nature of the good unless he has faith in the power of intellect to provide certainty of such a value. Our faith in intellect cannot give us the happiness we desire, however, because we are mortal beings and our value judgments reflect our dividedness. Socrates was in love with pure intellect and believed it had the power to provide certainty of the good by negating the mutability of existence; but nothing could be more uncertain than pure resistance, which is nothingness. Aristotle tried to solve the problem of nothingness by describing the good as a synthesis of resistance and existence, but his method seems no more certain than Idealism, since Supreme Being must constantly labor to overcome the difference between these antitheses in order to prevent them from flying apart into nothingness."

"Plato's method of obtaining knowledge of transcendent being produces the uncertainty of a Highest Good that is pure negation and cannot mingle for good in human affairs, while Aristotle's method produces the uncertainty of a Supreme Being that is pure action and cannot do anything but mingle, to the point of being unable to separate itself from the mutability of existence."

"Our faith in intellect is misplaced," Smith claimed. "Intellect is good—highly desirable—but it is not 'the good' because it is divided between its capacity for resistance and the goodness of existent values. There is great value in the life we now know, but we are also conscious of a value that transcends mortal existence and manifests itself in intellect as unhappiness or resistance, which is life itself. Thus certainty withdraws itself as soon as we attempt to ground our value judgments in resistance or existence."

"The philosophers put their faith in intellect and its capacity for resistance to the dividedness of sensuous existence, but resistance cannot provide certainty of any undivided value. And you feel this belief in the power of intellect is also evident in the church and its concepts of faith."

"We talk a great deal about 'faith,' which is certainty, but we tend to equate it with the same methods of obtaining certainty that are seen in philosophy. Thomas made no attempt to hide his attraction to Aristotle and the synthetic method, which he used to overcome the nothingness produced by Augustinian doctrine. He adapted Aristotle's description of being as a ratio of resistance and existence to the Christian worldview. He did not deny that existence is a corrupted value, but he claimed it was possible to overcome this corruption through the force of resistance channeled through faith."

"Which is where the confusion between faith and intellect comes in, presumably. Thomas's doctrine muddles the difference between faith and the qualitative force of resistance found in intellect."

"By equating faith with the capacity of intellect to resist the dark ages of nothingness through Aristotle's concept of Pure Act, Thomas drew the whole weight of the law down upon our heads. Goodness became a matter of pure action, either in the realm of synthetic theology or charity. But then his concept of faith became an intolerable burden to someone like Luther. That poor fellow tried with all of his might to obtain the certainty promised in pure devotional action—beat himself more than any other monk, deprived himself more, undertook his prayer duties so diligently that they piled up in arrears and almost crushed him. And still he could not find the peace he was looking for."

"In Luther we see the tendency to gloominess and pessimism that seems characteristic of the Northern temperament," I suggested.

"It is entirely possible that the differences in our value judgments about faith can be attributed at least in part to racial and ethnic differences," Smith agreed, "or even to something as simple as a lack of sunlight in the winter months, which can have a profound effect on the psyche and genetic disposition. It is true that the Reformation took root mostly in northern regions—even in Luther's native land. And this may be partly due to the pessimism that seems ingrained in those who live in less temperate climates."

"A lack of sunlight may darken our perspective generally and make us less sanguine about the possibilities of action, and this makes it difficult to find a satisfactory identity in Thomas's theory of value."

"In any case we know that many sincere believers felt oppressed by Thomas's equation of certainty with pure action. They felt an existential need to look for certainty elsewhere, as seen in the emphasis on 'grace alone' in reformed doctrine. Now in Luther, this resistance to Thomism did not lead to any specific methodology. Luther did not try to institute a church of his own, which may be why there is no sign of an affinity for Greek theories of value in his doctrine. But a more traditional response to Thomas was seen in the 'pure doctrine,' which equated faith with pure resistance. It was becoming clear as the Middle Ages waned that Scholasticism was leading to a degenerate form of teaching that tended to trivialize faith, as seen in the notion of the bank of holy merits. Calvin used this degeneracy against Catholicism by equating faith with the force of resistance found in intellect and the seeming capacity of this resistance to purify doctrine."

"Calvin opposed Thomas's concept of transcendent value as pure action with the negative power of pure resistance and divine wrath. In short, you see the 'pure doctrine' as a Platonic response to Scholasticism."

"Calvin claimed to have no truck with the Greeks because he was eager to draw a sharp contrast between himself and Thomas. Supposedly his 'institutes of religion' were based solely on the text and not on philosophy or its concepts of value. And it is true that none of the outward trappings of Idealism are seen in his doctrine. But he does single out Plato as the one philosopher for whom he feels some sympathy, and his doctrine also has a fundamental similarity to Idealism—which is the faith it exhibits in the power of pure resistance to provide certainty of transcendent value."

"The pure doctrine does not have the cosmology distinctive to Idealism, but both methods reflect the notion that pure intellect has sanctifying power."

"Calvin was not as forthcoming about the exact nature of the transcendent being as Thomas, for the reason already stated, but he agreed with Plato that it is a force of absolute resistance to existent values, and this leads to the conclusion that there can be nothing of real value in existence, since the first rule of reason is that it cannot contradict itself. This is why his doctrine has the same inherent limitations as Idealism: it negates all existing values and leads to nothingness."

"Luther was not much more comfortable with the pure doctrine than synthetic doctrine, if I remember correctly."

"The pure doctrine is foreign to any good German who loves his forests and mountains and flower boxes and beer, since it negates all sensuous pleasures as if they were nothing. But it has more serious consequences as well—it puts a firewall between faith and experience. It deprives the believer of the possibility of confirming his certainty through anything he can actually *do*. If it is true that we are totally depraved and there is absolutely no human action that has any value in the eyes of the creator, then we cannot know the power of divine love through any act of kindness or generosity or through the willing negation of any selfish desire."

"We cannot see the actual effects of faith in existence because the doctrine draws a curtain between faith and existence through its love of pure resistance. Thus the negative force of the pure doctrine detracts from the certainty that is sought in faith."

"It divides faith between pure action and pure negation in very much the same way that philosophy was divided; but then it cannot provide certainty of any undivided value. Faith is distinctive if it has the power to enable the believer to go beyond the limitations of intellect—the power to provide the gladness and desirable identity that cannot be found in intellect or its methods. But it loses much of its distinctiveness and attractive power whenever an attempt is made to conflate it with reason."

"But are you implying, then, that Thomas and Calvin lacked faith?"

"Far from it," he replied. "My point is simply that their faith—if it was certainty of a transcendent power—could not have been the same thing as the certainty they sought in intellect and its methods of judging value. Faith and theory are two separate things. Our institutional descriptions of faith had vitality at the outset because they were new, because they were rooted in a revitalizing resistance to the limitations of existing valuations, and because of the genius of their creators. But that vitality tends to dribble away down through the ages as various partisans seek affirmation in their dividing power."

"The word 'faith' becomes polluted with party spirit."

"This change is mortifying, since the sign of faith is the unity of the Spirit. The highest value known to man is life, a perfect unity in the sense that it cannot be divided and still be life. To be in unity, then, is to reflect the Spirit of life, as is clearly stated in the text. Intellect cannot produce unity through its methods of describing faith because intellect is a dividing power; as long as we cling to institutional doctrine, we will continue to be divided. Unity becomes possible, however, when we put aside our love of judgment and make the value of life our guiding light. By this light, it becomes clear that we are no 'better' than our fellow believers; that their lives and their concepts of value are no less valid than our own and should not be an occasion for division."

"This is why the comparative case was banished," I suggested. "All mortals are equally mortal; no one is entitled to boast about his theory of value if our standard of value is life. And it is interesting to note that the founder of the faith did not attempt to glorify intellect. Instead he humbled himself for the sake of love."

"He did not seek equality with God through the power of intellect, which was the original sin—he did not attempt to glorify *himself*; instead he glorified God by pouring himself out for the sake of others. The cross is the sign of the glory of unselfish love, not of intellect or the love of judgment seen in philosophy. This sign cannot be used to make some mortals seem more important than their fellow beings or raise up one institutional doctrine at the expense of some other—but what a glorious sign of value it was! All systems of value are rooted in judgment; this reflects the fact that the men who create those systems are under judgment and tend to project their deficiencies onto God. But the sign of love indicates something literally unthinkable to man in his natural state—a God who transcends judgment; a God who is gracious, who is love in his very essence."

"The cross indicates how to obtain life because it led to the sign of life."

"We are trying to obtain life through judgment," Smith agreed. "We are conscious of our mortal limitations, and we are also aware that judgment has power in the world—the power to raise men up or cast them down; thus we attempt to use this power to obtain the thing we desire most, which is an immortal identity. Now of course judgment cannot give us what we want. It is impossible to obtain an undivided identity through its dividing power. But the cross indicates the existence of another way to obtain what we desire that could not have been imagined until the cross itself appeared. Apparently there is another realm of reality that is not visible to men, another 'kingdom' that transcends the realm of judgment—the kingdom of love. This immortal kingdom cannot be accessed by any self-seeking means, such as the value judgments seen in institutional doctrine. The only way to obtain it, apparently, is to take up his cross and follow him into the realm of life."

"The divide in the realm of life is not between intellect and matter, as the philosophers imagined, or between resistance and existence, but between the desire to glorify ourselves and the love seen on the cross; between the selfishness seen in our theories of value and a love that is willing to pour itself out for the sake of another."

"All theories of value are based upon love; they all reflect our own desires, our notions of what is valuable and good. But the cross 'shows us what love truly is.' It has no mixed motives. It is sincere, pure. We cannot obtain the unity of the Spirit of life as long as we cling to our self-glorifying doctrines because those doctrines enshrine mortal desires. Unity becomes possible, however, if we cling to the sign of love; if we become willing to lay down this mortal life with all of its innate selfishness and dividedness in order to obtain access to something incomparably greater—the realm of life itself."

"The same gracious power that reconciled us to God can also reconcile us to our fellow believers and produce unity, but first we must put away our love of judgment."

"We must stop trying to redeem ourselves and allow ourselves to be redeemed; we must give up the impossible notion that it is possible to justify our existence through intellect and its theories of pure action or pure doctrine and invest our faith instead in the power that transcends human understanding—the power that is not seen as power on the cross. As long as we attempt to root faith in judgment, we will be divided, since judgment is a dividing power; but it is possible to be reconciled by 'rooting and grounding our faith in love.' We cannot obtain the enchanting unity of the early church while we are clinging to the divided concepts of value seen in institutional doctrine—but it is possible to recapture that gladness and generosity of spirit by remembering the nothingness of the early church and its resistance to the world and its love of judgment."

"We attempt to use our descriptions of faith to obtain being in the world when it is the very nothingness of the cross that points the way to life."

"If faith really is the means of obtaining life and a desirable identity, then it should seem as fresh to us as hot bread out of the oven; as a walk on a fall morning after the first frost with the aroma of bacon in the air; as one of those moments with friends and loved ones when all of the encumbrances of life seem to melt away and we see them in a new light. But I do not know that this is the case with the word 'faith.' My impression is that our tiresome infatuation with intellect has deprived this word of its hopeful significance and turned it into something rather small and uninspiring."

"To sum up, faith is far more precious than reason, in your view. Faith provides a way to go beyond the dividedness of reason and obtain knowledge of transcendent value; but then it follows that the inclination to conflate faith with reason devalues faith."

"Abraham is the model of faith, and his faith was singularly unreasonable from a worldly point of view. There is no sign of doctrine in Abraham or of the methods of judging value seen in Greek philosophy. It was not because of reason that he laid Isaac on the altar. Indeed, sacrificing Isaac was the most irrational thing he could have done, by mortal lights, since he loved him more than anything else in the world. But he obeyed because he believed in a God who is gracious; he believed God would honor his promise and restore his son. Now if God is gracious—if God is characterized by unselfish love and a spirit of generosity—then it was not irrational to think, as Abraham did, that his son would be restored. Faith does not negate intellect or reason. But intellect cannot arrive at this conclusion by its own light."

"Abraham's action can be considered reasonable if it was rooted in faith in a gracious God. Otherwise it was sheer madness."

"By the light of reason there was no way out of the dilemma in which Abraham found himself. He was commanded to lay the son whom he loved on the altar for the very reason that he loved him—he had to sacrifice what he loved in order to atone for his sin with Hagar, which showed a lack of faith; which indicated that he did not put God first in his heart. He could not obtain the immortality he desired by trying to preserve the life of his son because he was a mortal man who had sinned. He either had to appease the wrath of God and give up his posterity or attempt to save Isaac."

"There was no other choice according to the rules of judgment. Reason for its own sake provides no satisfactory solution to the dilemma. But a way out was supplied by his belief in the *graciousness* of God—in the willingness of God to restore his son to him in some way if he was willing to believe and to obey."

"The point of the story is that God provides a way out when no other way can be found—when we have boxed ourselves into an impossible situation by attempting to take matters into our own hands and justify ourselves by divided means. 'God is love,' according to the text, and the gracious kingdom of love lies beyond the harsh boundaries of intellect and its concepts of value. It lies beyond the thinking of men because our thinking reflects our own dividedness. Abraham could not have conceived of the happy ending of the story. What happened when he acted on faith in a gracious God literally exceeded his imagination. But this is precisely why he is considered the father of the faith. Abraham's faith is a large faith, an expansive faith, because it is rooted in love and not judgment. It is not stingy or grasping, like the pictures of faith seen in too many of our institutional doctrines. It is open, generous, free."

"Faith obtains transcendent significance when it reflects the graciousness of a God who is love in his essence and who is willing to supply a way out of the foolish predicaments we create for ourselves when all hope seems gone. It is just at that point that the reality of a transcendent realm is revealed and the curtain of death destroyed."

"Abraham may seem strange and exotic to us today, but we must understand that there is no difference between his dilemma and the dilemma we face every day—whether to take up the gentleness and humility of the cross or the sword of judgment. We can see the sword of judgment and its power; we have wielded it and are aware of its devastating effects. We know it has the power to single us out as singular men. But we also know that this sword cannot give us what we are looking for—an immortal identity. The only way to obtain such an identity is to lay down the sword, just as Abraham laid his son on the altar. It was not through Isaac that Abraham obtained what he wanted; it was through the king of love that was born from Abraham's line. And we too must put our faith in the power of something greater than reason and judgment if we want life."

"We must put our faith in the graciousness of God in order to overcome the dividedness of our own value judgments. But then the problem you see in institutional doctrine is that it obscures the potential sweetness of faith by attempting to ground it in reason."

"Doctrine reflects a faith in the power of reason, not love. And the doctrines that result from this palsied faith cannot be compared with the great faith seen in Abraham—which was not a safe faith, or a face-saving faith that could be circumscribed with sharp pencils and arguments, but a faith that was fearless and willing to attempt the impossible. Abraham was willing to sacrifice the son of his old age because he believed in a God that exceeded the thinking of men. Faith that is based on the power of reason cannot exceed our own thinking, however; our limitations. Such a faith is not bold or great-spirited because all concepts of value are rooted in self-love—in the love of what we ourselves love—and not in the self-emptying love seen on the cross."

"But what about the creeds, then?" I said, suddenly feeling some anxiety over this enthusiasm for boldness. "They don't divide believers. In fact if I understand them correctly, their purpose was to forestall divisiveness."

"There is a degree of graciousness in the creeds," Smith agreed. "A deliberate attempt seems to have been made to state a minimum of widely agreed-upon facts in order to promote unity while also establishing a standard of orthodoxy and avoiding the pitfalls of interpretation seen in certain persistent revisionisms."

"This does not sound like an unqualified endorsement, however."

"I am happy to endorse the statements made in the creeds," he replied laughing. "I agree with them, and the creeds are certainly preferable, in my view, to any institutional doctrine that divides us over disputable matters and theories of value derived from Greek philosophy. But I do find myself somewhat puzzled by the prominence of the 'I' in those fine-sounding credo statements of ours. What is the bumptious little pronoun doing there? It has nothing to do with the admirable factuality of the creeds themselves. Thus the only way it can obtain significance is through a presumed difference between itself and those who do not accept such statements as fact."

"There is a force of resistance in the 'I' that implies a judgment about faith, and this judgment is at odds with the expansiveness you would like to see in faith."

"The creeds establish a dividing line between those who accept the facts they enumerate at face value and others who may not be quite so certain. But this strikes me as a superficial judgment. Life is a long and winding path, and not everyone arrives at his destination in the same timely fashion. Some of us are naturally credulous and find it easy to accept the credo statements at face value, even when we have no idea of what is meant by such abstruse formulations as 'begotten, not made.' Others may feel a positive enthusiasm for the restraint the creeds exhibit, since it is difficult to improve upon them as conciliatory summations of doctrine, as was shown by the addition of a single word."

"But not everyone fits neatly into these niches," I admitted.

"I myself was inclined to wonder about the accuracy of the creeds at one stage of my life. The doctrine of the trinity in particular was a stumbling block to me. I have long since come to realize the importance of the doctrine and admire the elegance and ingenuity with which it is presented—an indirect argument; but I am not so sure that I have any more certainty now of the existence of the gracious power described in the creeds than I did when some of their doctrines seemed incredible."

"You're suggesting that it is possible to believe in the transcendent power that the creeds describe in a factual way while also struggling with some of the specific doctrines in the creeds, in which case they do not necessarily facilitate an accurate value judgment about faith."

"The creeds do not reflect the passionate faith of Abraham. They are rather narrow documents, after all; rather insipid and uninspiring for the very reason that they restrict themselves to seeking consensus in statements of fact. Someone who came to the creeds without having read the text would have no inkling at all that God is said to be merciful and kind. The creeds present facts about the incarnation but say nothing of the tenderness of the manger; they tell us about the historical reality of the cross but not its significance—the gracious power it is said to illuminate. They have nothing to say about the solicitude of the shepherd for the sheep, and yet what could be more significant to the sheep than this?"

"The very factuality of the creeds tends to exclude the great *tenderness* of the text, which to the sheep may be one of its most important attributes."

"The Gospel narratives are full of tenderness, which accounts for much of their appeal. But it is important to remember that tenderness is linked inextricably to nothingness. The overwhelming tenderness of the cross cannot be separated from its nothingness, from his willingness to die broken and naked for our sake and the abuse he endured from those in power. But the purpose of using intellect to make value judgments about 'faith' is to overcome our feelings of nothingness; to make ourselves seem strong and obtain a forceful identity in the world."

"Not a great deal of tenderness can be found in institutional doctrine," I admitted with a laugh.

"We are afraid of nothingness, which is why we long to make ourselves seem important through some demonstration of power; which is why we continue to cling to the sword of judgment long after its futility has been revealed. But the very difficult lesson to be learned from Abraham is that the power of God is made strong in our weakness. Abraham's willingness to lay his son on the altar makes him seem foolish to the world, since Isaac was his only hope; but it was an act of great strength if it reflected faith in the power of a gracious God."

"It indicates a willingness to defy the order of judgment that is seen in the world in order to glorify such a God."

"The problem with judgment is that it is based on appearances—and on that basis Abraham seems foolish. The whole point of faith is that there is an unseen realm of reality which is not accessible to judgment, a gracious realm that transcends judgment. Thus the attempt to use judgment to valorize faith leads to ungracious results. This can be seen in the use of the miracles as a test of faith. The problem with the miracles is that they reflect an intersection of the mortal and immortal realms. They can be seen in the mortal realm, and recognized as great demonstrations of power, but the immortal power that makes them possible cannot be seen as itself in the outward demonstration."

"The miracles reflect the *graciousness* of God, and therefore they should not be used to judge the faith of others."

"They reflect God's kindness, his limitless compassion. You remember what Isaiah had to say about the Messiah. He was not going to come with a sword of judgment to establish a new kingdom like David's; his transcendent power was going to be seen in miracles of healing and kindness. There is no word about the Messiah gathering up his armies to conquer the enemies of Israel. His sign was to be healing the sick, giving sight to the blind, preaching good news to the poor. The transcendent power seen in the miracles is a power that desires to preserve and build up life; that desires to relieve suffering and give happiness. No such Messiah is seen in any other culture or literature because he is literally unthinkable from the human point of view. There is no selfishness in him, and men are selfish beings."

"There is a hidden message in the miracles—that love is more powerful than the diseases and devastation found in this realm of judgment; that the kingdom of life is nothing like the world. But then we make a mockery of this power when we use the outward demonstration of power to judge the faith of others."

"The greatest miracle of all was the raising of Lazarus from the dead, literally a life-giving miracle. It is possible, of course, to obtain a formidable identity in the world on the basis of this demonstration alone—to use the outward appearance of power to justify our 'faith' and make it seem important and powerful. And indeed, this seems to have been the cause of the triumphal entry. But the problem with using the miracle to justify ourselves through reason and judgment is that reason does not have the power to raise Lazarus from the dead."

I laughed. "Our faith in judgment is misplaced. By the power of judgment, what happened to Lazarus was impossible. Some power greater than judgment was necessary in order to achieve the miraculous outcome that was seen."

"This power is not visible in the miracle itself, in the outward demonstration of power. There is a clue to its nature, however, in the simple words 'he wept,' which indicate great tenderness. This weeping of his may make him seem foolish to the world, because the world bases its value judgments on appearances of power. Supermen and superior men are not permitted to weep; they must appear to be invincible in order to obtain the precedence they desire. Nor are the pages of our doctrine-makers generally drenched with tears of sorrow and compassion. But the strange thing about this foolish weeping of his is that it may seem more powerful to 'the sheep' than the miracle itself."

"It is a sign of what they are looking for—a God who is tenderhearted; a God who is compassionate and different from the world and its love of judgment."

"To the eyes of real faith, the miracle itself is not surprising; if God is God, then it does not seem strange to see men raised from the dead. But what may be more surprising and enchanting is the fact that he wept. The very thing that makes him seem foolish to the world may also make him seem impossibly desirable in the eyes of those who are looking for a shepherd. His weeping provides them with important information. For one thing, he has friends. He cares about mortals and takes a vital interest in their happiness, unlike the gods of Greek philosophy, who use men for their own purposes. Also it seems he is a little like the sheep—he can be moved to tears; he can identify with their sorrows. Finally, he is not afraid of the *foolishness* of sorrow. He does not feel compelled to hide his tears because the world and its shows of power are meaningless to him—and this is compelling to the sheep, who cannot obtain power by their very nature."

"So what you're saying is that his weeping becomes an encoded sign of resistance, a sign of a type of power that is hidden from the world and its value judgments."

"It indicates the existence of a different kind of kingdom from the kingdoms of this world. There is an ontological order in the world created by the power of reason and judgment. We may be enamored of this order in its many forms when it seems to justify our existence and furnish a forceful identity—but it is important to remember that the one who raised Lazarus from the dead had 'no place to lay his head.' His kingdom was not of this world. It was the kingdom of life, and this makes it difficult to make value judgments about faith, since all such judgments are based upon outward appearances of power."

"Those appearances of power appear in the mortal realm, and therefore their significance is limited. They have little or nothing to tell us about the realm of life."

"Anyone who says he has no place to lay his head is a radical, and any movement based on this principle is a resistance movement. The graciousness of his kingdom had nothing to do with the religion of the Pharisees, who used the dividing power of law to glorify themselves, or with the rule of reason advocated by the Greek philosophers, who used law to justify divided concepts of value. And unfortunately he probably would still have no place to lay his head if he returned today—not even in the church that bears his name; not until that church gives up its love of judgment and begins to reflect the graciousness of the cross."

"So to sum up, it is possible to base 'faith' on two completely different views of the miracle. We can look upon it as an outward demonstration of power that can be used to justify faith in God; basically this involves an attempt to use the miracle to ratify our identity at the expense of others. But the miracle can also feed faith by demonstrating the graciousness of God—his tenderness and loving-kindness. And this second type of faith is a little more difficult to pin down through our methods of judging value."

"Such a faith cannot make any outward show of power because it is rooted in a power that lies beyond itself. But it can provide the certainty that cannot be found in intellect. Indeed, I experienced an amusing demonstration of this paradox just the other day in a conversation with my perfidious grandson. He has begun to study earth science, you know, and for some reason I was seized with the urge, as we sat in these very chairs, to give wings to his fledgling understanding by enlightening him about the role of chlorophyll in the greenness of our forests."

"I take it he was not impressed."

"The little rascal saw through me with alarming ease. It seems he is in love with the woods and would rather wander aimlessly down autumn trails, dreaming about who knows what, than to attempt to absorb the brilliant doctrines of his masters. And I think I am able to see why he was not impressed with my little demonstration of power, now that I have recovered somewhat from the shock of rejection. Such knowledge seems powerful to me—but there is no good reason why it should seem powerful to *him*. There is no reason why the apparent facts about chlorophyll should impress someone who is in love with the woods, as if our concepts of value were as valuable as the thing itself."

"Perhaps you were simply trying to help him become well-informed."

"Oh, there may have been some smidgen of disinterest in my eagerness to impart my great knowledge to the boy; but I suspect there was something else, too—my vanity. Our knowledge about chlorophyll makes us feel powerful because it discredits anyone who disagrees with us; but Jeremy is in love with the woods, and this love makes it perfectly plain to him that I have very little power, in spite of what I think I know about chlorophyll. I cannot make the trees turn green in summer; I have no control over the quality of the green that is seen in them. Their pleasures are perfectly indifferent to my desire to obtain an imposing identity through judgment."

"But surely there's nothing *wrong* with wanting to know such things."

"Such knowledge is not harmful in itself, but it leads to small and divided values when it is used to compare ourselves with others, since there is one comparison in which no mortal can excel—the same one that causes us to seek certainty in our doctrines in the first place. Jeremy has knowledge of something that lies beyond judgment. After all, his love for the woods is not *nothing*. His resistance to doctrine may strike us as being rather foolish; and yet he seems quite content with his love, while all of my boastful talk about chlorophyll does not seem to have the power to fill up the empty space inside."

"Jeremy has faith in the pleasurable power of the woods, which is quite certain, while faith in the doctrine of chlorophyll is rooted in a divided power and cannot give us the happiness we desire. But a trickier question arises when we are dealing with religious doctrine, it seems to me. In a nutshell, is it possible to have faith in the power seen in the desirability of life without accepting the doctrines that describe that power?"

"I am not attempting to justify skepticism," Smith replied. "Far from it. But I am not certain that our value judgments about faith add anything to faith itself. And it strikes me that in many cases they are simply inaccurate. A famous example is 'doubting Thomas.' It seems he felt compelled to keep on asking those foolish questions of his, and this questioning attitude may seem to indicate a resistance to belief. And yet Thomas was also the one who declared a willingness to lay down his life for the one he loved."

"This willingness to give his life suggests a faith of some kind."

"Thomas's skepticism may not be what it seems. He appears to be someone who was capable of a great love and who was willing to make the greatest sacrifice that love can make. Meanwhile some of us who confidently recite the creeds on Sunday morning and are proud of our faith do not seem very tenderhearted and are unwilling to give up anything at all for the sake of love—even the position of the candlesticks on the altar."

"There is a stark contrast between Thomas's openhearted gesture and the grasping attitude that is sometimes evident among the faithful," I conceded. "But I had not thought of Thomas as being tenderhearted."

"I don't know if he was, either," Smith admitted. "My point is simply that the evidence counsels us to reserve judgment. There is a hint of an affectionate nature in the question he asked when he heard his 'master' was going away. This question can be interpreted to mean that Thomas was so attached to him that he wanted to have a roadmap to where he was going, not realizing it was not a place at all—that he was experiencing separation anxiety. We cannot say for certain that this was true of Thomas, but we do know that an affectionate nature is not inconsistent with the psychology of skepticism. Affectionate people can be hurt by the world and its facile value judgments. They know a great power through the strength of their attachments, but the certainty of such knowledge cannot be demonstrated outwardly and is not always valued by those who are in love with themselves and the power of judgment."

"They learn to adopt an *appearance* of skepticism, perhaps, to protect themselves from the hardness of the world. But to be fair, this is not why he is called Doubting Thomas. He doubted the sign of life—the very sign that is the cornerstone of faith."

"True—but permit me to suggest that this, too, may be a sign of a strong attachment and not necessarily coldhearted skepticism. Perhaps it indicates that he simply could not bear the thought of going through the separation one more time. He would not allow himself to believe because he was afraid of losing his 'master' again. Or, on a more mundane level, it could indicate the jealousy that often attaches itself to a strong attachment. Perhaps he was offended that the others had seen the 'master' and not himself—and this offense gave rise to the resistance he exhibited."

"It *could* indicate these things. You're not trying to convince me that Thomas really was tenderhearted. All you are saying is that these possibilities are within the realm of human psychology. They introduce a degree of uncertainty into our ability to make value judgments about Thomas and his seeming hard-heartedness. And this uncertainty should tell us that it is better to reserve judgment."

"There is nothing we love more than to link faith to judgment, since there is nothing we desire more than to overcome our nothingness. But what judgment tells us about someone like Thomas may simply be wrong. Reason cannot provide knowledge of any undivided power because reason is a dividing power. And reason cannot empower us to make value judgments about the faith of others with certainty because it depends upon outward appearances of power, while the heart and its true feelings cannot be seen."

"So what troubles you, then, about our discussions about faith is that they may actually drive the sheep away from the shepherd. They come to us looking for bread, and we feed them a stone."

"Thomas was not judged for his unbelief; he was allowed to touch the wounds. And it is only by those wounds that we are healed—not by any value judgment we might make about 'faith.' To be allowed to touch the wounds is to discover that mercy is real and has power; and those who are wondering if there is anything of value in faith may be able to find what they are looking for if we allow them to touch our wounds as well. This gracious act gives them the freedom to learn a great secret about us—we are vulnerable; we fall short of the glory of God and do not deserve to be glorified. This freedom comes at some cost to ourselves, since it requires us to lay down our lives and our love of judgment for their sake. But it gives others an opportunity to see beyond our fears and insecurities and catch a glimpse of the gracious realm of life."

There did not seem to be anything more to say. I could not continue to pretend to be baffled any longer by his resistance to the word "faith." The air was getting chilly, as often happens in September when the sun goes down, so I went inside to fetch a car blanket for him to throw over his arthritic knees. And there we sat for some time in silence, observing the remains of summer.

Chapter 10

Indomitable Being

It was mid-October by the time I managed to visit Smith again, a cloudy but cheerful Friday afternoon, oaks, maples, birches all a-blaze under a blue-gray icy sky. A couple of fragrant apple logs were burning in the fireplace, casting a flickering light on the stacks of books, pads and papers lying everywhere and even under foot.

I found him seated at an antiquated PC, pondering a half-filled screen—a circumstance that caused a slight arrhythmic jar.

"Are you working on something?" I said trying not to sound overly interested.

"You got me thinking the last time you were here," he replied.

"What's the topic?"

"'God is dead,'" he said cheerfully.

"What! You must be joking."

"Not at all. The concepts of the good that were precariously built upon the love of intellect have suffered a shattering fall. We must either turn away from such foolish contrivances or give up all hope of finding our way out of our current predicament."

"You mean the God of *philosophy* is dead—the belief that intellect is the good."

"We confused the good with the goodness of intellect and its capacity for resistance to divided values. But resistance cannot provide knowledge of any undivided value for the very reason that it is resistance—which is why our modern philosophers decided to negate the good and try to find happiness in resistance for its own sake."

"Hence 'God is dead,'" I concluded as I popped the top off some homemade brew I wanted to share. "It seems our faith in intellect was misplaced. Intellect is capable of making value judgments about what is good through its qualitative force of resistance, but it cannot overcome this same resistance and obtain knowledge of transcendent value. And this makes it difficult to believe in the old equation of intellect with the good."

"Intellect and judgment cannot give us what we want because we desire life. The philosophers revealed an awareness of the greatness of this value when they attempted to justify their value judgments on the basis of their ability to describe *being*. There is something mysterious about this word, something that intimates transcendent value, and they thought they could obtain knowledge of this value through judgment. But the transcendent resonance that attaches itself to 'being' comes from life, not intellect—and it is impossible to obtain knowledge of this value through any dividing power."

"Life is an undivided value for its own sake, while intellect is a dividing power; thus intellect cannot be used to obtain knowledge of the value of life."

"The philosophers used the word *being* to blur the difference between intellect and life. Plato said that the unhappiness or force of resistance found in intellect indicates consciousness of a transcendent state of being—'the good'—and claimed it was possible to overcome our unhappiness by totalizing this force of resistance and negating sense. For Plato, the transcendent value intimated in the word 'being' can be found in pure intellect, pure resistance, because Plato thought that 'being' was intellectual in nature. But if the essence of being is life, then his love of pure resistance cannot provide the knowledge he desired—because mortal life is not without value."

"It is not possible to obtain knowledge of the value of life by negating present existence as if it were nothing, since, as you are fond of saying, mortal life is nothing other than life. Idealism cannot lead to knowledge of the transcendent value intimated in being by glorifying intellect as a transcendent value. In fact it leads to nothingness."

"Plato realized there was something pure about being, something that was not like the world and its unhappiness, but he equated this purity with intellect and its capacity for resistance; and pure resistance does not have the power to provide knowledge of any undivided value. Nor was it possible to overcome this problem by describing being as pure action, which of course is what Aristotle tried to do. He seemed to have a clearer sense of the transcendent resonance of being than his teacher when he said that Supreme Being is 'nothing other than life itself'—but he too was infatuated with intellect. Supreme Being may indeed be life itself, but Aristotle described present being as a synthesis of material and intellectual causes; and this is an intellectual value."

"This synthesis is a *concept* of what life is, based on the notion that the First Cause is the same thing as the qualitative force of resistance found in intellect—that it is intellect in its essence; that intellect takes precedence to life, causes life to come into being. But you feel the value of life implied in being should take precedence to intellect in our understanding of what is good."

"Two distinct meanings for the word 'being' can be traced in Aristotle. In its most exalted sense, it is life itself—it is that which is absolutely different from the limitations of mortal existence. Here Aristotle seems to have glimpsed a great truth, however fleetingly. But in the practical sense, 'being' is virtually the same thing as our own existence, since Aristotle claimed that the First Cause overcomes its resistance to matter in order to manifest itself as Pure Act. The purveyors of the synthetic method wanted to have it both ways. They wanted us to believe that the transcendent is intellect in its essence, a force of pure resistance to divided values, just as Plato described it, and yet at the same time they also wanted us to believe that 'being' can be found as itself in existent values."

"Which is impossible if being is life, since mortal life is not the same thing as life itself. The only way Aristotle can overcome the negative result of totalizing intellect and its capacity for resistance is by characterizing being as Pure Act—but then it loses the differential quality of goodness."

"Intellect produced descriptions of being that were divided between action and negation because intellect is a dividing power. And this dividedness led to a downward spiral in philosophy after Descartes inadvertently broke the linkage between being and the transcendent being through the cogito. The possibilities of the old methods of judging value had been exhausted by his time through the war between the Schoolmen and both the 'pure doctrine' and Renaissance Neoplatonism. Idealism and Realism could not have been revived in their original form, since it was obvious to everyone that they led to divided results. But Galileo breathed new life into philosophy by making it seem that science had the power to reveal the nature of being where the old methods had failed."

"His astonishing cosmology suggested the possibility of obtaining transcendent knowledge through science for its own sake—through clear observation of the heavens that God had made. And Descartes seized upon this idea by linking those purifying powers of observation to pure intellect."

"The Schoolmen attempted to arrive at an understanding of the goodness of nature through their reciprocal method of reasoning, without direct observation or with only partial observation of the things themselves. This led to descriptions of nature that could be fantastically complicated and abstruse and bore no clear relation to what actually exists. Scholasticism had also been used to support the Ptolemaic cosmology, which accounts for some of the institutional resistance to Galileo, in addition to certain diplomatic missteps of his own. Thus Galileo's discoveries made it seem possible to wipe the slate of science and philosophy clean and start over. They generated almost infinite optimism that science could be used to obtain the happiness that had eluded the philosophers as well as those doctrine-makers who had wedded Greek philosophy to their theology."

"Hence Descartes stated that his intention was to purify science by using pure intellect to expose the errors produced by Scholasticism. But his love of pure intellect led to the same problems as Idealism in the end because pure intellect results in nothingness."

"Descartes believed that God had created the universe, which led to a much more positive view of the value of nature in Rationalism than in Idealism and left room for the notion that knowledge of transcendent being can obtained through science. But like Plato, Descartes was in love with pure intellect and its seeming power to produce clear and unambiguous value judgments about being. This love led him to claim that it was possible to purify science of the murkiness caused by Scholasticism by using pure intellect to negate its constructs of value—but pure intellect cannot produce any positive value judgment about the nature of being on its own, since it is the same thing as pure resistance."

"In Descartes' mind, God was pure intellect; thus the cogito seemed to establish a direct link to the goodness of God through the capacity of intellect for a purifying resistance to mixed description of value. But it introduced the same old divide into the new science because the 'I' of the cogito is clearly pure Subject."

"It is one thing to use pure intellect to negate the creaking constructs of being seen in Scholasticism—this Descartes was able to do quite efficiently, since Subject with its intuitive powers plainly tells us that those constructs have little or nothing to do with reality. The cogito brought the great superstructure of Scholasticism crashing down in ruins, although it had been toppling for some time. But it is impossible to overcome the nothingness or absence of being that results from negating that construct through the cogito itself, which is rooted in the power of intellect and its capacity for resistance."

"If we assume that intellect is the essence of the transcendent being, as Descartes did, then some sort of construct is necessary in order to do what he set out to do—link the goodness of God to nature through intellect—because the qualitative force of resistance found in intellect is different from sensuous existence."

"It becomes necessary to build a bridge between the goodness of intellect and the goodness we perceive in existent values. The divine intellect must be read directly into existent values in some way in order to justify the concept that intellect is capable of deciphering the nature of the good through the goodness of nature. And this Descartes was unable to do because his ideal of pure thought divides intellect from sense. The result of the cogito in actual practice was not the religious illumination sought by Descartes—the proof of the existence of God he thought his method would render. Instead the cogito led to the highly formal concept of natural science seen in the Enlightenment and a stout resistance to any type of direct teleological inference."

"In fact to Deism, an utterly amorphous conception of God; a God who is beyond human reckoning. So Descartes translated Plato's love of pure intellect into an attack on Scholasticism. He did not discount the goodness of existent values; all he discounted was the synthetic method of describing that goodness. But his method led to the same problem as Idealism because he assumed that 'being' was intellectual in nature."

"It is not known just how clearly Descartes saw the similarities between himself and Plato, but we do know he was attracted to the same method of obtaining happiness that Plato has come to symbolize—the concept that it is possible to obtain knowledge of transcendent being by totalizing the force of resistance found in our unhappiness with existent values and valuations. He did not exhibit the supercilious contempt for nature seen in Plato, which accounts for his great sweetness—Descartes is one of the most lovable of philosophers—but he did share Plato's love of pure intellect and the notion that it has the power to purify being by resisting object-centered constructs of value."

"But the same force of resistance that made the cogito seem powerful also prevented it from coming to any substantive conclusions about the nature of being."

"The only way science can use nature to make any positive value judgment about transcendent being is through a construct of intellect and sense, as is seen in cause-and-effect reasoning. But of course this was just the sort of thing the cogito negated. The actual implementation of Descartes' method led to the same negative results seen in Plato. For example, his famous discourse on the passions is essentially negative. In Descartes' view, the passions are something that disturb the tranquility of pure intellect and must be chased away by laying bare their root causes through the power of the cogito."

"The actual result of his method is not a *positive* value judgment about the nature of being or the good based upon observation of nature. It is the negation of nature and sensuous being as something that gets in the way of the happiness of pure mind."

"The result is purely negative—happiness is predicated on curing ourselves of the so-called passions by understanding that they are nothing more than the manifestation of purely sensuous processes; by using this insight to control them, eradicate them from our existence. Now of course the problem with this approach is that we are sensuous beings. Even if it were possible to understand the root causes of the passions in the way proposed by Descartes—and I am not at all sure that it is—even then his own proposition of reality makes it impossible for us to obtain the happiness we desire because we cannot negate our bodies through the strength of our minds."

"This is the same old problem that Aristotle alluded to when he called us 'thinking things.' It is not possible to go beyond our thing-ness through the negative power of intellect and its force of judgment."

"In Descartes' view, the passions were evil and pure intellect was good. But this is simply a new form of dualism—dualism in scientific clothing. The passions are not necessarily evil. They may disturb the putative tranquility of pure mind, but they should be valued for that very reason. What would human life be without passion? Empty and dull. What—should we give up Shakespeare and Beethoven for the sake of pure mind? Should we give up the cross? No, our thing-ness, as you call it, is not without value. It seems we are made to be passionate, and without passion life is like an empty glass, all form and no content."

"I almost hate to bring this up because I don't want to appear to be agreeing with you, but the same problem you see in Plato and Calvin with regard to love is also evident in Descartes' learned discourse upon the passions. It seems love is nothing more than one of those pesky passions to be eradicated for the sake of pure mind—but one could certainly argue that love is a 'passion' worth hanging on to."

"One certainly could. Love stirs up the mind, which brings it into conflict with Descartes' shining ideal of pure intellect. But then the price we pay for the vanity of the cogito—for presenting ourselves to the world as purely intellectual beings—is too high. The dispassionate nature of the cogito when it departs from the realm of pure theory and actually enters into being became all too evident in the Enlightenment, which is why it was overthrown by Romanticism in the end."

Indomitable Being

"Descartes succeeded in slaying the age of figures that preceded him through naturalism, but the new age he inaugurated was no less divided than the old because the cogito leads to pure form and highly restricted results."

"This problem can be seen in a more literal way in his foray into physics. If we can understand physics, the motions of things, then we have solved a great puzzle and obtained a good deal of wisdom about the nature of being; but the physics produced by modern science are no less divided than the descriptions of being seen in Plato and Aristotle. Descartes' grid-like geometry is ingenious in its simplicity, which makes it very fetching as an analytical tool; but this same simplicity prevents him from obtaining the transcendent understanding he desires. His analytical geometry appeared to justify the idea that knowledge of motion could be obtained through math and rational numbers—the *mathis universalis*, through which an attempt is made to establish a link between the seeming clarity of mathematics and the goodness of nature; in short, to make nature seem like a rational value. But the problem is that analytical geometry cannot tell us anything of much value about nature for its own sake."

"Its results were so limited that they led to the reaction seen in Newton and a shift in science in a direction that would not have been pleasing to Descartes."

"Newton and his synthetic geometry caused the cogito to go into eclipse for a time, until the difficulty and determinism of the differential calculus caused a negative reaction of its own and a full implementation of the cogito in Rationalism. But this second phase of Descartes' program also led to highly limited results. The cogito was transmuted into the Enlightenment ideal of pure observation; the task of the naturalist was to produce a description of nature in which all resonances of Scholasticism had been carefully stripped away, as Foucault reminds us, and all that was permitted to remain was a purely formal system of classification based upon optical differences."

"But this rigid form of naturalism is actually an exclusion of being. It is nothingness in the sense that any direct intimation of the influence of transcendent being on nature has been ruled out in order to fulfill the asceticism demanded by the cogito."

"The power of the cogito was funneled into a new kind of science that was not based on cause and effect reasoning or even experimentation but on the capacity of Subject to demonstrate resistance to Scholasticism by restricting himself to pure observation of the physical characteristics of natural objects. But the resistance of this new science to constructs of value prevented it from making any connection between the observed object and the 'I' of the cogito. It is impossible to connect the 'I' and its capacity to think and make value judgments to the goodness of the objects found in nature except by a construct where intellect is already somehow present in those natural objects."

"All the 'naturalist' can do to intimate the goodness of transcendent being is to create a vast superstructure of resemblances between the objects found in nature which appears to add up to a great chain of being—and this brings us back to Thomas and his famous complaint, since the great chain of being is nothing more than a metaphor."

"Idealism and Rationalism both led to nothingness, or the absence of 'being,' because they were both rooted in a love of pure intellect and its force of resistance. There is one very important difference between them and the nothingness they produced, however. Plato reserved the venue of 'being' for the transcendent being. His Ideals *might* be nothing—or then again, their seeming nothingness might indicate the resistance of this being to human ways of thinking. But nothingness takes on a more sinister connotation through the cogito. 'I think, therefore I am' shifts the venue of philosophy from transcendent being—which is an immortal value—to the mind of the philosopher himself; to mortal men. And in that case, the nothingness produced by Rationalism becomes linked to our own mortality."

"On one hand, this change made the cogito seem fresh and new; it insulated Rationalism from the known problems of Idealism and invested it with the optimism of the new science. But there was nothing left over from the nothingness produced by Rationalism after Descartes set aside the Ideals."

"The cogito deprived philosophy of the gracious covering of 'the good.' Being loses its transcendent significance and becomes contingent upon the philosopher's own capacity to think and to unravel the mysteries of nature through the power of science. The cogito literally gives precedence to intellect over life. Rationalism was no more capable of overcoming the nothingness caused by pure intellect than Idealism—but the nothingness resulting from the cogito was Descartes' own; the nothingness of mortal existence. And this led to the destruction of philosophy and being in the end."

"Descartes unleashed the dogs of nothingness by making Subject and its capacity to think the essence of being. No longer was the goodness of being hidden in the mind of an immortal being; it was transferred to the minds of men. And this great change opened the door for the possibility that all of our concepts of being are simply nothing."

"The cogito, which was born in pure devotion, led to pure skepticism by equating the capacity of Subject to doubt with being itself. It was supposed to reflect the resemblance Descartes thought he saw between pure intellect and transcendent being; it was supposed to become the basis of a new science that would make a straight highway to God. But the cogito also intimated the possibility of obtaining the transcendent value intimated in being through intellect for its own sake, without the guiding light of a transcendent being. And this raised the possibility that the source of our misery was our belief in a transcendent being; that the impediment to happiness seen in former methods of describing being could be attributed to the presumed difference between the goodness of the transcendent being and our own existence; that the solution to the dividedness of philosophy was to cast God out of our thinking and pursue happiness by more direct means."

"Writers such as Voltaire and Hume took up the force of skepticism about Scholasticism's descriptions of being seen in the cogito and began to turn it into skepticism of being itself."

"It was clear that man was making great advances in science, and many leading thinkers of the day believed he was capable of liberating himself from the chains of the old ways of thinking about value as well as the 'great abomination' of religion and enter into a new era of happiness through the power of intellect for its own sake. Nothingness began to take on a life of its own through its opposition to the dividedness of the descriptions of transcendent being seen in Descartes and Newton. This trend reached its logical conclusion in Hume, who claimed the freedom to formulate a new philosophy without having to bow to the tyrannical determinism of Newton's cause-and-effect clockmaker—or indeed, of any transcendent being."

"So what is seen in the modern age is a loss of faith in the power of intellect to prove the existence of a transcendent being and a corresponding heroic skepticism nurtured by the advances that were being made in science."

"We are witnesses to the end of the age of philosophy and the attempt to obtain happiness through knowledge of being. Philosophy was unable to produce a satisfactory description of this value when it linked being to transcendent being, an immortal power, and then the cogito led to the negation of philosophy by locating being in the minds of mortal men and exposing the potential nothingness of our concepts of being."

"Kant tried to stem the tide through his synthesis of being and nothingness, but this method of judging value had the unintended effect of making nothingness seem even more imposing than being in the end."

"Kant wanted to dispel the negative impact of the cogito on science as well as the skepticism seen in Hume. He concluded, with some justification, that this skepticism was a result of the link described by Descartes between pure intellect and transcendent being. This link leads to skepticism, in Kant's description, specifically because the transcendent being is transcendent. It is impossible to obtain knowledge of transcendent being if this being is pure intellect—a force of pure resistance to existent values."

"So Kant put the last nail in the coffin of 'being' by offering to set aside transcendent being and look for knowledge of being in the mind for its own sake."

"The purpose of the method was to combat skepticism by setting aside the transcendent being and its resistance to the limitations of human thinking and trying to identify traces of such a being in the way we *think* about being. Like Aristotle, Kant based his theory of value on the goodness of nature. Our awareness of this goodness makes it seem possible to discern certain 'categorical imperatives' in the judgments we make about nature and about life—to identify a method of indirectly tracing the influence of transcendent being on our concepts of value. But Kant's first premise undoes his own method. It is impossible to set aside the transcendent and also attribute goodness to nature."

"The differential connotation of 'the good' is lost entirely. Aristotle's theory of value was based on the idea that nature is good because the transcendent being has overcome the difference between itself and matter; that the goodness of the divine intellect is manifested directly in the values that actually exist. If we set aside the transcendent, we lose the core rationale for that goodness."

"Kant was desperate to avoid the taint of Scholasticism and the enchanted notions of nature it produced. He wanted to appear to be as modern and as much of a naturalist as the self-appointed naturalists of the Enlightenment. But he also wanted to go beyond the nothingness of their descriptions of nature and use science to draw some definite conclusions about transcendent value—to obtain a 'Transcendental Aesthetic.' And it is impossible to justify such an aesthetic on the basis of the goodness of nature once we have agreed to set aside the transcendent. "

"Kant's method deprives the philosopher of the ability to look at nature as a direct manifestation of the goodness of God, as did Aristotle and Thomas. It sacrifices the underlying rationale of their theories of transcendent value for the sake of appearing to take a purely scientific approach to philosophy. But taking the transcendent out of being also makes it impossible to justify his value judgments about being. Those value judgments obtain 'transcendental' significance only if the transcendent being really does exist and its qualities can be seen in existent values."

"Aristotle and Thomas saw nature as a ratio of divine intellect and matter; to remove the transcendent from the ratio is to revert to materialism and expose the nothingness of any concept of being. Kant thought that setting aside the transcendent would remove the obstacle of nothingness caused by the cogito and make it possible to reconstruct being. But this premise is faulty for two reasons. First, the only way the synthetic method can read transcendent significance into nature is through a construct of intellect and matter. And more importantly, if the ratio of value outlined by Kant exists purely in the human mind, then it becomes tainted with the mind's own mortality."

"Nothingness becomes something more than the lack of substance produced by the love of pure judgment; it raises the specter of nothingness itself—of a complete break with the past and the attempt to find happiness in knowledge of being."

"Kant thought he was limiting the power of nothingness by setting aside the transcendent, but in reality he made it possible to see nothingness in a new way—as a power that was capable of producing happiness by annihilating philosophy and the dividedness of its concepts of being. And this is what is seen in Nihilism. God is quite literally dead to philosophy because it is impossible to obtain an undivided description of the transcendent value intimated in being through intellect and its dividing power; either by linking concepts of being directly to the transcendent being, as was seen in Greek philosophy, or by attributing being to our own thought-existence and our capacity to obtain knowledge of transcendent value and happiness through science."

"If intellect is incapable of providing an undivided description of the goodness of being, then perhaps 'being' does not really exist. This led to the notion that it is possible to obtain happiness by negating being and embracing nothingness. But then a new form of dividedness appears, since nothingness makes us conscious of the value of life."

"Life reemerges in a new light after Nihilism and the negation of our concepts of being—as a value that is highly desirable in its own right. The demise of philosophy provides an opportunity to look at value in a new way and go beyond the dividedness of our value judgments about what is good. But we must be careful, because this is not possible by the light of intellect alone. History teaches us that we cannot obtain the knowledge we desire by glorifying intellect and its differential power. We must begin by agreeing with the Nihilists that 'god is dead.' Nothing can be gained by trying to reinstitute philosophy or equating intellect with the good. In order to go beyond Nihilism, we must go beyond the vanity inherent in this equation and make life our highest standard of value."

"At that point it becomes possible to distinguish between the vanity seen in philosophy and the power revealed to us through the desirability of life; a power that, in your view, provides knowledge of what is good in its own right. But I still find this troubling. Are we discounting intellect? Is there still a place for the sweet light of reason in your antithetical scheme of things?"

"Reason is highly valuable and can even be sweet when it reflects faith in the graciousness of God—but reason loses its sweetness when we glorify its dividing power and use it to make our theories of value seem important. Reason is capable of great sweetness if it tells us that all human reason is a fallen value and cannot progress beyond its fallenness by its own lights. Reason is a valuable power if it tells us that we cannot expect to obtain the happiness we desire or knowledge of what is good through any power found in reason for its own sake; that the concepts of the good seen in Plato and Aristotle are divided and this dividedness cannot be overcome because of the nature of intellect itself. Reason is a valuable power if it sees that the law is spiritual because it reflects the value of life, not because it glorifies intellect or judgment. Reason is valuable if it tells us to throw away worldly reason and turn the other cheek, which is the logical conclusion of believing that 'all things work together for good to those who love God.' Reason is valuable if it counsels us that the only way to obtain the identity we desire is to remain humble and gentle, since we are mortal, and any attempt to glorify ourselves or our theories of value will lead to unsatisfactory results."

"But reason cannot lead to these conclusions of its own accord. It is *faith* that makes this sort of reasoning possible."

"Without faith these conclusions seem highly unreasonable. If God is not love, and if love is not sovereign in the universe, than it is foolishness to turn the other cheek. It is insanity to aspire to be 'completely humble and gentle' if God is not love, since these self-negating modes of being are rooted in the premise that they reflect the transcendent power of love. It is insane to say 'the race is not to the swift' unless we believe there is something more to life than the vanity of the world and its value judgments. Nothing could be less reasonable than the Beatitudes if God is not love.

Blessed are the meek! Such soulful notions are sheer foolishness to the wisdom of men. Don't our greatest philosophers tell us that the way to obtain happiness is to take up the sword of judgment and glorify our concepts of value? Doesn't the superman tell us that the path to transcendence is through the will to power?"

"Faith and reason are not of equal value, then, in your view. Reason reasons according to its own lights, and reason in mortal men is limited by their own mortality. It cannot give us the knowledge we desire. The only way to go beyond the unhappiness that we bring upon ourselves through our love of intellect and its force of resistance is to have faith in a gracious power that transcends its limitations—the power of divine love."

"The sign of love indicates that we must give up our mortal lives in order to obtain knowledge of immortal value. This is foolishness to human reason, which counsels us to attempt to obtain this knowledge by building up the life we already have. But it is not foolishness if God is sovereign and 'God is love.' In that case it is vanity to cling to mortal life, vanity to attempt to glorify ourselves and our concepts of value. We desire a transcendent identity—we desire life—and the only way to obtain such an identity is to lay down the divisive passions of this mortal world."

"The problem with reason is that we are conscious of the great value of life, but the life we actually see is mortal life," I suggested. "It is as if we were looking at life projected on the screen of our own mortality. Our excessive love of intellect produces bondage to that mortality and cannot overcome this limitation except through faith in a gracious God who is willing to overlook our shortcomings and give life."

"There are some who would have us believe that the power of reason as seen in Greek philosophy is sweet. But then why was there bitter enmity between the followers of Plato and Aristotle? If reason has the power to provide knowledge of transcendent being, then why does Plato conclude that the good is pure intellect while Aristotle describes it as a coming-together of intellectual and material causes? These two concepts of value reflect the dividedness of intellect itself; how then can they be sweet?"

"There is a kind of sweetness in the glorious rhetoric of the Greeks, but their actual concepts of 'being' seem rather small and divided, especially now that we have decided to stop resisting the reality of their dividedness."

"I am no foe of reason," Smith assured me. "There is perfect pleasure for me in the sweet, flowing reasonableness of the Beatitudes, which are sweet because they reflect the desirability of life; perfect pleasure in Ecclesiastes and its honest appraisal of life as we actually know it. But I do not find this same sweetness in Plato and Aristotle. What I see is two men engaged in a desperate struggle to prevail on the battlefield of philosophy; two men who allowed themselves to become enslaved to divided identities, not so much because they themselves were divided, but because they had to embrace dividedness in order to seek domination."

"So then you agree with those like Boethius who felt that they were not as different as they seemed; that they were not irreconcilable."

"Yes, but not for the same reason as Boethius. He wanted to glorify intellect and philosophy, which is why he was eager to smooth over the divide between Plato and Aristotle. But what I mean is that the dividedness of their theories of 'being' reflects their excessive love of intellect, not the reality of their own lives or being. They made caricatures of themselves in order to play the heroic role of protagonist in the story of philosophy. This was necessary because human beings are not in fact heroes; they cannot obtain the perfect knowledge of being sought by philosophers by heroic measures because they are mortal. And this fact is borne out by the mutually self-limiting descriptions of being seen in philosophy."

"They have to divide the good in order to appear to be heroes of philosophy and to have conquered the good."

"Plato and Aristotle were not as divided as their stories made them seem. Plato was clearly drawn to the beauty of nature. Indeed, his great enthusiasm for beauty was the inspiration for his philosophy. But in order to dominate on the plains of philosophy, in order to distinguish himself from those who went before him, Plato put himself in the position of having to defend the insane notion that pure intellect has the power to provide knowledge of the value of beauty—a position that forced him to negate the existent beauty that he loved and pretend it was nothing."

"He had to pretend to despise the very thing he loved in order to take up the sword of judgment on behalf of pure intellect. Since the beauty of nature is 'very good,' this narrative obligation results in a highly divided identity."

"And the same thing is seen in Aristotle. He was no less attracted by the notion of pure intellect than Plato—by the transcendent value seemingly implied in this purity. Aristotle plainly stated that the good is intellect and that happiness consists of pure contemplation of this good. But he was not unaware of the weaknesses in Plato's theory of value—especially the fact that pure resistance results in nothingness—nor was he any less eager to dominate. He thought he could overcome the problem of nothingness by seeking substantive knowledge of the good in the goodness of nature, but this design compelled him to describe nature as a construct of intellectual and material causes."

"As soon as such a construct comes into being, it is no longer pure intellect. It loses the appearance of purity that Aristotle himself was eager to obtain."

"Vanity and the desire to dominate caused Plato and Aristotle to impose limitations on their public identities that were not really there. They labored mightily to obtain transcendence through intellect and its dividing sword of judgment—but this is impossible because a dividing power cannot render undivided results. Therefore pure, sweet reason can be found in the statement that 'all is vanity' and the heroic efforts of men a 'striving after wind.' It is impossible to obtain the transcendent identity we desire by glorifying ourselves and our concepts of value for the simple reason that we are mortal beings."

"This teaching is sweet because it reflects a right understanding of the difference between the realm of life and mortal life—a sane consciousness of our mortal limitations and of the paradox that anyone who seeks greatness in the mortal realm has a small identity in the kingdom of life."

"There are those who would like to turn back the clock and restore an ancient regime in which reason was revered more than life itself. It is difficult to see what is to be gained from such an endeavor, since we know that reason depends upon judgment, which leads to divided results. But we should feel free in our postmodern age to leave the bitterness of the old world behind and press on to a more hopeful goal. The god of the philosophers is dead; they themselves have declared it. But for this very reason it now becomes possible to look forward to something better than the unhappiness of the past."

"It is no longer possible to delude ourselves into thinking intellect and its methods of reasoning can give us the happiness we desire—we cannot enslave ourselves to this notion any longer—which means we are in a position to go beyond philosophy and seek happiness in a new concept of value."

"There is a way to go beyond the sterile vanity of the superman—and that is to embrace our foolishness, our inability to give ourselves what we desire by mortal means. I recall that we were talking about tenderness the last time you were here. Tenderness is one of the greatest pleasures known to man, perfectly sweet, but it is important to understand that the tenderness we cherish is linked to the foolishness we abhor. All of philosophy is an attempt to overcome the foolishness of mortal existence and obtain an appearance of power. Unfortunately philosophy and its concepts of being lead to nothingness in the end—literally to Nihilism and the will to power, in which there is no tenderness at all. Postmodern man finds himself in the foolish position of having to admit that his methods of describing being come to nothing; and yet there is a paradoxical type of consolation in this uncomfortable predicament—because tenderness and foolishness are linked."

"It is just when we stop trying to seem powerful that tenderness becomes possible. Otherwise the will to dominate inhibits the flow of tender feelings."

"Tenderness is one of our most highly cherished literary values, especially in the hands of such masters as Homer and Shakespeare and Austen, but the greatness of the pleasure it provides is correlated to our foolishness as mortal beings. The most tender moment in the *Iliad* also happens to be the most foolish, since even a good man cannot outrun his fate. Hector does not have the power to save himself by the sword, but he is redeemed in the affection of many readers by the tenderness they feel as they behold his foolish predicament. If we measure value by outward appearances of power, then Achilles must be the hero of the story, since he dominates on the battlefield. But the tale rises above its endless gruesome battle scenes and the limitations of the will to power through the great tenderness engendered by Hector's demise; through his indulgent attitude toward Paris and Helen; through his willingness to be drawn into a conflict that he himself does not endorse in order to protect his city and family."

"We love him because of the selflessness that is not very evident in Achilles—because of his largeness of spirit. Certainly it seemed that way to Shakespeare, who made his feelings known by having him killed in an ambush."

"Achilles is no less foolish than Hector—indeed, the case can be made that he is a good deal more foolish, considered as a man. Achilles is a rather small man; petty, arrogant, sensuous, self-absorbed. He is able to mask his foolishness behind his sword, his heroism on the battlefield, but he cannot escape it. And in a sense this is fortunate for us. If Achilles had any of Hector's magnanimous qualities, then he would add fuel to our vanity and the cherished notion that might and right go hand in hand—a notion that comes from our fear of nothingness, our desire to justify ourselves through judgment."

"The reality is that Achilles lacks those qualities, and yet he can dominate by the sword. Homer does not give us the luxury of indulging in the fantasy that we can obtain a desirable identity through the will to dominate."

Indomitable Being

"Hector cannot dominate in this instance—cannot defeat a warrior who is under direct protection of a goddess. There is a great deal of foolishness in his situation, particularly in the way he died, but the tender feelings he inspires justify him in spite of the fact that he cannot conquer. And of course he is also justified by the status he enjoys in the mind of Jove. It is for Hector's sake that the conflict has been allowed to drag on for ten long years. A divine judgment must be delivered eventually, and that judgment must be in favor of the principle that it is wrong to steal another man's wife; but Jove is very reluctant to deliver this judgment because of his fondness for Hector."

"Which suggests the possibility of an unseen realm of identity and of reality itself. Achilles dominates Hector on the battlefield but not in the mind of Jove. What seems real in our solid world is not what's really real—is not the end of the story."

"It becomes possible to go beyond the annihilation of philosophy when we give up the god of philosophy—the god of mortal judgments—and focus our attention on the power that makes itself known to us through the desirability of life, a power that cannot be seen by mortal men; that hides itself from their vanity. Men do not have the power to give life, nor can they obtain it by their own means. 'All men are like the grass'—this is pure, sweet reason. Life is literally beyond the grasp of men; but in this beyond there are intimations of a hyper-reality not immediately accessible to intellect or judgment, a transcendent realm where Achilles cannot dominate because of his selfishness; where our notions of value are turned upside down and the meek inherit the earth."

"We are somehow conscious of the reality of this realm—of its great value—which is why we cherish a Hector, a Cordelia, an Anne Elliot. The sweetness of their tenderness reflects a realm of being that is not accessible through reason per se."

"If we judge by appearances, then it may seem to us that Achilles has won. The superman has obtained the domination he so desperately desired in the prevailing culture and has annihilated any thought of the existence of a transcendent being. 'God is dead' to the wise men and prophets of our age, the Zarathustras who are not drawn to their soapboxes against their will, like Moses or Ezekiel, but actively entertain the notion of themselves as Zarathustra. But life cannot come from that which is not life. Nothingness destroys the concepts of being seen in philosophy, but it cannot lead to knowledge of the value of life because life cannot come from nothing. Therefore those who cling to the tender power made known to them through the value of life have an opportunity to go beyond the smallness and superciliousness of the superman."

"But they must begin by agreeing with him that 'god is dead'—that it is not possible to obtain access to this higher realm of being through intellect; that judgment cannot give them the sweetness they desire."

"If they love the tenderness of Hector, then they cannot find what they are looking for in philosophy. It is not possible any longer to satisfy our desire for identity by clinging to the notions of being propagated by the philosophers; all that our self-appointed supermen can do today to aspire to a transcendent identity is to make themselves seem like Achilles—hard, cold, arrogant, cruel. And yet the great sweetness of tenderness points to another way to obtain what we desire. We can go beyond the poverty of Nihilism by giving up the illusion of heroism seen in the superman; by embracing the foolishness that he attempted to conceal in outward shows of power and reimagining what it means to be human and to have value."

"You are suggesting that it may be better to cede the battlefield to the overman and embrace the foolish feelings that are caused by his apotheosis than to try to overcome him by reinstating 'being.'"

"Nietzsche was right when he said that the world and its descriptions of value are motivated by the will to dominate, in which case it is impossible to overcome our foolishness and obtain the precedence we desire without giving up Hector's tenderness. There is another way to obtain gladness and a desirable identity, however; a strange way, to be sure, but one that reflects the reality of our existence—and that is to give up the romance of the hero; to give up the desire to see ourselves in an exalted light, which leads to the ridiculous situation seen in Homer, where someone like Achilles appears to prevail and obtain being while Hector descends into nothingness."

"It might be better simply to accept our foolishness than to attempt to overthrow the overman, even though this has now become a distinct possibility; better to seek identity in resistance to vanity itself than in resistance to the vanity of our fellow beings."

"A new identity is possible after we have been defeated by life itself in the struggle for domination, but first we must put our trust in the tenderhearted power revealed to us through the great desirability of life instead of the will to power. There's an example of this new type of identity in David, weeping foolishly in his chambers for the son who betrayed him. When he first became king, David embodied the old covenant, which provided men with an opportunity to justify themselves and obtain life through the sword of judgment. They were promised to prevail as long as they were obedient to the law, and the effects of this promise were seen in David and his seeming invincibility."

"As long as he followed the law, he had no problem conquering his enemies. But one thing he could not conquer was his appetite, and this led to his downfall in the end."

"David rose to unimaginable heights from humble origins. He vanquished the enemies that had terrorized Israel for generations. He was a hero in every sense of the word—not just in the trivial sense seen in Achilles—because he was someone who wanted to do right; who feared and trusted in God and not his own power; who loved the law that reflects the desirability of life; who was not self-centered but filled with a spirit of poetry. Then he fell from his lofty perch in a most spectacular fashion—at which point everything began to fall apart. No longer was he invincible. His kingdom became characterized by treachery and treason, to the point where his own son betrayed him."

"Eventually he sank to weeping like a 'fond and foolish' old man for that same traitor-son, to the profound embarrassment of his captains."

"His weeping showed weakness and foolishness to the world, which is why his captains despised it. A king does not have the luxury of showing weakness when his first responsibility is to protect his kingdom from its enemies. This made his weeping seem doubly foolish. And yet from another perspective David never seems quite so appealing as he does in his inconsolable grief. David is weeping not only for Absalom but for his own weaknesses, for the foolishness that he exhibited when he allowed his desire for Absalom's mother to make him an enemy of God and deprive him of his heroic status."

"His weeping reflects more than the loss of Absalom—it reflects the loss of the romantic notions he had about himself and what a good king he would be."

"David in his chambers is a wreck of himself, a pathetic old man who has been the direct cause of his own demise and has no one to blame but himself. But because of the great tenderness of the scene he also becomes a *glorious* wreck. He goes to some place that lies beyond the poetic imagination, beyond the psychic limitations seen in his captains and their fear of exposure; some gracious realm of consciousness where he is no longer afraid to seem foolish to the world, where he has given up the vanity of depending on himself and his own righteousness."

"He obtains a more nuanced identity than he had when he was merrily slaughtering Philistines and dancing before the Ark."

"David as a young king is the world in its greening time, full of itself and its possibilities. This is a time when we do not know ourselves and our limitations, when we are full of dreams about what we can accomplish through our virtue. But virtue has a double meaning. It is possible to obtain precedence through strength—the will to power—but it is not possible for us to be virtuous by the standard of desirability seen in life because we are mortal beings with mortal desires."

"In short, we find as we grow a little older that we are not the virtuous heroes we wanted to be," I agreed with a sigh.

"We desire things that do not build up life, that are not wholesome and do not reflect the perfect love seen on the cross, and we are not always able to resist these things because we live in bondage to the grave. We become disappointed in ourselves. But even then it is possible to obtain a desirable identity—by giving up our desire to seem heroic; by giving up the will to power, which is the first step in making ourselves available to the tenderness seen in David. Vanity is impossible for him as he weeps in his chambers, but for this very reason he also has a clearer picture of who he is and what the obstacles are to happiness. When we begin to see ourselves in this way—in all of our foolishness—at that point it begins to become possible to put aside the will to dominate and seek a more gracious identity than is seen in the superman or in the world."

"It becomes possible to seek identity in graciousness itself—an identity that reflects the value of life and the difference between this value and our own existence. So 'God is dead' in the sense that our methods of obtaining a transcendent identity lead to nothing in the end. We know beyond any reasonable doubt that our methods of describing being cannot avail us or give us the transcendent identity we desire, since there is no method for obtaining life. But then is it a matter of seeking knowledge of the 'who' of transcendent being, as opposed to the 'how' of our methods?"

"I see you want to play journalist," Smith said good-naturedly. "I am inclined to doubt that the dialectic of 'how' and 'who' can give us what we are looking for. But fortunately I am far too tired to undertake any such discussion now—and perhaps by the time we meet again I will have experienced a reformation."

Chapter 11

A Case of Mistaken Identity

It was the day before Thanksgiving, icy and gray, and I was dragging myself along the scenic route when suddenly I felt an urge to drop in on Smith and wish him a happy holiday. So I picked up a small pumpkin and fresh cider at an orchard on the outskirts of town and headed for the old cottage in the valley.

Smith seemed amused when he saw me standing in the screened-in porch with a hang-dog expression.

"What—back for more?" he said.

"Can't stay," I mumbled, handing him my packages. "Just thought I'd stop by and say hello."

"That wife of yours is expecting you, I suppose."

"Not really. She thinks I'm at a department meeting, which mercifully has been canceled."

"Well, then; come in for a minute and warm up. I have a nice little fire going in the fireplace."

"Good place for it," I said, stepping listlessly into the house. "Say—what have you got to drink?"

Smith poured us each a glass of sherry from the rough old gray jug he kept on the mantle (which just at that moment struck me as a bit of an affectation). "The how and the who," he said picking up on our last conversation as if a full month had not gone by in the interim. "Three little letters, all jumbled together."

"And signifying nothing."

"The two words do seem to be related, however."

"They're alphabetically compatible," I suggested.

"Indeed, signs of intimate relations," he said with a laugh. "To know is the most intimate relation of all, and our thirst for knowledge indicates a strong desire for intimacy. But unfortunately the relations we seek through intellect are rooted in our resistance to unhappiness, which makes intimacy impossible. Subject-centered philosophers attempted to obtain a relation to transcendent being by totalizing that force of resistance, but pure resistance is just the opposite of intimacy. Plato's Highest Good is far off and forbidding—it is impossible to imagine an intimate relation to such a being. Meanwhile the synthetic methods appear to be relational by their very nature, since they describe a coming-together of reciprocal causes, a God who is Pure Act and immanent in existence. But this is not a true relation either, since 'being' becomes the same thing as ourselves and our existence."

"It loses its transcendent character, its difference—in which case the method cannot provide a relation to transcendent being," I said, a little too forcefully.

"The philosophers wanted to be known as men who enjoyed an intimate relation to the transcendent value intimated in 'being.' They sought to obtain this flattering identity through intellect and its capacity to make value judgments about being—but intellect is not a relational power and cannot provide any knowledge that is truly intimate. Plato had an unusually close encounter with the good—for a philosopher—when he saw that the beauty of nature indicates the existence of a transcendent being. Since beauty can provide a good deal of happiness, it occurred to him that it might be possible to obtain the good of happiness itself by using intellect and its qualitative force of resistance to disclose the nature of the being that is responsible for the existence of beauty. But the power that draws us to beauty is a force of attraction, while resistance pushes us away."

"As is seen in the fact that Idealism wound up negating beauty in the end. A relation must be based on some power other than resistance," I acknowledged wearily.

"Intellect *appears* to be capable of providing knowledge of transcendent value because the force of resistance to unhappiness found in the mind can be totalized as pure intellect. This is what made it seem so appealing. To Plato's mind, pure intellect seemed like a transcendent value for the very reason that it was pure. But the knowledge provided by pure resistance is not relational; indeed, it is inimical to relation. Plato founded Idealism on the love of beauty. This love can provide knowledge of transcendent value in the sense that the beauty of nature is far more desirable than anything made by man. It can even be said to render a degree of intimacy with transcendent being, since to know the great pleasure of beauty is to know something about the nature of that being—which is, apparently, to give pleasure. But Plato was not in love with beauty for its own sake. He thought it was possible to use the love of beauty to obtain a transcendent identity."

"He wanted to use the love of beauty to justify a theory of value—to glorify intellect and its concepts of being; to resist the identities seen in other philosophers and other theories of value. But then Idealism loses its relational power and becomes the divisive force we see in philosophy."

"Plato was in love with intellect and its force of judgment, its seeming capacity to raise some men up at the expense of others and provide them with a transcendent identity. He tried to justify this love by claiming that intellect is the essence of beauty, and that the joy experienced through the love of beauty can therefore be perfected by totalizing intellect and its capacity for resistance. But any attempt at totalizing resistance leads to a loss of the transcendent state of being sought in philosophy. In Plato, this can be seen in two ways. First, pure resistance devalues the beauty that actually exists and deprives the philosopher of the happiness it occasions. But worse, equating transcendent being with pure resistance also deprives him of the intimacy sought in knowledge by turning the good into a withering force of resistance to his own humanity."

"Plato undermines the goodness of beauty by equating intellect with the good. To know that goodness is to obtain a degree of intimacy with the good—but if there is no real goodness in beautiful things, as Plato claimed, then no such intimacy is possible."

"Plato was seduced by the strong force of resistance found in pure Subject—the 'who' of being, as it were. Subject obtains this resistance in two ways: first through its unhappiness with existence, and also through its very distinctiveness—the difference between it and all other beings. The confluence of these streams of resistance deceives Subject-centered philosophers into thinking they can obtain the joy of a transcendent identity by using their unhappiness with existence to distinguish themselves from others. But this is impossible if nature and existent values are 'very good.'"

"They cannot obtain a transcendent identity by attempting to negate the goodness of nature when that goodness is perfectly obvious."

"The word 'who' indicates a living being, but no one can obtain knowledge of a living being through the dividing power of judgment because life is an undivided value; because life cannot be divided and still be life. Philosophy cannot make us happy by glorifying intellect and judgment when our unhappiness indicates the fact that we ourselves are under judgment. We are unhappy because we are mortal beings who are conscious of the value of life—conscious of the difference between this great value and our own existence. Plato could not obtain knowledge of this immortal value by equating 'being' with intellect and his own capacity for resistance when he himself was mortal. All he really knew through his method of judging value was his own dividedness."

"Plato seems to have had an impatient longing for transcendence as well as a love of pure values, and these affections are reflected in his concept of the Highest Good. You see the descriptions of transcendent being in philosophy as projections of the limitations of the philosophers themselves."

"The concepts of value seen in philosophy represent an attempt to overcome the unhappiness of mortal existence through the power of judgment—but judgment does not have any such power. Men are under judgment because they are mortal, because they fall short of the glory of God, which is his immortality; but then their value judgments about what is good indicate nothing more than their own dividedness. Plato cannot, for example, obtain a transcendent identity by totalizing the resistance found in his unhappiness with mortal life because mortal life is not without value. It is not 'the good' if the light is life, but it is marvelous in its own right and far surpasses the understanding of men."

"Mortal life is not the opposite of life, which is what Plato's theory of value implies—the opposite of 'being.' The difference between life and mortal life does not justify the dualism seen in Idealism, which comes from the equation of pure intellect with the good, and the corresponding notion that material existence must be evil."

"Since 'being' intimates life, the only way to obtain intimate knowledge of this value is through a relation that reflects the value of life itself—a living relation. The types of relations supplied by intellect are intellectual relations, not living relations. It is impossible to obtain a living relation to transcendent being through intellect when we ourselves are mortal beings—when transcendent being literally transcends our existence. Such a relation becomes possible, however, through the power that makes itself known in the desirability of life. This power is relational by its very nature. It is not a dividing power; it is a force of reconciliation. And it is gracious. It willingly provides the means to obtain a living relation that cannot be found in the minds of men."

"An unselfish love is naturally gracious, and this quality is more useful to us if we desire an intimate relation to transcendent being than the force of resistance seen in the concept of the 'who.' In short, graciousness is more valuable than judgment. Not a great deal of graciousness can be seen in the philosophers and their eagerness to judge one another, but true graciousness is seen on the cross."

"The cross does not glorify the power of intellect or the value judgments seen in philosophy; it glorifies sincere love. The divided loves seen in philosophy were not unselfish. Plato and Aristotle claimed to be able to obtain possession of the good through their methods of describing value—that is, their love of knowledge was acquisitive and not disinterested. And this acquisitiveness worked against the intimacy they were seeking in knowledge of 'being.' To invert Socrates' dictum, it is impossible to enjoy a relation to something we already have. If we possess the good, then we cannot also have a relation to the good. Possession negates intimate relation."

"The selfish desire to make ourselves seem equal to the good through possession of the good deprives us of the possibility of intimate knowledge."

"This intimacy requires us to give up the vanity seen in philosophy and acknowledge the difference between ourselves and an immortal God; to give up our methods of obtaining knowledge of the good for something far more valuable, which is a living relation. The notion of such a relation is highly desirable. One of the most pleasant things about paradise before the fall is the image of God himself walking with his creatures in the garden—before the sight of God became fatal to mortal eyes. They enjoyed perfect intimacy with a being who is pure light; whose holiness is filled up with the sweetness of life; who is tenderhearted and unselfish and does not judge by appearances but by truth."

"The relationship is intimate because it is unhindered. No selfishness had yet intruded itself upon their consciousness and caused them to fall from grace."

"They enjoyed intimacy because their minds were not yet clouded by vanity; because they had not yet fallen for the lie that it is possible to make ourselves equal to God through the power of intellect and judgment. The way to regain this intimacy, then, is not to delude ourselves with the excessive love of intellect seen in philosophy, or to imagine that we are capable of obtaining possession of the good, but to take the lowest seat first; to humble ourselves and frankly acknowledge the difference between our broken humanity and the holiness of immortal God; to give up the selfish love of judgment for the sake of something far greater—the gracious love seen on the cross."

"Intimacy can be restored, but not through any method of glorifying our concepts of value."

"Intimacy requires us to rend our garments and stand naked before God; to give up the theories of value in which we attempt to conceal our mortal weakness in order to gain access to a realm of value that transcends our own limitations. There is a delightful example of this intimacy in the story about Abraham bartering for the lives of his brother and family. No confusion is seen in Abraham over the difference between the creator and the creature, no pridefulness or posturing about his ability to obtain what he desires by his own means. He does not come to challenge God or to claim possession of the good for himself; he comes to humbly beg him to change his mind for the sake of those who have not given themselves over to idolatry."

"He knows he does not have the power to spare their lives, and this knowledge makes him humble."

"His attitude of complete humility is the key to the intimacy suggested by the scene. He is granted the extraordinary privilege of being able to bargain with God. Not only that, but God appears to be willing to relent. God thinks highly enough of Abraham and his humility that he exhibits a willingness to change his mind and alter his judgment. Now presumably God knows in advance that Abraham's bargaining will not lead to the end he desires. Not even ten faithful souls can be found. But there is a marvelous intimacy in the forbearance shown toward Abraham and the willingness to consent to each diminishing minimum that he proposes."

"As if God were not aware that Abraham is trying to bargain with him. The graciousness of this picture of transcendent being is seen in his willingness to let Abraham think he is gaining his point."

"God is willing to bargain with someone who desires to preserve life. This is nothing like the selfishness seen in Plato and Aristotle, who wanted to glorify themselves at the expense of those who did not share their concepts of value. They considered equality with God as something to be grasped through the power of intellect—they demanded it by claiming to have obtained knowledge of the good. What they sought is impossible, since intellect cannot obtain knowledge of the transcendent value of being through its dividing power. But the charming intimacy of Abraham's story becomes possible if we are willing to remain humble; if we do not seek equality with God but openly acknowledge that God is God and men are mortal."

"So the intimacy seen in the Garden was possible as long as the absolute difference between God and men was observed; as long as men understood the difference between immortal being and themselves and did not fill their heads with conceited notions of obtaining equality to God through intellect."

"They enjoyed this great intimacy as long as their delight was in God. The destruction of intimacy came about when they forgot to seek joy in glorifying God and decided to glorify themselves; when they tried to obtain parity with God by investing themselves with the knowledge of good and evil. The obvious problem with this desire is that they were not equal to God. They were mortal. And the immediate consequence of seeking equality with God was the knowledge of their mortality, their dividedness, and a double loss of intimacy."

"They became enemies of God, and their fear of judgment made them enemies of each other as well."

"Now from this perspective, the most obvious problem with the 'who' questions is that we are not God. We are not transcendent beings, and it is impossible for us to obtain knowledge of transcendent being through intellect and its capacity to ask such questions because our concepts of value are tainted with our own mortality—as becomes evident in the dialectic of 'who' and 'how,' where 'who' is said to represent pure Subject and its capacity for resistance, and 'how' indicates the need to ground this resistance in an existent value in order to overcome its nothingness."

"The only way to obtain possession of the good through intellect is to divide it, since intellect is a dividing power—but then intellect cannot give us the intimacy or the transcendent identity we desire."

"Our methods of judging value are a type of spiritual sloth. Plato fell in love with pure intellect because it appeared to provide possession of the good—because possessing the good meant that it would no longer be necessary for him to labor to obtain knowledge of what is good. The synthetic method reflects the same desire for rest and ease, since its middle terms are believed to be fixed by the ratio of intellect and matter. In the mind of Aristotle, it was possible to ascend to parity with Supreme Being by identifying the point where its force of resistance seems to vanish in the goodness of existent values."

"Plato and Aristotle both wanted to complete their labors and rest in their value judgments about what is good—but this desire to rest is an enemy to intimacy."

"They both had their own intellectual pleasures and notions of value, and they tried to equate these valuations with the good. They tried to obtain a transcendent identity by glorifying the things they themselves cherished—but this made it impossible for them to have the highly desirable intimacy intimated in knowledge of the good. To have this intimacy, it is necessary to labor. It is necessary to be willing to stretch ourselves and make ourselves open to new concepts of being and of what it means to have value."

"The 'who' questions cannot lead to intimate knowledge any more than the 'how' questions if the 'who' we desire to know really is a transcendent being. They must remain unanswered in order for an intimate relation to become possible—otherwise they reflect our own limitations."

"I find the notion of the 'who' much more appealing than the Highest Good," Smith admitted. "It suggests something more than pure intellect—it indicates a Someone, a personality, in which case an intimate relation to transcendent being becomes possible. My reservation is that there may be a tendency to conflate this 'who' with pure subject and its capacity for resistance. The notion of 'who' can lead to divided concepts of value when it is equated with the difference between itself and 'how'—the difference between 'I' and 'am,' pure subject and pure being. If the purity of transcendent being is sought in that difference, then the 'who' questions can become infected with the same nebulous quality as the Highest Good. They lead to metaphorical interpretations of the statement 'God is love,' as seen among those theologians who were influenced by Nietzsche. And then they turn love into an intellectual endeavor and deprive it of its relational power."

"In that case the 'who' becomes the same thing as intellect and its capacity for resistance; and resistance is not a relational value."

"This is one case where the disciple was not like his master. He appears to have been enthusiastic about the Great Negation because it restored faith to the first rank of philosophy, but his concept of discipleship was rooted in the relational power of love. And indeed, if we think of the 'who' as the power found in the desirability of life, then our concept of value is not divided between 'who' and 'how.' God is love, and 'to love is to know God.' The two interrogatives are like a mirror gazing back upon themselves, since the 'how' cannot be known without knowing 'who,' and knowledge of the 'who' cannot be obtained without acting upon 'how.'"

"But isn't this just where we fall down again?" I complained. "Is it really true that we can obtain knowledge of what is good through anything we ourselves can do? We may have been made that way at one time, but we certainly seem to have fallen like a stone. A great collective cynicism has overtaken us through the notion that there is nothing beyond self-interest and no reason to study great writers or learn about the past. The shopping mall has become our place of worship; justice is for sale in the courts and the op-ed pages; too many of our children have no respect for authority and waste their lives watching television, an open cesspool that has now replaced the hearth in our affections. I don't know if it is still reasonable to think of ourselves as having the potential to obtain intimate knowledge of transcendent being through 'how' questions after raising up such an impressive triumvirate of antichrists as Hitler, Stalin and Mao; men who made the depravity of Nero seem relatively mild, men who did not quail at having the most hateful and pitiless acts done in their names. It has become all too easy to see ourselves as a vile race, I'm afraid, our hearts full of black and evil thoughts."

"I see you are somewhat inclined to pessimism today," Smith commented. "Perhaps it is the late autumn pall. And of course the negation implied in pure resistance can seem quite appealing at such times, since it suggests the possibility of dispensing with the perplexities of existence and starting over; of leaping over existence to something entirely fresh and new. The 'who' of pure Subject is definitely the more *promising* of the questions philosophy asks because its force of resistance seems to indicate infinite possibility. But the problem with seeking happiness in its annihilating power is that pure resistance is a negative value. It deprives us of the possibility of obtaining intimate knowledge of transcendent being through anything we can actually do."

"But I was under the impression that 'no one is good.'"

"This is true—if the good is life. By this standard, mortal life is a mixed value; evil clinging slyly to the good and goodness mixed up fatally with evil. The statement 'no one is good' indicates resistance to the flattery implicit in the title 'good teacher'—the notion that philosophers are capable of becoming masters of the good. No one can become a master of the good if the good is life; no mortal is deserving of such a flattering identity. But this does not mean that there is no goodness in mortal life. It does not mean, for example, that there is no such thing as a good teacher who desires the welfare of his students and is devoted to giving them a good education. In fact he himself was just such a teacher. To interpret his resistance to the flattery of 'good teacher' as a negation of existent values is to deprive his teachings of their goodness."

"It is to turn the story of his life into a hollow drum, a metaphor of goodness with no substance. Still, I can't help wondering if there is any goodness in *me*. I've been finding it harder and harder to get to sleep at night—seems I cannot put out of my mind all the slings and arrows of life or the ways I have hurt others and continue to hurt them."

"I would be the last person in the world to dismiss existential resistance, since it is real," Smith replied. "There is great value in resisting the vanity of wanting to be known as 'good teachers.' It is in such resistance that the seeds of true relation are found with our students, who are not inferior beings but fellow mortals on the path of life. And to extend your point, it is also true that there can be real value and great sweetness in the humility that refuses to accept praise from men—refuses to pretend to be good—since this humility indicates an awareness of the value of life. There is another type of resistance, however, that uses similar language to yours and is not necessarily existential—a resistance rooted in intellect and its capacity for judgment. This resistance seeks the identity of having obtained intimate knowledge of transcendent being by negating existence. According to this harsh doctrine, nothing that mortals do has any value in the eyes of transcendent being or any power to provide knowledge of what is good. But in that case, what do we make of Abraham? Why was he allowed to bargain with God?"

"This 'harsh' doctrine negates the sweetness of the intimacy of Abraham's relationship with God."

"Those who embrace the doctrine do not always exhibit the humility seen in Abraham. Indeed, they believe that the doctrine of their own depravity has the power to transform them into teachers of the good! Something similar is seen in Socrates. He loved to make himself seem humble and self-effacing, but to some extent this was part of his rhetorical strategy. His description of the Highest Good as a force of pure resistance to existent values implies that he must be a lowly being, since there can be no doubt that Socrates is made of matter. It *suggests* a deep humility and awareness of the difference between himself and 'the good'—but in reality it is something quite different, for it turns out that he does not think meanly of himself at all. In fact he believes he has obtained direct knowledge of the good through his method of describing being."

"Hardly anyone thought more highly of himself than Socrates, who believed he had a divine right to impose his concept of value on others. But surely this is not the case with those who think of themselves as being totally depraved!"

"There can be vanity in this formulation as well—when it is used to distinguish ourselves from others; to make ourselves seem more intimate with the transcendent being than our fellow beings, more knowledgeable about what is good. If we say we are totally depraved because we are genuinely appalled at our state of being and desire to take the lowest place first—as, for instance, when the apostle calls himself the worst of sinners—then such a sentiment is the opposite of vanity. It reflects a consciousness of the value of life through a willingness to consider ourselves less important than our fellow mortals; through the gracious gesture of putting others first and not indulging our natural desire for precedence. But when we deceive ourselves into believing that the very concept of total depravity has the power to confer some sort of special status and transform us into 'saints,' then we are not following the path of lowliness that leads to intimacy. We are following the path that raises men up and divides them."

"It is difficult to obtain intimacy with others when we consider ourselves to be superior to them. But at least the lovers of pure doctrine attributed the purifying power that turns sinners into saints entirely to God. The Schoolmen claimed we could overcome the difference between transcendent being and fallen existence by our *own* actions. In fact Thomas said this miraculous feat could be accomplished through love. So how can you be sure you are not talking about the same sort of construct of value?"

"I make no pretense to be good," Smith replied with a laugh. "It has often seemed wonderful to me that others cannot see into my mind, thus enabling me to preserve whatever small shred of dignity I might still have, however undeserved. I am fully aware that even my best intentions and actions are not wholly untainted by selfishness; and while I know many people who are far better than myself, such as my dear wife, still my own experience, as well as the world and its lugubrious history, provide ample confirmation for me of the teaching that 'no one is good.'"

"In which case it is impossible to obtain goodness through the work of love."

"It is impossible to *become* good—to overcome the difference between life and mortal life—through any good that we can do. But doing good can provide *knowledge* of what is good. I heard that someone in our little community put an anonymous holiday gift in the mailbox of Barbara McCreary last week. Now this was a very kind gesture. Barbara, having recently lost her husband, and having two children at home to care for, will naturally find some of her anxiety relieved. And the gift is all the more generous for having been given anonymously. Absolutely no desire for credit was attached to the gift, and so she is free to enjoy it without the burden of obligation. Now does such a gift make the giver 'good'? Is it possible, through such a gift, to obtain equality with God? No; the very fact that it was given anonymously indicates an awareness that any such thought is vanity. But is it possible to obtain knowledge of what is good through such a gift? There is no question in my mind that this is the case. True religion is taking care of widows and orphans and keeping a tight rein on the tongue—the first showing the active side of love, which succors those in need, and the second showing love's negative side, which prohibits us from seeking to build ourselves up at the expense of others."

"Love is both pure action and pure negation, as you are fond of claiming," I said a little uneasily, wondering how he had happened to stumble upon that particular example. "We can see the active side of love in the charitable act, and this act can provide knowledge of what is good if it is good to relieve the suffering of others, while the call to discipline the recalcitrant little muscle reflects the force of pure resistance seen in the law, which is summed up in the command to love one another."

"Knowledge of what is good is obtained both through pure action and pure negation if we conceive of transcendent being as the power revealed to us through the desirability of life. We find out what is good when we act charitably because even mortal life is a very great value, which is why satisfaction and a desirable identity can be found in giving happiness to others and actively building up life; which is why we love redemption stories. But knowledge of what is good can also be obtained through the negative force seen in the commandments. If we do indeed put a restraining order on the devious little muscle that longs to glorify ourselves, we find that we are far happier in the end."

"In the long run, there is greater happiness and satisfaction in resisting the temptation to proclaim our good deeds than in the instant gratification that comes from succumbing to this temptation. And this truth is revealed to us through the desirability of life, which makes us conscious of our limitations and counsels us to shun any attempt to make ourselves look 'good'; which teaches us to be patient and not demand immediate rewards for any good thing we might have the good fortune to be able to do."

"It is impossible to become 'good' if our standard of goodness is the power revealed to us through the desirability of life, but it is entirely possible to obtain knowledge of what is good if we 'do justice, love mercy, and walk humbly with our God,' behaviors that reflect the gracious value of life. Such behaviors cannot make us 'good,' but they can provide knowledge of what is good through their very graciousness; and this knowledge can enable us to go beyond the nothingness we bring upon ourselves through the vanity of thinking that our methods of judging value have the power to make us happy."

"Your resistance to the equation of the good with intellect does not negate the possibility of reasoning about what is good. All it negates is the vanity of thinking of ourselves as 'good teachers,' as masters of the good."

"It appears that the only way to become a good teacher is to know we are not 'good teachers,'" Smith chuckled. "Reason is not annihilated by this acknowledgment, which reflects a right understanding of the value of life and the difference between this transcendent value and our own existence. By the light of life, it seems entirely reasonable that mortal beings cannot obtain what they desire by claiming to have obtained the goodness of transcendent being. Reason was glorified in philosophy in order to glorify mortal men, but reason is nothing more than the handmaiden of knowledge in the realm of life. Indeed, it is the handmaiden of love—just the opposite of what the 'good teachers' taught."

"We should employ reason to leaven our existence, but we should not make intellect our light. 'In him was life, and this life was the light of the world.'"

"I am not comfortable with the notion that the logos is reason. Where is the justification for this concept in the text itself? When the word was made flesh, he did not glorify reason or intellect, like the Greeks. In fact much of what he said seems highly unreasonable apart from the sovereignty of love. Nor was it because of reason that he went to the cross; it was because God so loved the world that he was willing to sacrifice his own son. There is nothing reasonable about the cross. It is 'foolishness to the Greeks' because the Greeks glorify reason and the cross seems highly unreasonable—the son of God lays down his crown for the sake of mortals. And it is a 'stumbling block' to the Jews because the Pharisees glorified the law and their outward conformity to its standards."

"So love provides the key to wisdom that cannot be found in intellect and its concepts of value," I concluded, shaking my head—a gesture which unfortunately Smith misinterpreted.

"Oh—I know exactly what you're thinking," he replied, wagging a bony white finger in my direction. "You are wondering how a pompous old ass like me can sit here pontificating about 'love' when he is just as intolerant as ever and living like a misanthropic anchorite in his cottage in the woods. And I agree with you. I am not a 'good teacher.' What I am is nothing more than a miserable old sinner. The older I get the less I think I know about what is good—indeed, about anything at all. But I do know one thing: the more I cling to the world and its vanity, the more miserable I become. It is only when I let go of the world and its false promises of happiness—let go of judgment—that I begin to experience any joy or peace or the intimacy that is the antidote to despair."

I wanted to assure him that I had not been thinking any such thing, but the responses that came to mind seemed all too likely of being misconstrued. So we sat in silence for a few minutes as the warm south wind blew in the pines and leafless maples.

"I suppose I should go," I said at last. "We have twenty guests coming tomorrow, and I am the designated turkey chef."

"Poor fellow; my daughters make me quite lazy."

Smith walked me to the door. I did not want him to think that I agreed with his harsh self-assessment, so I made an awkward attempt at embracing him. Then I wondered all the way home what he thought of such a ridiculous gesture.

Chapter 12

Life and Culture

I FOUND Smith in a relaxed if pensive mood late one December afternoon, serenely observing the rain and sleet.

"You seem absorbed," I said, stamping my feet in the entryway.

"I'm waiting for the snow. Snow and more snow, and blustery winds; that is the sweet promise of December."

"Still listening for that voice in the storm, I take it."

"Oh, I heard it long ago. 'Vanity, vanity; all is vanity.'"

"So much for culture, then," I sighed. "The galleries, the theaters, the concert halls all plying their bright trade—all drowned in a sea of rainy gloom."

"Let us hope that *culture* runs somewhat deeper than such whited sepulchers as that," he replied with a smile.

"You feel that such things are not what they seem?"

"They claim the exalted mantle of 'culture,' but they base this claim on appearances of power; and thus they are not likely to draw very deep."

"But this is unfair! The arts have to present an appearance of power by their very nature. A baker may be a good craftsman, but no one wants to see his bread hanging with the masterworks at the Met."

"Unfortunately I no longer seem to be able to find what I am looking for in such valuations," Smith replied with a sigh. "It is true, of course, that anyone can tell the difference between a lowly loaf of bread and a masterful painting, which appears to resist the worm of death in the splendid fortress of the museum; thus a hierarchy is established in the mind in which the creative artist obtains transcendence through an outward demonstration of power. But perhaps this is why we are fortunate to have the cold storms of December—to remind us of our colossal vanity."

"You or I have a much better chance of making a good loaf of bread than a tolerable painting, but that difference is not the same thing as *culture*, I take it."

"I am not at all certain that our efforts to glorify art are any more conducive to 'culture' than a lowly loaf of bread. To cultivate is to break up the earth and plant a seed and take care of it in the hope that it will become a living thing; thus it seems to me that culture must depend ultimately on some power that cannot be seen. But cultural identities are based entirely upon outward appearances of power—and anything that surfaces in the mortal realm is divided."

"You are thinking of the metaphorical significance of culture; its root, if I may make a bad pun."

"You may, and you have. To cultivate is to facilitate life; this is culture of the highest order. And the word 'culture' may very well be deserving of the devotional attitude it inspires in the hearts of men when it reflects the standard of desirability found in life. But most of what is *called* culture is rooted in an attempt to obtain a transcendent identity through the power of judgment—which is impossible, since judgment cannot nurture any living value."

"Men cannot produce culture through judgment if 'culture' really does have the transcendent resonance of life," I summed up.

"Cultural identities are based on the belief that it is possible to obtain transcendence through judgment and its force of resistance to the unhappiness of existence, but this same resistance also leads to divided values because of the difference between intellect and sense. Romanticism with its love of nature came into being through resistance to the limitations of Rationalism and the love of pure reason, just as the Enlightenment was rooted in resistance to the mixture of empiricism and religion seen in Newton and the Baroque revival, and the Neobaroque in resistance to the Neoplatonism of the Renaissance, and Neoplatonism to Scholasticism, and so forth and so on. The resistance supplied by these cultural identities made them seem powerful in their own time, but resistance is a dividing power and cannot satisfy a desire for life."

"Which is why they were all overturned in the end. And now our love of resistance has led to the dead end of Nihilism and the negation of 'being'—to resistance for its own sake, or the futile attempt to obtain transcendence by *denying* the value of life."

"In the end, devaluing life is the only possible way for mortal men to obtain the transcendent identity for which they pine through their own means," Smith replied with a chuckle. "At first we thought we could ascend to the level of transcendent being through our methods of describing being. This is impossible, since 'being' is an immortal value. Then Nietzsche got the clever idea that there was another way to obtain transcendence—by negating the difference between ourselves and transcendent being; by embracing our own existence, our nothingness, and putting the good out of our minds. But this too is impossible, because living beings cannot negate the goodness of life."

"Nietzsche thought it was possible to annihilate the difference between life and mortal life by negating the value of life. But this led to the rather morbid results seen in Modernism, since life is too great a value to be negated."

"Nihilism is just what Nietzsche said it was—a fact of modern existence. It reflects an awareness that philosophy and its pursuit of knowledge of being and 'the good' cannot give us what we desire. Plato and Aristotle equated transcendent being with intellect in order to validate their value judgments about being. For a long time we were able to deceive ourselves into thinking that their methods of describing being had the power to make us happy; but 'being' intimates the value of life, which is not the same thing as intellect at all; a gracious value, absolutely desirable for its own sake. And the value judgments seen in philosophy fell so far short of this great value that it has now become impossible for us to look at them and even imagine they can satisfy any great desire."

"Something fundamental has changed in our attitude toward philosophy," I agreed. "It seems we are not able to take it seriously anymore. It has lost the vital role it once played in culture and now seems to be content to consign itself to the margins of discourse, where it can 'play' and not be bothered with real life."

"Nihilism represents the end of the cycle of identities supplied by philosophy and the force of qualitative resistance found in intellect—the annihilation of philosophy itself and its power to capture our imagination through its value judgments about transcendent being. It is no longer possible to reinstate philosophy and its pursuit of the good of happiness after Nihilism when Nihilism constitutes an acknowledgment that all of our concepts of what is 'good' are hopelessly divided. But neither is it possible to negate the goodness of life, as Nietzsche told us we must do in order to become supermen. The attempt to negate life does not lead to the happiness of knowing transcendent value; it leads to morbidity and mawkishness by seeking such a value in mortal beings."

"So Nihilism, then, would be the very opposite of culture, in your view—it represents an attempt to glorify men by negating life."

"The attempt to use intellect to obtain knowledge of transcendent value led to Nihilism in the end because we ourselves are mortal beings and our value judgments about 'being' reflect our own dividedness. By the end of the Renaissance it was becoming obvious that the rebirth of classical philosophy was not going to produce the happiness desired by men, since its concepts of being were hopelessly divided between sense and intellect. Descartes and his fellow scientist-philosophers managed to stave off the end of philosophy for a while by substituting good science for the explicit pursuit of 'the good'; but this effort also was doomed to failure. Scientific philosophy turned out to be no less divided than the Greeks between resistance and existence. Intellect and sense are different values, and this difference cannot be overcome through any description of being that attempts to glorify intellect."

"Philosophy lost the gracious covering of 'the good' when it turned its attention to science, and nothingness began to rear its ugly head. If all of our concepts of transcendent being occur simply in our own minds, as Descartes' dictum indicates, then it becomes impossible to suppress the possibility that those value judgments might just be nothing, since we ourselves are mortal beings."

"The cogito enshrined the capacity of intellect to doubt its own concepts of being, but then this doubt began to overwhelm being through our own nothingness as it became evident that scientific philosophy was incapable of rendering any undivided value judgments about transcendent being. Hegel tried to slay this doubting Hydra by describing nothingness as the limit of our concepts of being, a clever ploy that made us think there was some sort of middle ground between being and nothingness. And indeed, it is possible to imagine such a limit if nothingness represents nothing more than intellect and its force of resistance. But in direct relation to 'being,' nothingness also reflects our own mortality—and there is no middle term between life and mortal life."

"Nothingness can be conceived as a *limit* of being only as long as it reflects transcendent being, an immortal value, and its resistance to our limitations, which is how Hegel used the term. But if we really do set aside the transcendent, as the Transcendentalists proposed, for the sake of pure science, then nothingness becomes the same thing as our own mortality."

"Nietzsche seized upon this contradiction to create the firestorm of Nihilism—but it was not a perfect storm, because it was rooted in the same vanity as Plato and Aristotle and their excessive love of intellect. Since Hegel failed to make us happy through his synthesis of being and nothingness, Nietzsche claimed it was possible to go beyond the limitations of philosophy by totalizing nothingness and negating any thought of being. All we need to do is to embrace our own mortality and the transcendent principle that seemed implicit in the survival of the fittest—the will to dominate. But it is not possible to make ourselves happy by embracing our own mortality when we are conscious of the value of life."

"Nietzsche positioned himself as the antithesis of philosophy, but he overestimated the power of intellect in the same way as the philosophers. It was not because of any lack of power in ourselves that we were unhappy, according to Nietzsche; it was because we were seeking our bliss in something that does not exist—the transcendent being that was the object of philosophy. But he thought we could make ourselves happy by using intellect to negate being—and this is impossible, since life is a very great value and cannot be blotted out of the mind."

"Intellect does not have the power to do what the superman must do in order to obtain the transcendent identity he desires. Any attempt to glorify himself by negating the value of life simply exposes the limitations of his concept of value. The superman must wage unrelenting war against 'being' and 'the good' in order to justify his claim to have obtained domination on the battlefield of philosophy, but excluding that goodness leads to highly divided values. A reasonable visitor to one of our modern museums might well wonder what is wrong with attempting to represent the beauty of nature in art and why no such art ever seems to find its way into the hollowed halls of Modernism, no matter how skillful it might be. But any representation of such pleasures would imply that they are 'good,' and this violates the rigid absolutism of the age."

"Representation of the beauties of nature is excluded because it is contrary to the ideology of Nihilism. The overman cannot obtain a transcendent identity through absolute resistance to the good if there is goodness in nature; thus anything that reminds us of this goodness must be sacrificed on the altar of his vanity."

"Nihilism was supposed to produce transcendent values in culture and the arts, but in reality it led to devastation and the negation of culture. Just as the superman's love of absolute resistance to being translates into morbidity and cold abstraction in the museum, so it produces resistance to plot and characterization in literature, values that run counter to the idea that 'being' literally does not exist and all stories are meaningless; so it annihilates poetry by insisting on the negation of rhyme and meter, which obtain transcendent resonance by reflecting the sweetness of life; so it annihilates music by negating the value of melody, harmony and rhythm, as if music could be music without them."

"It is impossible to obtain the *transcendent* identity sought by the overman by attempting to negate the good because the goodness of such things cannot be negated."

"In that sense, a lowly loaf of bread may actually be more valuable than much of what passes for 'culture,'" Smith commented. "Bread is capable of fully satisfying our cravings with pleasant flavors and aromas—but what is the desire that we are attempting to placate by glorifying culture? The philosophers sought the identity of masters of 'being.' This suggests that they wanted to be known as immortal beings—as men who had overcome the mutability of existence. It was impossible for them to obtain knowledge of the transcendent value intimated in 'being' through intellect because intellect is a dividing power. They did not obtain the immortal identity they desired; their philosophy did not rise to the level of culture. And then Nietzsche came along and pretended to have an entirely new vision of culture. No longer was culture going to be rooted in the immortal value of 'being.' Instead the superman was going to negate being and embrace his own mortality, his nothingness. But then why does he call himself a superman?"

"Such an identity is not exactly *nothing*," I said with a laugh. "It would seem he has not in fact succeeded in embracing nothingness if he wants to obtain a transcendent identity. Plato and Aristotle thought they could obtain an immortal identity through intellect, but intellect cannot facilitate life. Nietzsche thought he could obtain such an identity by negating life—but then life itself becomes the limit of his happiness."

"Nietzsche cannot make himself happy by negating being when it is specifically the immortal identity of the superman that he desires. It was not enough for him, apparently, to frolic in the fields with Dionysus, drinking and wenching to his heart's content, oblivious to any thought of 'being'; like Plato and Aristotle, he was consumed with an Apollonian desire to obtain precedence in the hearts and minds of his fellow beings. The superman may have gone beyond the dividedness caused by philosophy's preoccupation with being by negating being, but he cannot obtain a transcendent identity by embracing nothingness when the value of life is self-evident."

"He enslaved himself to a highly divided identity in which there is no joy and not much pleasure."

"The superman is a cold identity, made up of largely of acid and conceit. Nihilism was supposed to lead to a state of pure existence in which he was perfectly at home with himself, but in fact it ensnared him in the bitterness of his own mortality. He modeled himself on Prometheus, that shimmering creature of the poetic imagination who liberated humankind from the selfishness of the gods—but Prometheus had a hope that leavened his suffering, since he was immortal and believed the life-renewing forces of time and change would lead to a reversal in his fortunes. There can be no such hope for the superman after he negates the good, however;

there can be nothing but unrelenting misery as the goodness of life feasts on the limitations of his love of nothingness."

"So you believe that his limitations have now been exposed?"

"Modernism is tottering on the brink of extinction, and has been for some time. The same worship of naturalism that led to Nihilism is now in the process of overthrowing the superman by illuminating the value of life. There can no longer be any doubt that the superman has a small and divided identity and cannot obtain the domination he desires in culture. He has had more than a century to demonstrate his knowledge of transcendent value—more time than the virtuosi of the Enlightenment or the nature-lovers of Romanticism—but no such value has emerged in the modern age. And no such value can emerge from Nihilism and its negative ideal of absolute resistance to the good."

"The goodness of life cannot be denied and cannot be negated; therefore the overman cannot obtain the transcendence he seeks through Nihilism. I must say, however, that he still seems to be clinging to that rock of resistance as tenaciously as ever in my little neck of the woods."

"This is always the case at the end of the age," Smith observed. "Cultural identities obtain hegemony through the consent of the governed; therefore they cannot be overturned until they reach a critical mass and their limitations are fully exposed. This is why cultural change is difficult to see for those who happen to be living through it. Kant was not fully aware of the change that was imminent and of which his own writing was the most prominent sign. He cloaked his radicalism in sheep's clothing because the Enlightenment was in its institutional phase—but the prevailing culture faded away with shocking rapidity once its limitations became self-evident."

"The same seems to be true of all such identities. At one point they seemed inconceivably powerful—and then suddenly they were spent. But this suggests that whatever follows Nihilism will probably be no more lasting in the end," I noted.

"If culture reflects the value of life, then it requires resistance to prevailing cultural identities, which are rooted in vanity," Smith agreed. "Beethoven was born at the zenith of the Enlightenment, when its dividedness was becoming obvious, and stretched and strained with his contemporaries to break its bonds through the Romantic spirit that was beginning to gather force to produce such magnificent works as the *Eroica*, which reflected Goethe's vision of a heroic synthesis of Medieval and Neoclassical cultures. But he did not stay in that historic moment for long; he lost faith in the revolution when he saw it personified in Napoleon and moved on to something more wonderful in the 'Ode to Joy' and *Missa Solemnis*, which are rooted in the desirability of the immortal realm."

"He was not afraid to let go of something as great as the funeral march with its romantic melancholy for the possibility of obtaining something greater. But then I take it that art is not *inimical* to culture," I teased.

"No—but artists cannot aspire to this exalted value if they are laboring under the delusion that they are supermen," Smith rejoined. "There is no such thing as a great artist who believes he is great. Great art requires greater humility. No one can reflect the transcendent value implicit in 'culture' unless he is profoundly conscious of his own limitations and the foolishness of glorifying men or their art. Therefore no one who claims to be a superman can rise to the value of culture."

"A great artist must set his heart on something higher than the praise of the world in order to obtain an identity that reflects the value of life. He cannot glorify himself and also aspire to 'culture' when he himself is mortal."

"Never was any artist more infused with a high opinion of himself and his powers than the superman, and never were the limitations of mortal beings more obvious than in the Modern age. The superman is dead—but culture becomes possible again through the demise of his frank egotism. The attempt to make the superman seem like a transcendent being revealed the difference between life and mortal life, but his failure to live up to the high opinion he had of himself does not mean that culture is dead. It is quite possible to go beyond the limitations of Nihilism by giving up the vanity seen the superman; by acknowledging the difference between life and mortal life and using art to glorify the transcendent power that makes itself known through the desirability of life."

"The dismal results of Nihilism present a stark choice between the vanity of the overman, which leads to highly divided values, and the desirability of life itself, a value that cannot be used to flatter any man."

"The way to go beyond the annihilation of culture seen in the modern age is to give up the will to dominate that characterizes the superman. Nietzsche was right about philosophy: it was motivated at least as much by the will to dominate as by the desire to obtain knowledge of 'the good.' But he was wrong when he claimed that the superman could go beyond the limitations of philosophy by embracing domination for its own sake. Open domination cannot give us what we desire any more than domination for the sake of 'the good' because we are conscious of the goodness of life."

"Nihilism cannot go beyond the limitations of philosophy when it remains within the realm of philosophy and the will to dominate."

"Like all concepts of value rooted in pure resistance, Nihilism seemed desirable when it was simply a theory. But Nihilism cannot remain in the realm of theory forever and also obtain the domination upon which the superman predicates transcendence. At some point it becomes necessary for the superman to come out of his coy pose of pure resistance and make his value known in a concrete way in order to validate his claim to domination—and then it also becomes impossible for him to hide the limitations of his theory of value."

"Nihilism sought domination, and this required it to remain within the realm of philosophy and discourse. It is impossible to rise to transcendent value as long as we are clinging to the dividing power of intellect in the hope of dominating our fellow beings."

"This is just what we saw in Job," Smith noted. "He could not obtain the answer he was looking for as long as he insisted on remaining in dialogue with his friends—as long as he allowed himself to be seduced by the mirage of obtaining domination through intellect and its dividing power. In the end he found it necessary to get up and walk away from human discourse; literally to walk away from the fatal temptation to use the mind and its qualitative power to justify himself. And only then did he obtain access to a transcendent realm of understanding. Only then did he become conscious of the difference between life and mortal life, a difference that is obscured by the pride of intellect."

"So a connection appears between culture and the storm after all."

"The cold storms of December do not flatter us in any degree. They are honest counselors, perfect strangers to vanity and the impossibly high opinion we have of ourselves, to the foolish little struggles for identity that seem important to us as we act out our destined roles on the stage of life. The sheer otherness of moaning winter winds can help us to clear our minds of all of the tricks we use to distract ourselves from our fear of nothingness—but only if we are willing to hear it for what it is; only when we have the good sense to experience a healthy jolt of fear and trembling."

"Only then do we become capable of catching a glimpse of the truth about ourselves."

"A howling winter storm has the power to plow up the hard crust of vanity in which we encase our fragile egos—if we are willing to hear it on its own terms and its utter indifference to our illusions of power. This process is painful, since it forces us to come to terms with the reality of existence; with our foolishness as mortal beings, which is hateful to our vanity. And yet it is just at this point of self-awareness that we become good soil for the seed of culture and capable of bearing good fruit."

"Culture, then, requires us to turn away from the world and give up the vanity of our love of judgment for the sake of life."

"The philosophers were fully aware of the transcendent value implied in 'being,' but vanity prevented them from digging deeply enough into the difference between this value and themselves. They thought they could obtain knowledge of this value through intellect, which is impossible, since intellect is a dividing power. Nihilism negated philosophy when it negated 'being'—it is no longer possible to pretend to ourselves that philosophy has the power to make us happy or give us the identity we desire. But the voice in the storm indicates transcendent possibilities even after the death of philosophy, a way to move past the morbid dreariness of the modern age. The restoration of culture begins with a willingness to see the truth about ourselves; to give up the notion that we are capable of justifying ourselves through judgment, and to seek gladness instead in the power that makes itself known through the desirability of life."

"The power of the storm reminds us of our nothingness, but it can also make us aware of the existence of a power that transcends our understanding and is capable of giving the joy that cannot be found in philosophy or its methods."

"The philosophers diagnosed our unhappiness as a lack of intellectual purity, which they sought to remedy by making value judgments about 'the good.' According to Plato, we are unhappy because we have been separated from the good of pure intellect by the addition of matter to the form of our being. This diagnosis led to the dividedness seen in philosophy and to Nihilism in the end. But there is another diagnosis which leads to an entirely different conclusion—that our excessive love of intellect is the *cause* of our unhappiness; that this love makes us impure by dividing us from the tree of life."

"We thought the knowledge of good and evil would make us equal to God, an immortal being, but in fact it disclosed that we are mixed beings and made us unhappy."

"It seems we confused intellect and its power to make value judgments about what is good with the goodness of transcendent being—which is its immortality. Vanity caused us to glorify intellect, a power we ourselves had, and to choose the knowledge of good and evil over the tree of life. But the fault is not in intellect, which is highly desirable for its own sake—in fact quite astonishing. The fault lies in our excessive self-love; our desire to use intellect and its capacity to judge what is good in order to lift ourselves up to the level of transcendent being."

"On the other hand, this choice does not speak particularly *well* of human intellect," I noted with a laugh. "They knew they would die if they ate from the tree of the knowledge of good and evil, and yet they deliberately chose this knowledge over life."

"They already knew what was good—they lived in paradise and had access to the tree of life. They had perfect pleasure. The knowledge of evil, which they gained through disobedience, was that they were mortal and absolutely different from God as measured by the light of life. They discovered that life is absolutely desirable for its own sake—life is good, and evil is that which falls short of this exalted value. The moment they obtained this knowledge they became ashamed because it was knowledge of their own nakedness, their powerlessness to give themselves the one thing they desired most; in fact the very thing they were seeking when they succumbed to temptation."

"They wanted to obtain equality to God, but through disobedience their eyes were opened to the real difference between their existence and immortal being."

"The sword of judgment came in between them and the tree of life; and then they lost the ability to see the value of life clearly and began to confuse this value with their own mortal lives. They confused intellect and its force of judgment with 'the good'—life itself with 'being'—because they themselves were under judgment—they were mortal. Vanity misled them into thinking judgment had the power to render the happiness they desired, when in reality their own dividedness stood between them and this good."

"Vanity caused them to confuse their own mortal lives with the good, and the dividedness of the concepts of value seen in philosophy reflected this confusion."

"When the philosophers lost sight of the tree of life, they forgot to be ashamed of their nakedness. They boldly claimed that they could obtain the undivided value of 'the good' through intellect and its dividing power. They coveted the exalted identity of philosopher, of one who has obtained knowledge of the good, thinking this identity would answer their unhappiness; thinking it was possible to transcend themselves through the power of intellect. But then the same philosophy that they held so dear did little more than enflame their unhappiness by intensifying their dividedness."

"The more they labored to make themselves happy through intellect, the more divided and unhappy they became."

"They tried to find their way back to the tree of life by glorifying intellect and its force of judgment—which was the very thing that divided them from this tree in the first place. If we were divided from that tree through the vanity of wanting to obtain equality to God though intellect and the knowledge of good and evil, then it is impossible to find our way back to the tree through intellect and its concepts of what is good. All such concepts simply reflect our own dividedness, our mortality."

"There is only one way to regain access to that tree—and that is by laying down the vanity of our excessive love of intellect for the sake of life."

"Actually a more radical remedy was needed. It was not possible for us to lay down our vanity of our own accord because we no longer had direct access to the tree of life. We could not see the tree—our own mortality stood in the way—and therefore we were not fully aware that our notions of value were in bondage to the grave. In order to restore the true value of life to consciousness a new type of tree was necessary; a tree that removed the obstacle between us and transcendent being; a tree that showed us what we could not see for ourselves by the light of natural reason—that the way to obtain gladness and a desirable identity is to lay down this mortal life for the sake of something better."

"This new tree was the sacrifice that was necessary in order to reconcile us to immortal being, but it was also the sign we needed to see in order to understand the path of life, in order to go beyond the benightedness of our mortality."

"What we see on this tree is the act of willingly giving up the glory of the mortal realm and the illusion of power that judgment can provide for the gracious value of life, which cannot be obtained through judgment. Just as we lost our ability to see the value of life on account of our vanity and love of judgment, so the new tree restores this value by overcoming judgment through the power of love. The tree that restores life indicates that the way to obtain the identity we desire is to give up the sword of judgment and cling to the love of God; to take up the sign of love for ourselves and allow this sign to reinform our identity and our concepts of value."

"This tree has the power to restore the innocence we forfeited when we indulged in the forbidden fruit—the innocence of knowing only what is good, of knowing that we can obtain life by putting our faith in its justifying power and giving up our love of judgment, our desire to compare ourselves with others. And this is important because joy is impossible without innocence."

"True," Smith said. "When a child hears about the manger at this season of the year, his thoughts are not clouded with massive church buildings and budgets or self-important ceremonies or the various struggles that have occurred down through the ages over doctrine. He does not see committees or programs or wars waged in the name of religion; he does not see the miasma of unhappiness in which we become mired whenever we attempt to glorify ourselves at the expense of our fellow beings. All he sees is pure love in the humility and meekness of the manger."

"And that is the secret of his joy. All of those other things are merely shadows."

"Do you remember how we loved a good blizzard when we were young? We were free to extract every last drop of delight from howling winter winds and snowy drifts because we did not fear death. But then we became conscious of our nothingness and could no longer be satisfied with a child's foolish pleasures or the sincerity of his love. We began to look for ways to compare ourselves with others, as if such comparisons had the power to make us happy. We sought careers, built homes, mowed lawns, invested in the market, surrounded ourselves with impressive-sounding philosophies and doctrines, all in an attempt to show that we were not lacking in power, that we were important and deserving of respect. But the more we gained of the world the less we enjoyed the howling blizzard. Valuable property might be damaged! Status might be lost! And we who had become something were appalled at the prospect of our nothingness."

"We became too wrapped up in ourselves and our illusions of power to enjoy the power of the blizzard. Meanwhile those storms were always there, always waiting for us in their awesome majesty."

"We tend to lose sight of how pure the manger was in the age of Augustus—a sign of radical resistance. It seeks to conquer by sweetness rather than the sword; by kindness rather than judgment; by innocence rather than worldliness. We cannot taste the sweetness of this sign if we remain infatuated with intellect and its dividing power. Compared with such mighty identities as Rationalism and Transcendentalism and the Superman, a manger seems rather foolish. But this same foolishness is the key to obtaining what we desire, since we desire life."

"The meekness of the manger becomes a sign of hope when all other hope is lost. All of the grandiose identities supplied by intellect and its capacity for resistance have now been exposed in their nakedness—but then perhaps it becomes a little easier to see just how valuable this meekness really was."

"Strange, isn't it, how we long to be like children again at this time of year—to see what they see and feel what they feel—"

Smith grew quiet. I had a pretty good idea of what he was thinking. His wife, Jane, had died on Christmas Day two years earlier after a terrible bout with pancreatic cancer. She lived a month or so longer than predicted; Smith was convinced she had held on for the holiday she loved. I looked out the window and noticed that the rain had indeed turned to snow and was starting to blow heavily. One could hear the northwest wind gusting in the trees and branches tapping on windows.

The stove was beginning to ebb, so I went to fetch a log. As I did I became aware of the distinctive scent of Douglas fir. Looking around, I spotted a beautiful wreath near the door, decorated with bells and cones and waiting to be put up. I stared at it for a moment, unsettled by the recollection that Smith's wife had been a great maker of wreaths.

"That's quite a wreath," I said as I pulled a log out of the bin.

"Julie made it," Smith said without turning around.

"Funny, I saw Julie the other day at the post office. I was rather struck by how much she—"

"Looks like her mother?" he said with a chuckle. "Something in the eyes, perhaps."

"Yes—the eyes."

I stuck the log in the stove and went to fetch my now-dry coat, which was hanging on a wooden peg nearby. "Guess I'd better get going before the roads turn to ice. But of course we'll see you Christmas Eve."

"Oh, if I'm not in the way," he said absent-mindedly.

"Not at all. The kids always look forward to it. Really coming down now," I observed, squinting through the storm door. "Looks like I might have to get out the snow blower tomorrow."

"Perhaps," Smith said. He was not looking at me, but out the large den window, where the snow was catching an updraft from an overhang and flying wildly about. He seemed a million miles away.

www.ingramcontent.com/pod-product-compliance
Lightning Source LLC
Chambersburg PA
CBHW071445150426
43191CB00008B/1239